BUDDHISM AS PHILOSOPHY

D0225123

Buddhism as Philosophy

An Introduction

MARK SIDERITS

Published in the UK by
Ashgate Publishing Limited
Great Britain

Published in North America by
Hackett Publishing Company, Inc.
Indianapolis/Cambridge

Copyright © 2007 Mark Siderits

Published by

Ashgate Publishing Limited
Gower House
Croft Road
Aldershot
Hants GU11 3HR
England
http://www.ashgate.com

Hackett Publishing Company, Inc.
P.O. Box 44937
Indianapolis, IN 46244–0937
USA
http://www.hackettpublishing.com

British Library Cataloguing in Publication Data
Siderits, Mark, 1946–
Buddhism as philosophy : an introduction.
– (Ashgate world philosophies series)
1.Philosophy, Buddhism
I.Title
181'.043

ISBN 978–07546–5369–1

Library of Congress Cataloging-in-Publication Data
Siderits, Mark, 1946–
Buddhism as philosophy : an introduction / Mark Siderits.
p. cm.
Includes bibliographicsl references and index.
ISBN–13: 978–0–7546–5368–4 (Ashgate : Hbk : alk. paper)
ISBN–13: 978–0–7546–5369–1 (Ashgate : pbk. : alk. paper)
ISBN–13: 978–0–87220–874–2 (Hackett : Hbk : alk. paper)
ISBN–13: 978–0–87220–873–5 (Hackett : pbk : alk. paper)
1. Philosophy, Buddhist. I. Title.
B162.S53 2007
181'.043–dc22   2007011455

Typeset in Times New Roman by IML Typographers, Birkenhead, Merseyside.
Printed at Sheridan Books, Inc.
15 14 13 12 11   3 4 5 6 7 8

Contents

Preface

In this book I have tried to make clear the theories and arguments of the Buddhist philosophical tradition. If I have attained any measure of success, it is due to the help of many others. And so there is a long list of people to whom I must express my appreciation and thanks. First and foremost are the students who have taken PHI 208 through the years. Their comments and questions have helped me discern the underlying logic of the Indian philosophical debates, and have shown me connections between disparate topics that I would otherwise not have seen. I am glad to have had the opportunity to learn from them.

Much of the material in Chapter 10 was first presented when I gave the Matilal lectures in Indian philosophy at King's College London. I wish to thank Professor Richard Sorabji for making this possible. And a heartfelt thanks is due to all the students who showed up for late Friday afternoon lectures at the Strand.

Much of what follows reflects things I have learned over the years from colleagues and friends in philosophy and Buddhology. I have had the great good fortune to work in an analytically oriented philosophy department whose members are willing to entertain the possibility that Buddhist philosophers might have important contributions to make to the discipline. I have especially profited from my many cross-corridor discussions with Kenton Machina and David Anderson. I have learned much about Buddhist and Indian philosophy from conversing with Arindam Chakrabarti, Amita Chatterji, Georges Dreyfus, Jonardon Ganeri, Katsura Shoryu, J.N. Mohanty, Roy Perrett and Tom Tillemans. Thanks are also due to Chris Bartley and Chakravarthi Ram-Prasad for their advice and encouragement. And I owe a special debt of gratitude to Will Rassmussen, whose *upāya* resulted in a much improved final draft. I also found useful the comments of several anonymous readers.

The people at Ashgate have been extremely helpful. Sarah Lloyd has always been most supportive and encouraging, and Celia Hoare managed the production process. I also appreciated the many words of advice and encouragement from Rick Todhunter at Hackett.

Finally, I want to express my thanks to Esther for sharing her book at a crucial moment many years ago, an act of generosity the ramifications of which are still unfolding. And of course I owe a special debt of gratitude to Muji for keyboarding assistance.

Abbreviations and Translation Sources

AKBh: *Abhidharmakośābhāṣyam of Vasubandhu*, ed. Prahlad Pradhan (Patna: Jayaswal Research Institute, 1975).

BCA: *The Bodhicāryāvatāra of Śāntideva with the Commentary Pañjika of Prajñākaramati*, ed. P.L. Vaidya (Dharbanga: Mithila Institute, 1960).

BSB: *Bodhisattvabhūmi*, ed. Nalinaksha Dutt, Tibetan Sanskrit Works, Vol. VII (Patna, 1966), pp. 30–32.

M: *Majjhima Nikāya*, ed. V. Trenckner (London: Pali Text Society, 1948–60).

MMK: *Mūlamadhyamakakārikā*, ed. Raghunath Pandeya as: *The Madhyamakaśāstram of Nāgārjuna*, with the Commentaries *Akutobhayā* by Nāgārjuna, *Madhyamakavṛtti* by Buddhapālita, *Prajñāpradīpavṛtti* by Bhāvaviveka, and *Prasannapadā* by Candrakīrti (Delhi: Motilal Banarsidass, 1988).

MP: *Milindapañho*, ed. R.D. Vadekar (Bombay: Bombay University Publications 1972).

MPS (*Mahāprajñāparāmitā Śāstra*): Lamotte, Étienne, translator, *Le Traité de la grande vertu de sagesse de Nāgārjuna (Mahāprajñāpāramitāśāstra)* (Louvain, 1944–80).

NS, NSB, NSV: *Nyāyadarśanam of Gotama, with Vātsyayana's Bhāṣya, Uddyotakara's Vārttika, Vācaspati Miśra's Tātparyatika, and Viśvanātha's Vṛtti*, ed. Taranath Nyaya Tarkatirtha and Amarendramohan Tarkatirtha (Delhi: Munshiram Manoharlal, 2003).

PV, PVBh: *The Pramāṇavārttikam of Dharmakīrti*, ed. Ram Chandra Pandeya (Delhi: Motilal Banarsidass, 1989).

S: *Saṃyutta Nikāya*, ed. M. Leon Feer in 5 vols (London: Pali Text Society, 1884–98).

TB: *Bauddha Tarkabhāṣā of Mokṣākaragupta*, ed. and trans. B.N. Singh (Varanasi: Asha Prakashan, 1985).

TS: *Tattvasaṅgraha of Sāntarakṣita*, edited with the *Pañjikā* (=TSP) by Embar Krishnamacharya. Baroda: Oriental Institute, 1984.

VM: *Visuddhimagga of Buddhaghosâcariya*, ed. Henry Clarke Warren, rev. by Dharmananda Kosambi (Cambridge, MA: Harvard University Press, 1950).

VMS: *Vijñaptimātratāsiddhi: deux traites de Vasubandhu*, ed. Sylvain Levi (Louvain: 1925).

VV: *Vigrahavyāvartanī*, edited and translated in: *The dialectical method of Nagarjuna: (Vigrahavyavartini)*, eds E.H. Johnston and Arnold Kunst, trans. Kamaleswar Bhattacharya (Delhi: Motilal Banarsidass, 1978).

CHAPTER ONE

Buddhism as Philosophy?

The purpose of this book is, as the title suggests, to examine Buddhism as philosophy. Before we actually start doing that though, it might be good to first get a bit clearer about what each of these two things – Buddhism and philosophy – is. That will help us see what might be distinctive about studying Buddhism as a form of philosophy. And it is important to be clear about this, since there are some preconceptions about these matters that might get in the way of fully grasping how the philosophical study . of Buddhism works.

1.1

When people first encounter philosophy, they want to know what it is about. Other disciplines have their own subject matter: biology is the study of life processes, sociology is the study of human societies, astronomy looks at planets and stars, etc. So what is philosophy about? Those who are not new to the study of philosophy know that what makes philosophy a separate discipline is not its special subject matter. True, there are questions that we naturally think of as 'philosophical' in some sense. Questions such as, 'How should I live my life?', and 'How do we know anything?', and 'How did all this come to be?'. But the first question is also addressed by literature, the second by cognitive science, and the third by astrophysics. What distinguishes philosophy from other disciplines?

The answer has more to do with method than with content. What sets philosophy apart as a discipline is more its concern with how to answer questions than with the answers themselves. To study philosophy is to learn to think carefully and critically about complex issues. It is not necessarily to learn 'the answers' that the discipline has arrived at. This can make the study of philosophy frustrating for some. When we first study a subject, we expect to learn the body of knowledge that has been developed by that discipline. When we study chemistry we learn the atomic weights of the elements, when we study history we learn the causes of the First World War, etc. Only later, if at all, does one start looking into the methods the discipline uses within its field of knowledge. The study of philosophy is not like that. True, one might find out in an introductory philosophy course that Plato thought the soul must be immortal, or that Descartes held the one thing that can't be doubted is that the 'I' exists. But one also learns that not all philosophers agree with Plato or Descartes on these claims. Some students find this frustrating. Where, they want to know, are the facts that philosophy has established? In all the centuries that philosophy has existed, has it made any progress, come up with any answers?

1

One response to this question is that indeed philosophy has established something quite significant – that the truth turns out to be very complicated. None of the simple answers to the questions that philosophy examines is correct. This is an important (and unsettling) result. The questions that philosophers ask often seem like they should have simple and straightforward answers. Take, for instance, the question how the mind and the body interact. The state of my stomach causes me to have a desire, and then the resulting state of my mind brings about bodily motion in the direction of the refrigerator. How do these things happen? One thing that philosophical investigation of this question has shown is that we still don't know the answer. Even more detailed scientific study of the brain won't succeed (at least by itself) in explaining how this works. Yet we rely on the mind and the body working together in everything we do. So perhaps philosophy has established something after all – that under the surface of seemingly simple matters lurks surprising complexity. Getting to the bottom of things turns out to be devilishly hard work.

But there is another way to answer the complaint that philosophy hasn't established any facts. Someone who says this might be wondering, What is the point of studying philosophy? And the way the challenge is posed suggests that they think the point of studying some subject is to acquire a body of knowledge, that is, to add new facts to the facts they already know. So one response to the challenge might be to question this assumption. Perhaps the point (or at least a point) of studying philosophy is to acquire a set of skills. Specifically the study of philosophy might turn out to be one of the best ways to learn some critical argumentation skills: defining one's terms carefully, constructing good arguments in support of one's views, critically evaluating arguments (one's own and others'), responding to objections, and the like.[1] And these skills turn out to play a crucial role in many different areas of life. They are, for instance, extremely important to the practice of law. This would explain why the study of philosophy is recognized as one of the best ways to prepare for legal practice (something that was known in ancient Greece and in medieval India). Of course the issues that philosophers grapple with can be intrinsically interesting to anyone who is at all thoughtful and reflective. But on this way of thinking about philosophy, the benefit of grappling with them is not so much that one gets the 'right' answer, as that one learns to think more carefully and critically about complex matters in general.

To say this is not to say that the questions that philosophers ask are unimportant.

---

[1]A note about the word 'argument'. As philosophers use this term, an argument is just a presentation of evidence that is meant to support some conclusion. An argument always consists of two or more statements: a conclusion and one or more premises. The conclusion is the statement that the author of the argument is trying to get others (the audience) to accept. The premises are statements that the author thinks the audience is likely to already accept, and that the author thinks will show that the conclusion is more likely to be true. Giving an argument is one way of trying to persuade others of something. It differs from other forms of persuasion in that when it is properly done it engages the rationality of the audience – it leaves it up to them to determine whether or not this argument gives good reasons to accept the conclusion.

It's because people find these to be pressing questions that they pursue the difficult task of trying to answer them – and thereby develop their logical and analytic skills. So something more should be said at this point about what sorts of questions these are. Philosophical inquiry can be sorted into several broad areas. One such domain is ethics. This has to do with the general question of how we should live our lives. So it includes not just questions about the nature of morality (which is concerned with what constitutes right and wrong in the treatment of others). It also deals with questions about what sort of life might be the best life for persons. Now it is sometimes thought that questions of ethics and morality are questions for religion. And it is true that most religions have a great deal to say on these matters. But when people think of questions of right and wrong, good and bad, as matters for religion, they often have in mind the idea that a religion simply tells us how we ought to behave. So they are thinking of ethics and morality as a set of rules or command-ments. This is not what philosophers mean by ethics, though. As they use the term, ethics involves critical examination of competing views about how we ought to conduct ourselves. And this is something that one can do regardless of what (if any) religious beliefs one has. The medieval Christian thinker Thomas Aquinas was doing ethics in this sense when he tried to determine what conclusions we can draw about being virtuous from a certain view of human nature. But so was the nineteenth-century German atheist Friedrich Nietzsche when he asked how we should live our lives given that God is dead. What makes both of their discussions of ethical mat-ters philosophical is that both involve the critical examination of arguments.

Metaphysics is another major area of philosophy. The word 'metaphysics' gets used in several different ways. For instance, in bookstores the 'metaphysics' section is usually filled with books on astrology and the occult. But as it is used in philosophy, it simply refers to the disciplined investigation of the most basic features of reality. Where ethics concerns the question how things ought to be, metaphysics concerns the question how things fundamentally are, or what reality is basically like. Now we might think that questions about how things are, or what reality is like, should be left to the sciences. And it is true that if, for instance, we wanted to know what a certain chemical compound is like we should turn to chemistry. But metaphysical questions are much more basic or fundamental than those that science can answer. Chemistry can tell us what effects might be caused by mixing two chemicals. But it is a metaphysical question what the general nature of the relation between cause and effect is. Likewise the sciences tell us a great deal about the nature of the physical world. But it is a metaphysical question whether everything that exists is physical; this is not a question that scientists can or should try to answer using the methods of science. Some other examples of metaphysical questions include: What is the nature of time? Are there, in addition to particulars such as individual cows, universals such as a single *cowness* that exists in all of them simultaneously? Does there exist an all-perfect, eternal creator of the universe? Is there a self, and if so what might it be like? The pursuit of metaphysical questions like these has often led philosophers to related but separate questions in the philosophy of language, such as how it is that words and sentences have meaning, and what it means for a statement to be true.

Another important area of philosophy is epistemology or the theory of knowledge. Here the basic question is how we can know what things are like and what should be done. Inquiry in epistemology has often taken the form of asking just what it means to say that someone knows something or other. For instance, can someone be said to know something if they haven't ruled out all the ways in which they could be mistaken (even when they're not mistaken)? But epistemological inquiry may also take the form of asking what are the means or methods of knowledge. Sense-perception and inference (or reasoning) are popular candidates for reliable ways to acquire knowledge, but what about authority (taking the word of some trustworthy person), or reasoning by analogy? And if there are different means of knowledge, how are they related to one another? Does each have its own distinctive sphere, or do they all serve equally well to give us knowledge about the same objects? Does any one means of knowledge have precedence over others?

As you might have guessed given what was said earlier about the nature of philosophy, philosophers have developed a number of different theories in each different branch. And there is no general consensus as to which theories in metaphysics, epistemology and ethics are correct. There is general agreement that the simplest answers are wrong. Take, for instance, the ethical theory of subject-based ethical relativism. This is the view that whether an action is morally permissible or morally wrong depends on whether or not one sincerely believes that doing that action is wrong. All philosophers today would agree that this theory is false. But when it comes to more sophisticated theories in these areas, agreement breaks down. For every theory that has been proposed in metaphysics, epistemology and ethics, there are serious criticisms that have been developed by philosophers. Much of the practice of philosophy involves looking at these objections to a given view and seeing if it's possible to answer them. (It is through this process that philosophical theories have grown so sophisticated.) But in doing so one frequently discovers that there are important connections between the view one holds in one area of philosophy and the positions one takes in other areas. A particular theory in ethics might for instance turn out to be unworkable unless one holds a certain position on some metaphysical issue. Learning to see these sorts of connections is another important benefit of studying philosophy.

Not every culture developed its own philosophical tradition. But ancient Greece did, and this is the source of modern Western philosophy. And so did classical India. In each case the original impetus seems to have come from a concern to answer ethical questions. Out of dissatisfaction with the received view of how people should live their lives, there arose efforts at thinking systematically about these matters. But in both cases these inquiries soon led to major developments in metaphysics and epistemology. For philosophers became aware that if we are to determine how we ought to live, we need to be clearer about the nature of the world and our place in it. And this in turn requires greater clarity about what constitutes knowledge and what processes lead to it. People sometimes wonder if it could be just a coincidence that philosophy arose in two such different cultures at roughly the same time. Now we know that there were trade contacts between classical India and the Hellenic world. So it is at least conceivable that some ancient Greek philosophers and some classical Indian philosophers knew something of one another's work. But the two philosophical traditions appear to be genuinely distinct. They tackle the same basic questions in ethics, metaphysics and epistemology. And they employ the same basic techniques of analysis and argumentation. (This is why it is appropriate to call them both 'philosophy'.) Sometimes individual philosophers in the two traditions even reach strikingly similar conclusions. But this should not lead us to suppose that there was significant borrowing between one tradition and the other. We know after all that the same invention can occur independently in two distinct cultures. In mathematics, for instance, the zero was invented separately, in ancient India, and also by the Mayans of pre-contact meso-America.

1.2

Philosophy, then, is the systematic investigation of questions in ethics, metaphysics and epistemology (as well as several related fields). It involves using analysis and argumentation in systematic and reflective ways. This will do, at least for now, as an account of what we will mean by philosophy. What about the other term in our title, Buddhism? We might seem to be on safer ground here. While many people might lack detailed knowledge about what it is that Buddhists believe and what Buddhist practice involves, surely everyone knows that Buddhism is the religion that was founded in ancient India by the Buddha, subsequently spread throughout Asia, and is now attracting adherents in the West? Well, yes, but there's a load of mischief lurking in that word 'religion'. There is one sense in which Buddhism can accurately be called a religion, but there is another widely used sense of that word in which it would be a mistake. And clarity about this matter will prove just as crucial to our undertaking as will being clear about what philosophy is.

We often base our understanding of a word on familiar examples. In the case of 'religion', the familiar examples for most people in the West are Christianity, Judaism and Islam. These are all monotheistic religions: they each involve belief in a single personal being who is eternal, is creator of the universe, and is all-perfect. Not all religions share this sort of belief: Hinduism and Shinto are both polytheistic. It doesn't seem to be stretching things too much to group all the theisms together under one label, though. But particularly if the religion one is most familiar with is Christianity, one might also think of a religion as a 'faith'. To think of religion this way is to see it as a set of beliefs that one accepts out of a conviction that is not based on rational argumentation. Religion is then seen as falling on the 'heart' side of the head/heart, or reason/faith, divide.

In modern Western culture there is a tendency to suppose that certain questions are to be settled through the use of reason, while others can only be addressed through faith and feeling. This is the dichotomy between reason and faith, with reason seen as a matter of the head and faith a matter of the heart. Along with this dichotomy there is a related one between 'facts', seen as the sort of thing that the sciences discover, and 'values', seen as private, subjective commitments that are not open to rational investigation and scrutiny. Suppose we agree that using our reason involves thinking about things in a cool, careful, detached and deliberate way. Now it is probably true that some matters should not be decided entirely on the basis of calm, cool consideration of reasons. One's choice of life-partner, for instance, should probably involve considerable input from the 'heart' side. But it is not at all clear that 'head' and 'heart' constitute a strict dichotomy. And in any event, it is not obvious that the matters we consider religious (or 'spiritual') necessarily belong on the 'faith' side of any such divide.

One thing that all the theisms (monotheisms and polytheisms) have in common is that they each try to articulate some vision of the ideal state for humans. This ideal state is usually depicted as being quite different from the way that people would live their lives if left to their own devices. The latter 'mundane' (or 'worldly') state is depicted as inherently unsatisfactory, as fallen away from how we ought to be. And the ideal state is represented as a sort of salvation from this fallen state. When we think of a religion as dealing with 'spiritual' matters, it is this concern with attaining salvation, of escaping from an unsatisfactory way of being, that we have in mind. The concerns of religion are, in a word, soteriological. (A soteriology is a doctrine of salvation.) Now to think of religion as a faith is to suppose that soteriological concerns can only be addressed through a form of emotional commitment. It is to hold that reason and logical investigation are of little or no use in seeking salvation. Many people in our culture believe this. But this was not the view of classical Indian culture. (Nor was it held by the ancient Greeks, or by the philosophers of medieval Islam.) To many people in ancient India, including the Buddha, it made perfectly good sense to use our rational faculties in the pursuit of salvation. Of course this was not the only path that Indians recognized. The *Bhagavad Gītā*, a major Hindu text, teaches that there are four different paths; which path one should take depends on one's talents and predilections. But all four paths culminate in salvation, for they all instill knowledge of our true identity. The Buddhist tradition generally teaches that there is just one path to liberation, not four. But that path consists in the combined practice of philosophical reasoning and meditation. Indian Buddhists, like others in ancient India, thought that salvation from our unsatisfactory state was to be had through coming to know the truth about who we are and where we fit in the universe. And they thought that attaining such insights required the use of philosophical rationality.[2]

---

[2]This is not to say that Buddhism is a philosophy and not a religion. To say that would be to assume that it must be one or the other. It would be to assume that there is a strict dichotomy between reason and faith. Buddhists would be likely to reject that assumption. Their attitude toward soteriological matters might be usefully compared to one we often take today toward scientific matters. Most of us who are not scientists tend to take the more advanced theories of a science like physics on trust. But we know that if we were to receive proper training we would be able to assess for ourselves the evidence in support of those theories.

Buddhism is, then, a religion, if by this we mean that it is a set of teachings that address soteriological concerns. But if we think of religion as a kind of faith, a commitment for which no reasons can be given, then Buddhism would not count. To become a Buddhist is not to accept a bundle of doctrines solely on the basis of faith. And salvation is not to be had just by devout belief in the Buddha's teachings. (Indeed the Buddhists we will study would be likely to see belief of this sort as an obstacle to final liberation.) Rather, liberation, or nirvāna (to use the Buddhist term), is to be attained through rational investigation of the nature of the world. As we would expect with any religion, Buddhist teachings include some claims that run deeply counter to common sense. But Buddhists are not expected to accept these claims just because the Buddha taught them. Instead they are expected to examine the arguments that are given in support of these claims, and determine for themselves if the arguments really make it likely that these claims are true. Buddhists revere the Buddha as the founder of their tradition. But that attitude is meant to be the same as what is accorded a teacher who has discovered important truths through their own intellectual power. Indeed the person whom we call the Buddha, Gautama,[3] is said to have been just the latest in a long series of Buddhas, each of whom independently discovered the same basic truths that show the way to nirvāna.[4] This may or may not reflect historical fact. But the spirit behind this claim is worth remarking on. What it suggests is that the teachings of Buddhism are based on objective facts about the nature of reality and our place in it. And these facts are thought of as things that human reason can apprehend without reliance on superhuman revelation.

If we expect all religions to be theistic, then Buddhism might not qualify as a religion. The Buddha (that is, 'our' historic Buddha, Gautama) is not the equivalent of the God of Western monotheism. Nor is the Buddha considered a prophet, someone whose authority on spiritual matters derives from privileged access to God. Gautama is seen as just an extremely intelligent and altruistic human being. Indeed Buddhism explicitly denies that there is such a thing as the God recognized by Western monotheism, that is, an eternal, all-powerful and all-perfect creator. To most

---

[3]'Gautama' is the Sanskrit version of his name, 'Gotama' the Pali version. In addition there are a number of epithets that are used to refer to him: 'Śākyamuni' ('sage of the Śākya clan'), 'Siddhārtha' ('one whose aim is accomplished') and 'Tathāgata' ('one who has thus gone') are among the more common. 'Buddha' is not a name or epithet but a title: a Buddha is someone who has independently discovered the facts about suffering, its causes and its cure, and taught these to the world. Becoming a Buddha supposedly involves a long and arduous process of preparation. Someone who has chosen to enter into that process but has not yet arrived at the destination of Buddhahood is referred to as a *bodhisattva* (a 'being [destined for] enlightenment').

[4]Buddhists believe that everything that arises through conditions is impermanent. This would include the teachings developed by Gautama and transmitted through the traditions of institutional Buddhism. So eventually these teachings, and institutional Buddhism, will disappear. Facts like those that Gautama recognized will continue to obtain, however. So in time another Buddha may come along and recognize the significance of such facts for human salvation. This has supposedly happened many times in the past.

people this denial is tantamount to atheism. So if we are to count Buddhism as a religion, it will have to make sense to say there can be atheistic religions.

Of course the Buddha and classical Indian Buddhists acknowledged the existence of a multiplicity of gods. Should we then think of Buddhism as polytheistic, in the same sense in which many forms of Hinduism are polytheistic?[5] Perhaps we might if we wanted Buddhism to fit under a nice tidy definition of 'religion' that required some form of theism. But this would be somewhat beside the point as far as Buddhism is concerned. The gods that ancient Indian Buddhists believed in were (like the gods of ancient Greece and all the rest of pre-Christian Europe) finite beings, rather like human beings, only longer-lived and more powerful. More importantly, they play no role whatever in the quest for nirvāna. Perhaps worship and sacrifice to the right gods might win one various mundane benefits, such as timely rainfall to make the crops grow, or the health of one's loved ones. But the gods cannot bestow nirvāna on us. Indeed the fact that they also undergo rebirth (they may live extremely long lives, but they are still impermanent) is taken to show that they are no more enlightened than we humans are. Even an enlightened human being like a Buddha or an *arhat* (someone who has attained nirvāna by following the teachings of the Buddha) cannot bestow nirvāna on others. That is something that one can only attain for oneself; enlightened beings can only help others by giving them pointers along the way. And the point, for Buddhism, is to attain nirvāna, to bring suffering to an end. So for this spiritual tradition, the question whether there are any gods turns out to be largely irrelevant.

The doctrine of karma and rebirth is another matter. Classical Indian Buddhism accepted this doctrine. These Buddhists believed that death is ordinarily not the end of our existence, that after we die we are reborn, either as humans or as some other form of sentient being (including non-human animals, gods, and the inhabitants of various hells). Which sort of rebirth one attains depends on one's karma, which has to do with the moral quality of the actions one has engaged in. If those acts were primarily morally good, one may be reborn as a human in fortunate life circumstances, or even as a god. If one's life was full of acts done out of evil intentions, however, one might end up as a *preta* or so-called 'hungry ghost'. (These beings are so-called because they are only able to eat feces, and to drink urine, pus and blood.) Now this may sound like just the sort of thing that other more familiar religions offer: a promise of life after death, and a doctrine of retribution for one's sins. So is Buddhism really all that different from those other spiritual traditions? Is it really the case that it only expects us to believe those things for which there is objective evidence?

This is a good question. It may turn out that not everything Buddhists have traditionally believed can be rationally supported. This outcome is one of the possibilities that opens up when we examine Buddhism as philosophy. But before

---

[5]Indeed many of the same gods that we find in classical Hindu texts show up in the Indian Buddhist tradition as well. See A.K. Warder, *Indian Buddhism* (Delhi: Motilal Banarsidars, 1970, pp. 152–56).

saying any more about that, I should clear up some possible confusions about the doctrine of karma and rebirth. The first point to make is that as Buddhists understand it, karma is not divine retribution for one's sins. The laws of karma basically have to do with receiving pleasant results for acting out of morally good motives, and receiving painful results for acting with evil intentions. This prompts some to ask who determines what is good and what is evil. For Buddhists the answer is that no one does. Karma is not a set of rules that are decreed by a cosmic ruler and enforced by the cosmic moral police. Karma is understood instead as a set of impersonal causal laws that simply describe how the world happens to work. In this respect the karmic laws are just like the so-called natural laws that science investigates. It is a causal law that when I let go of a rock while standing on a bridge, it will fall toward the water below with a certain acceleration. No one passed this law, and no one enforces it. The laws of physics are not like the laws passed by legislative bodies. There are no gravity police. And if something were to behave contrary to what we take to be the law of gravity, that would be evidence that we were wrong to think it was a law. A true causal law has no exceptions. Likewise, the laws of karma are understood not as rules that can be either obeyed or broken, but as exceptionless generalizations about what always follows what. If we could keep track of enough persons over enough successive lives, we could find out what the laws of karma are in the same way that science discovers what the laws of nature are: our observations would disclose the patterns of regular succession that show causation at work.[6]

A second point to make about the Buddhist attitude toward karma and rebirth is that belief in rebirth does not serve the same function that belief in an afterlife serves in many other religious traditions. The fact that after I die I will be reborn is not taken to be a source of relief or consolation. And the point of Buddhist practice is not to do those things that will help ensure a pleasant next life and prevent a painful one. The truth is just the opposite. As we will see in more detail in the next chapter, the Buddha claims that continued rebirth is just what we need liberation from. (The reason, briefly, is that rebirth entails redeath.) One could set about trying to use knowledge of karmic causal laws to try to guarantee that one continues to exist in relatively comfortable circumstances. But on the Buddhist analysis that would just reveal one's ignorance about how things really are. And because such behavior was based on ignorance, it would inevitably lead to more of the suffering that Buddhism is meant to cure. The doctrine of karma and rebirth is not meant to make us feel better about the fact that we will all die. For those Buddhists who accept it, it is part of the problem, not part of the solution.

---

[6]It is widely held not just by Buddhists but by other classical Indian schools as well that the practice of meditation or *yoga* leads to the development of a number of extraordinary powers. One that is frequently mentioned is the ability to recall past lives, first of oneself and then of others. Someone who had such powers could tell us what the karmic causal laws actually are. For they would be able to observe which deeds in one life were regularly followed by pleasant rebirths, which by painful rebirths. Of course since every intentional act has some karmic effect, the patterns would be quite complex and difficult to discern. But it could at least in principle be done.

A third point about the doctrine of karma and rebirth is that this was not a view that was peculiar to Buddhism. Instead it seems to have been commonly accepted by spiritual teachers from before the time of the Buddha, and to have been part of the common-sense conception of the world for most Indians for most of the time that Buddhism existed in India. So when Indian Buddhists claimed that we undergo rebirth in accordance with karma, they were not making claims that would have struck their audience as novel or strange. Now when we think of a religion as something that makes claims that must be taken on faith, we have in mind claims that are not already part of common sense. So the fact that Buddhists accepted the doctrine of karma and rebirth does not show that Buddhism is a religion in the sense of a creed, a set of doctrines for which there is no evidence and that are to be accepted on faith. Perhaps Indians accepted this doctrine without good evidence. But if so, it was not because they were required to as practicing Buddhists.

The doctrine of karma and rebirth is not a part of our common-sense world-view. So it would be reasonable for us to ask what evidence there is that this doctrine is true. It would be reasonable, that is, if we are investigating Buddhism as philosophy. For in studying philosophy we are interested in finding out what the truth is. (We may not always find it, but that's our aim.) Things might be different if we were studying Buddhism as an historical artifact, as part of the study of the history of religions. Perhaps then we would simply note that Indian Buddhists believed in karma and rebirth, and set aside the question whether they were justified in their belief. Instead we might simply explore how this belief affected other aspects of Buddhism: their ethical teachings, for instance, or their artistic representations. There is a great deal we can learn by studying Buddhism and other religions in this way. By simply setting aside the question whether the teachings are true or false, and focusing on how different elements of the tradition might be related to one another, we can learn to see the inner logic of the system, how it hangs together as a system. This can help us see things we might otherwise miss. But it cannot tell us whether its teachings are reasonable. And this is something we might want to know when we study a religion like Buddhism. Buddhists claim that those of their teachings that run counter to common sense can be supported by rational arguments. Are they right about this? And if it turns out that some claim of theirs that strikes us as strange cannot be given rational support, how much damage does that do to the overall system? These are the sorts of questions that philosophical examination involves.

And this is how we will proceed with the doctrine of karma and rebirth. We will ask (among other things) if there are good reasons to believe it. If there are not, we will go on to see whether other important teachings of Buddhism would also have to go if this doctrine were thrown overboard. This might come as a shock, particularly if you think of a person's religion as something sacrosanct that others shouldn't question. How can we criticize beliefs that might turn out to be central to another person's whole way of life? But someone who asks this is forgetting something: Buddhist philosophers thought that their most important claims should be subjected to rational scrutiny. This is what made them philosophers. They certainly criticized the views of other Buddhist philosophers. And there was a great deal of rational criticism exchanged between the Buddhists and other Indian philosophers. So perhaps it would actually be dishonoring Buddhism not to subject its doctrines to rational scrutiny. To study it as no more than an item of historical interest, and not ask how much truth there is in its core teachings, might mean failing to take it seriously as an important human creation.

1.3

We have said enough for now about what philosophy is and what Buddhism is. And we have already begun to discuss what it might mean to study Buddhism as philosophy. There are a number of other things that need to be said on that score. One is that this study will be selective. Like any other religious tradition, Buddhism is an immensely complicated phenomenon. To study Buddhism as philosophy means primarily studying texts. Specifically it means studying those Buddhist texts that present philosophical theories and arguments. But this means leaving out of consideration many other sorts of Buddhist writings, such as those that specify the rules that monks and nuns must follow when they enter the Buddhist monastic order (the *saṃgha*), and those popular writings designed to present simple moral teachings to an audience of lay followers. Moreover, there is much more to Buddhism than its literature. And our focus on texts means these other areas will go largely untouched. We will not be examining the many different kinds of Buddhist artistic expression to be found in such fields as sculpture, architecture, painting, devotional poetry and drama. We will have very little to say about Buddhist institutions, their organization and history. We will say very little about the Buddhist practice of meditation, and nothing at all about such lay Buddhist devotional practices as stūpa worship. All of these aspects of Buddhism have been dealt with elsewhere, and there is no need to duplicate that scholarship here.[7]

There are, though, other studies of Buddhism that focus on many of the same topics that we will be examining. These are works that try to introduce Buddhism through a historical survey of its chief schools and their principal doctrines. Now we will try to trace a historical progression as well. But there will be less concern here than in the typical doctrinal history to say who influenced whom, what influenced what, in the development of key Buddhist teachings. Indeed at several points we will take things out of their historical order. This will happen where understanding conceptual connections takes precedence over working out the historical order in which ideas developed. But the most important difference between this work and histories of Buddhist doctrine is that the latter are more likely to present just the conclusions of the Buddhist philosophers. Our job will be to look not only at their

---

[7]An excellent resource that discusses many of these topics with respect to Indian Buddhism from its origins to its destruction in the late twelfth century CE is Warder's *Indian Buddhism*.

conclusions, but also at the arguments they gave in support of their conclusions. We will look at the objections that other Indian philosophers raised against the Buddhist views we examine, and we will consider the responses that Buddhists gave. We will try to come up with our own objections, and then try to figure out what (if anything) Buddhist philosophers could say to answer them. We will try, in short, to see how well Buddhist doctrines stand up to the test of rational scrutiny. Because we are examining Buddhism philosophically, we want to know what in Buddhist teachings represents the truth.

Now some of those teachings we can quite easily say are false. This is because some of the claims of Buddhist philosophers are based on views of the natural world very different from what our own sciences tell us about nature. For instance, some Buddhist philosophers hold that ordinary physical objects such as rocks and tables are made up of very large numbers of atoms of four different types: earth, air, water and fire. (Similar views are found in ancient Greek philosophy.) Now this idea that material things are made up of four different elements or kinds of stuff is one we know today is false. When ancient philosophers called water an element, they had in mind that there was just one fundamental kind of stuff present in every liquid. So the difference between water (that is, H_2O) and ethyl alcohol might just be a matter of how much fire element was present in addition to the water element. We now know that there are far more than four naturally occurring elements, and two liquids might be made up of completely different elements. Moreover, we know that each of these elements is in turn made up of more fundamental particles, until we reach what are now thought to be the most basic of these, the six kinds of quarks. So when Buddhist philosophers argue about a question like whether color is present in each of the four elements, we can say that the very question is misguided – no answer is likely to be true.

Does this mean that Buddhist philosophy can be dismissed as an outdated, pre-scientific view of the world? No. Here we can learn from what we find when we study ancient Greek philosophy. The Greek philosopher Aristotle believed that the earth is the center of the universe. We know that this is false, and yet Aristotle is still considered an important philosopher. What we have learned to do in studying ancient philosophy is simply set aside those parts that conflict with our modern scientific knowledge, and focus on what remains. This is a legitimate approach. When philosophy began, both in ancient Greece and in ancient India, it was felt that philosophers ought to develop a truly comprehensive world-view. For the same methods of rational analysis and argumentation that philosophers were developing in order to answer questions in metaphysics, epistemology and ethics, seemed to likewise be suitable for studying the natural world. So, for instance, Aristotle wrote treatises on biology and meteorology, and the Sāṃkhya school of Indian philosophy developed a theory of chemistry. Indeed most of our present natural sciences have their origins in philosophy. But they have since developed their own distinctive methods, and have become independent disciplines. Philosophy now focuses principally on issues in metaphysics, epistemology and ethics. This is why, when we today look at ancient philosophers, we tend to set to one side the details of their views about how the natural world works. For it usually turns out that even when these details are simply wrong, this has little or no effect on their views in the core philosophical areas of metaphysics, epistemology and ethics. This is how we will treat the Buddhist philosophers as well.

There is another element in the texts we will study that we shall also want to set off to one side. We will be examining texts in which Buddhists give arguments for their key claims in metaphysics, epistemology and ethics. But in some cases the reason given is basically an appeal to the authority of the Buddha. This sort of thing happens when there is a dispute between two different schools of Buddhist philosophy over some doctrine. One school may then point to some passage in the sūtras (the discourses of Gautama and his chief disciples) as grounds for accepting their position. Now this might count as a good reason to accept the view in question if you already thought that the Buddha's teachings were authoritative. But for those of us who do not automatically accept the authority of the Buddha, this cannot count as a good reason. So we will simply set such passages aside.

Most chapters in this book contain extracts, sometimes quite long ones, from primary sources in Buddhist philosophy, as well as extensive discussion. This means we will be reading passages from a variety of different Buddhist philosophical texts, beginning with the sūtras (the Buddha's own teachings), and ending with texts written some 1500 years later. Reading and understanding these texts will pose some real challenges. Because most of these were written for other ancient Indian philosophers, it is not always easy to see what the argument is, and how the author responds to objections. But we will start slowly, and you will have plenty of help on this. The point here is for you to learn to read and understand these texts on your own. That way, if you want to look more deeply into some topic in Buddhist philosophy, you will be able to do so without having to rely on anyone else's interpretations. Then you'll be better equipped to try to find out what the truth is for yourself.

One final point before we begin our study of Buddhism as philosophy. Some people might take the title of this book to mean that it will tell them what the Buddhist philosophy is. But as you may have guessed by now, there is no such thing as *the* Buddhist philosophy. At least not in the sense in which we are using 'philosophy' here. Given what the discipline of philosophy is, it should not be surprising that Buddhist philosophers disagree among themselves. By the same token, there is no such thing as the Christian philosophy, or the Jewish philosophy. There are philosophers who use the tools of philosophy to try to articulate what they take to be the basic truths of Christianity and of Judaism. But Aquinas and Kierkegaard disagree profoundly in their understandings of Christian teachings, and Maimonides and Spinoza likewise differ in how they approach the philosophical expression of Judaism. Things are no different when we come to Buddhism. While there are certain fundamentals on which all Buddhist philosophers agree, there are important issues over which they disagree. Sometimes these differences can make things quite complicated. So to help us keep track of things, it would be useful to have a basic taxonomy of Buddhist philosophical systems. We can start with the following basic division into three distinct phases in the development of Buddhist philosophy:

1   Early Buddhism: the teachings of the Buddha and his immediate disciples;
2   Abhidharma: the development of rigorous metaphysical and epistemological theories growing out of the attempt to give consistent, systematic interpretations of the teachings of early Buddhism;
3   Mahāyāna: philosophical criticism of aspects of Abhidharma doctrines, together with an alternative account of what Buddhist metaphysics and epistemology should look like.

Both the second and the third phase saw the development of a number of different schools, reflecting different approaches to the philosophical challenges being confronted. For our purposes the important schools will be:

2a.   Vaibhāṣika (Sarvāstivāda)
2b.   Sautrāntika (Dārṣṭāntika)
2c.   Theravāda (the form of Buddhism presently practiced in much of South East Asia)
3a.   Madhyamaka (the philosophical basis of much of Tibetan Buddhism)
3b.   Yogācāra (Buddhist idealism)
3c.   Yogācāra-Sautrāntika (Buddhist logic, the school of Diṅnāga).

We will look at each of these schools in turn, seeing how their views developed out of the work of earlier philosophers, and trying to understand and assess the merits of their arguments. But we will start, in the next three chapters, with the fundamentals that all Buddhist philosophical schools agree on, the basic teachings of early Buddhism.

Further Reading

For a discussion of the historical relations between ancient Greek philosophy and classical Indian philosophy, see Thomas McEvilley, *The Shape of Ancient Thought* (New York: Allworth Press, 2002).

CHAPTER TWO

Early Buddhism: Basic Teachings

In this chapter we will explore the basic teachings of early Buddhism, the teachings of the Buddha and his immediate disciples. This will serve to introduce a set of core principles that all Buddhist philosophers accept. In later chapters we will examine how various Buddhist philosophers developed these core teachings in different ways. But before we get to those basic ideas that are common to all schools of Buddhism, it might be useful to say a few words about the life of the Buddha.

2.1

Apart from his career as a teacher, there is little that is known with much confidence about the details of Gautama's life. Until recently, scholars were fairly certain that he lived from 566 to 486 BCE. But recent research suggests that his death may have been as late as 404 BCE. So if we accept the traditional claim that he lived for 80 years, then perhaps his life was lived wholly within the fifth century BCE. He was born in the city-state of Kapilavastu, the home of the Śākyas,[1] in what is now the western part of Nepal, near the Indian border. He grew up in relatively comfortable circumstances. But in early adulthood he chose to abandon the settled life of a householder and became a wandering renunciant or *śramaṇa*, someone whose life is dedicated to finding answers to certain spiritual questions.

The *śramaṇas* of sixth and fifth century BCE India represented a new phenomenon in Indian religious life. They rejected key elements of the prevailing Brahmanical orthodoxy as inadequate to their spiritual concerns. The Vedic religion that they challenged was centered on a set of texts, the *Vedas*, that the Brahmin priests considered supernatural in origin and authoritative. These texts enjoin performance of various rituals and sacrifices, both to uphold the cosmic order and to obtain various benefits for the person in whose name the ritual or sacrifice is carried out. But the new set of ideas associated with the notions of karma and rebirth made these older religious practices seem unsatisfying. If after I die I shall just be born into some new life, what point is there in trying to make my present situation more comfortable? Shouldn't I be more concerned with the lives to come after this one? Indeed what exactly is the point of going on to life after life? Is that cycle to go on forever? The Vedic religion seemed satisfactory as long as people held on to conventional views of human life and human happiness. If we each have just this one life on earth (and perhaps an afterlife thereafter), then it might make sense to devote it to things like

---

[1]Hence the epithet he later acquired, 'Śākyamuni' or 'sage of the Śākyas'.

15

sensual pleasure, wealth and power, and the social standing of a virtuous person.[2] But with the advent of new ideas about the nature of human life, the old answers no longer seemed to work. And so the *śramaṇas* sought a new account of human happiness and how to attain it.

Among the many *śramaṇas*, there were some who claimed to have found a solution to the problem of human existence, and offered to teach it to others. Their answers differed, but most shared the idea that true happiness could only be found by overcoming our ignorance about our true nature. And most also agreed that the truly ideal state for us must involve liberation (*mokṣa*) from the cycle of rebirths. The *śramaṇas* also explored a wide variety of techniques for attaining this ideal state they sought. These included various ascetic practices – performing austerities such as fasting, remaining utterly motionless for long periods, abstaining from sleep, and the like. They also included various meditational or yogic practices: learning to calm the mind and focus it in one-pointed concentration, exploring a variety of altered states of consciousness, and the like.[3]

Like other new renunciants, after abandoning his life as a householder Gautama sought to find a suitable *śramaṇa* teacher. According to our oldest accounts, he studied with several, and mastered the theories and techniques they taught, but found these inadequate. He then struck out on his own. Coming across an isolated forest grove, he resolved to devote a full night of concentrated effort to solving the problem of human suffering. Employing a variety of yogic techniques, he entered into four successive stages of meditation, and thereby acquired three sorts of knowledge: recollection of his own past lives, understanding of the general laws of karma, and knowledge of what would come to be called the four noble truths. This knowledge signaled his enlightenment (*bodhi*), his attainment of nirvāna or liberation from rebirth. Having thus attained his goal, he considered whether or not to teach his discovery to others. At first he is said to have been deterred by the difficulty and subtlety of the truths he had discovered. But he eventually concluded that there were some who could grasp these truths and thereby profit from his discovery. So he

---

[2]While the *Vedas* did not teach rebirth, they were not entirely clear on the question of an afterlife. Brahmanical culture of the time also recognized three possible goals in life: sensual pleasure (*kāma*), material wealth and power *(artha)*, and virtue and social repute (*dharma*). For each of these goals there was thought to be a special science concerning methods for obtaining it. And a literature developed around each of these sciences. So the *Kāma Sātra*, for instance, is the foundational text for the traditional science of obtaining sensual pleasure.

[3]While the *śramaṇa* movement may have started as a protest against Brahmanical orthodoxy, the Vedic tradition eventually responded to this challenge by developing a number of its own systems for attaining liberation or *mokṣa*. These included such philosophical schools as Sāṃkhya, Nyāya and Advaita Vedānta. These schools are referred to as 'orthodox' because they accept the authority of the *Vedas*. In this they differ from Buddhism and the other 'heterodox' schools (such as Jainism), which deny that the *Vedas* have any special authoritative status. Through the orthodox schools the Brahmanical tradition was in effect countenancing *mokṣa* as a fourth possible goal in life, in addition to the original three of *kāma*, *artha* and *dharma*.

embarked on the career of a Buddha, one who has solved the problem of human suffering through their own efforts (without reliance on the teachings of others) and imparts that knowledge to others out of compassion.

There is another, far more elaborate account of Gautama's life before his enlightenment. On that account, Gautama is a prince, his father, Śuddhodana, being a powerful and wealthy king. Gautama's conception is immaculate, and he is born not in the normal way but by emerging from his mother's side without breaking her skin or otherwise causing her pain. Immediately after birth he takes seven steps in each of the four cardinal directions; the world roars in response, and blossoms spring up under his feet. A seer tells Śuddhodana that the infant will grow up to be either a Buddha or a world monarch. He will become a Buddha if he sees four things in his youth: an old person, a sick person, a corpse, and a wandering renunciant. If he does not see all four he will become a world monarch. Śuddhodana wishes to ensure that his first-born son becomes a mighty king, so he has Gautama raised in a luxurious palace surrounded by only young, healthy and attractive people. Gautama grows up in these surroundings, marries and has a son. Yet on four successive days while out hunting he sees each of the four sights. He then resolves to become a *śramaṇa*, and makes his escape from the palace at night. He spends several years with a succession of teachers, but only after striking out on his own does he succeed in attaining the goal of liberation. Upon attaining enlightenment, it is Māra, the evil god of death, who tries to persuade him not to convey his discoveries to the world. Other gods then intercede to protect him from Māra's powers and ensure that there is a Buddha in the world.

This more elaborate account of Gautama's early life is the basis of popular depictions of the Buddha in Buddhist art and literature. But this version of the story only emerges several centuries after the Buddha's death. And it clearly reflects the common process whereby the life of a sect's founder comes to be draped in legend. We know, for instance, that Gautama cannot have been a prince nor his father a king, since Kapilavastu was not a monarchy in his day. Likewise the Buddha was quite insistent on the point that he was no more than an ordinary human being. This would seem to explain why the tales of miracles surrounding his birth and enlightenment are absent from the earliest accounts of Gautama's life. Only much later did some of his followers, perhaps out of missionary zeal, transform the story of his early life into a hagiography. Still there are things we can learn from these legendary accretions to his biography. Consider the tale of the four sights, for instance. Why might those who shaped the legend have chosen an old person, a sick person, a corpse, and a *śramaṇa* as the sights that would spur a pampered prince to renounce his life of luxury? Clearly because the first three signify the fact of human mortality, and the existential crisis that results from this fact, while the fourth represents the possibility of averting the crisis. This point will prove useful when we try to understand the Buddha's teachings on suffering.

2.2

While there is not much we know with certainty about Gautama's life before his enlightenment, we know a great deal about his career as a teacher after enlightenment. For instance, we know that he first taught his new insights when he encountered five former companion renunciants at Sārnāth, near Vārānasī.[4] We will examine the record of that encounter later, but it might be helpful to begin with an overview. It seems that these renunciants followed a path of extreme asceticism, but when Gautama left them and struck out on his own he abandoned such practices. So they now suspect him of having lapsed into a dissolute life. He thus begins by describing the path he has discovered as a 'middle path' between the two extremes of asceticism and the life of sensual pleasure. He then describes this path as a 'noble eightfold path', listing its eight component practices: right view, right intention, right speech, right action, right livelihood, right exertion, right self-possession and right concentration. This leads naturally to the enumeration of the four noble truths, since the claim that there is such a path is the fourth of the four truths. The four are, in summary form:

1   There is suffering.
2   There is the origination of suffering: suffering comes into existence in dependence on causes.
3   There is the cessation of suffering: all future suffering can be prevented.
4   There is a path to the cessation of suffering.

Now the second truth is later elaborated in terms of a twelve-linked chain of causes and effects, the first of which is ignorance. And the ignorance in question will be explained as failure to know three characteristics of reality: impermanence, suffering and non-self. It is thus significant that the Buddha goes on to teach the five renunciants the doctrine of non-self, and moreover that he argues for non-self on the grounds that all the constituents of the person are impermanent. Finally, according to the sūtra that recounts this first teaching, it ended with all five *śramaṇas* attaining enlightenment.

To summarize, in this early episode in the Buddha's teaching career we find reference to the following doctrines and ideas:

- the Dharma as a middle path,
- the eight-fold path,
- the four noble truths,
- the twelve-linked chain of dependent origination,
- the three characteristics of existence.

---

[4]The Buddha's teachings are referred to collectively as the Dharma. (This use of the word is often translated as 'law'; we will encounter other uses of the same Sanskrit term.) The Buddhist tradition refers to the encounter at Sārnāth as 'the first turning of the wheel of the Dharma'.

Let us now look at these in more detail. The doctrine of the four truths plays a central organizing function in the Buddha's teachings, so we should begin there. The first truth, that there is suffering, seems clear enough. And it would be hard to deny that it is true: there is all too much suffering in the world. But this raises the question why the Buddha should have thought it necessary to point it out. In fact, Buddhists claim this truth, properly understood, is among the hardest for most people to acknowledge. This is the first of the four truths because the Buddha thinks it is something about which ordinary people are all in denial. To see why, we need to understand just what is meant here by 'suffering'. And here is where the legend of the four sights becomes relevant. What it tells us is that by this term Buddhists do not mean ordinary pain, such as what we feel when we are injured or sick. Instead they mean existential suffering – the frustration, alienation and despair that result from the realization of our own mortality. Remember that according to the legend, Gautama would not have become a Buddha had he not encountered the facts of old age, disease, decay and death until late in his life. What is it about these facts that makes their recognition significant? Well, we each want our own lives to go well. We want to be happy. And when we want happiness, what we want requires a sense that our lives have meaning, value and purpose. Of course different individuals are made happy by different sorts of things. But when something makes someone happy, that's because they take it to say good things about who they are and where they are going. The difficulty is that once we are forced to acknowledge our own mortality, it becomes difficult to sustain the sense that events can have significance for my life. How can anything contribute to the meaning of my life when in the long run I shall be dead, with the world going merrily on its way without me? Now we all know at some level that some day we will die, yet we still seem to live our lives on the assumption that death can be indefinitely postponed. It is when events show this assumption to be false that existential suffering arises.

Here is one point at which you might think it makes a difference whether or not we accept the doctrine of karma and rebirth. Indeed you might think that the account of existential suffering that has just been given only makes sense if we deny this doctrine. And since the Buddhists accept the doctrine, you might suspect that they must mean something else by 'suffering' than existential suffering, the sense of alienation and despair that comes from recognizing the implications of our mortality. After all, if we live another life after we die, my death can't be the end of me. And if what I do in this life determines what sort of life I get next time around, wouldn't what happens to me now always have meaning for my future existence? So why would existential suffering arise for someone who accepted karma and rebirth? The Buddhist will reply, though, that these suspicions merely illustrate how difficult it can be to grasp the true nature of suffering. The tradition distinguishes among three different layers within the notion of suffering, each more subtle than its predecessor: suffering due to pain, suffering due to impermanence, and suffering due to conditions. It is the last of these that is meant to explain why the fact of rebirth itself constitutes a kind of existential suffering. But to see why Buddhiists think this, we need to say something about the first two ways in which they claim we experience suffering.

The first includes all those experiences that we would ordinarily classify as painful: being cut, burnt or struck, having a toothache or headache, losing a prized possession, not getting the job we'd set our hearts on, and the like. Note that even with such simple cases as a toothache there are actually two levels to the negative nature of the experience. First there is the feeling of pain itself, the immediate sensation of hurting. But there is also the worry that we commonly experience when we have something like a toothache: what does this painful feeling say about who I am and where I am going? Even when we don't put it to ourselves in so many words, this sense of 'dis-ease', of not being at home with ourselves, can permeate our lives when we have some nagging pain, undermining even our enjoyment of ordinary pleasures.[5]

The second form of suffering includes all negative experiences deriving from impermanence. This has much wider scope than one might suspect. As we will later see in more detail, Buddhists claim that everything that originates in dependence on causes must also cease to exist. And since all those things we ordinarily care about are dependent on causes, it follows that they are all impermanent. Now the pain of a toothache could be counted among the experiences that derive from impermanence. We get toothaches because healthy teeth are impermanent. But it is not just getting something we don't want, like a toothache, that is included here. Getting something we do want also comes under the category of suffering as impermanence. Of course it seems counter-intuitive to classify getting what you desire – a car, a job, a child, the esteem of people you care about, happiness for a friend – as a negative experience. But this is why Buddhists call this kind of suffering more subtle than the first. There is suffering in getting what one wants because the desired object is impermanent. So the happiness we feel is always tinged with anxiety about losing it. Indeed the feeling of happiness we derive from getting what we want is itself impermanent. When the novelty wears off, so does the feeling of happiness. Which is why we seem to always be in pursuit of something new. This explains the pattern we follow: always formulating some new goal, some new object of desire, when we get what we previously wanted (or give it up as unattainable). And when we begin to notice this pattern in our behavior, the happiness we feel on obtaining something new begins to drain away.

The last point leads naturally to the third level of suffering, suffering due to conditions. By 'conditions' here is meant the factors that are said to be responsible for rebirth (namely the intentions or volitions that motivate actions and cause karmic fruit). So suffering due to conditions refers to the suffering that results from rebirth. But to revert to the question we asked earlier, why should the mere fact of rebirth

---

[5]'Dis-ease' might be a better translation of the Sanskrit term we are discussing here, *duḥkha,* than is 'suffering'. This term is formed from the prefix *duḥ,* which is related to the English 'dis', plus the noun *kha,* which came to mean 'happiness' or 'ease'.

count as a form of suffering? Some specific rebirths might be quite unpleasant. But if we knew the karmic causal laws, we might be able to avoid those and obtain only rebirths in relatively fortunate circumstances. Why would that still count as suffering? The answer is encapsulated in the fact that re-birth also entails re-death. When we think that rebirth would help us avoid the suffering that is due to our own impermanence (that is, our mortality), we are forgetting that rebirth means re-encountering that very impermanence we wish to escape. Once we take this into account, the prospect no longer seems quite so inviting. Indeed the idea of perpetually going through this cycle – being born, living a life, losing that life and then starting anew – can only inspire a kind of cosmic ennui: what could possibly be the point? What we are now faced with is the requirement that there be an endless succession of future lives in order to sustain the sense that the life I am now living has a point. But if this life gets its point from the next, and that from its successor, and so on, will this really work? Perhaps the doctrine of karma and rebirth, instead of undercutting the claim that sentient beings are subject to suffering, actually reinforces the point.

It might be natural to wonder if the Buddha was not unduly pessimistic. Surely life is not all doom and gloom. And perhaps with a little luck and some good sense, one can live a life that is predominantly characterized by happiness. Of course the Buddhist will respond that this is just what nirvāna amounts to. But the opponent will say that seeking nirvāna seems a rather drastic step. For this requires abandoning much of what is usually thought to give life value: sensual pleasure, wealth and power, and virtue and repute. Surely at least some people can live lives that are happily devoted to such conventional ends as family, career and recreation. The Buddhist will respond that such pursuits can sometimes give pleasure and happiness. Buddhists do not deny that people sometimes experience pleasure and happiness. They claim, though, that pleasure and happiness are deceptive in nature: being in these states leads us to believe that they can be made to endure, when in fact, for the reasons sketched above, they cannot. And in the long run, they claim, those reasons dictate that the happiness one obtains from such pursuits will be outweighed by the suffering. The pursuit of happiness will become a kind of treadmill, and the sense that we are on this treadmill leads to alienation and despair. For anyone who is at all reflective about their life, it is inevitable that the happiness in their life will be outweighed by the suffering.

Here is one last question before we move on: might anti-depressants help? Modern medicine has created a class of drugs designed to help people who have lost all sense of enjoyment in their lives. And the more subtle sense of suffering that we have just been discussing sounds somewhat like this condition. Could a simple pill be an alternative to the arduous task of seeking enlightenment? Here is one possible way the Buddhist might respond to this question. First, they might claim that no pill can alter the facts. Taking a pill might alter how we assess those facts, but that is another matter entirely. For what the pill might actually do is foster an illusion, create the sense that we can continue to ignore those facts. Suppose that by taking an anti-depressant we could avoid the sense that the happiness-seeking project is an endless treadmill. We might then be looking at the same facts that led the Buddha to his analysis of suffering, but we would be seeing those facts in a different light. The Buddhist would claim, though, that our assessment of the facts would be unrealistic. Taking the pill would simply re-instill the illusion that conventional happiness is attainable in the long run. And this, they would hold, is no alternative to facing the facts squarely and taking the appropriate action: seeking nirvāna.[6] It is an interesting question whether the assumption they would then be making is true.[7]

2.3

While the first of the four noble truths points out the existence of suffering, the second is meant to explain how it originates. The underlying idea at work here is that by learning the cause of some phenomenon we may become able to exercise control over it. So the Buddha gives a detailed account of the factors he claims are the conditions in dependence on which suffering arises. This account, the twelve-linked chain of dependent origination, is traditionally understood as describing a sequence that takes place over three successive lives. In one life there occurs (1) ignorance (namely ignorance of the fact that all sentient existence is characterized by impermanence, suffering and non-self), and because of its occurrence there occur (2) volitions (*saṃskāra*), understood as the active forces in karma. It is in dependence on these volitions in the one life that there occurs (3) consciousness in the next life. That is, rebirth (in the form of the first moment of consciousness in a new life) occurs because of the desires that led to the performance of actions in the past life. On this consciousness in turn depends the occurrence of (4) a sentient body. That is, it is due to that first moment of rebirth consciousness that the organized matter of the fetal body comes to be a sentient being. On the existence of the sentient body in turn depend (5) the six organs of sense (the organs of the five external senses plus an 'inner sense' that is aware of inner states such as pain). On these depend (6) contact or sensory stimulation. And given sensory stimulation there arises (7) feeling, that is, the hedonic states of pleasure, pain and indifference. Feeling in turn causes (8) desire, and desire leads to (9) appropriation (*upādāna*), the attitude whereby one takes certain

---

[6]This is not to deny that anti-depressants can be genuinely helpful for those suffering from clinical depression. The Buddhist claims that the happiness-seeking project cannot be sustained in the long run. While this might seem like a depressing analysis, remember that they also claim there is a better alternative to that project, namely nirvāna. And they think we should make the effort to seek that better alternative. Someone who is clinically depressed might not be capable of making such an effort. Their sense of the futility of it all might render them unable to do anything to better their situation. A Buddhist might then say that anti-depressants would be useful in their case.

[7]Assume that by taking a pill one could permanently prevent the subtle sense of suffering from arising. Assume as well that the Buddha's analysis is correct, that the happiness-seeking project really is an endless treadmill. Would it actually be better to not take the pill, face up to the facts, and seek nirvāna? The Buddhist claims it would be, but why? What assumption would their answer seem to be based on? And is that assumption correct?

things as being 'me' or 'mine'. In dependence on appropriation there originates (10) becoming. This consists of the volitions that bring about the next rebirth, as well as the psychophysical elements making up the sentient body in that rebirth. In dependence on this there is (11) birth, that is, rebirth into the third life. And in dependence on birth there is (12) old age and death, here standing for all existential suffering.

There are obviously some difficulties in this list. For instance the tenth condition, becoming, seems to involve a repetition of the second, volition, and the fourth, sentient body. It also seems odd that birth into the third life should be listed as a separate condition, while birth into the second life is not. There is another version of the list that omits the six organs of sense, and instead has the sentient body serve as the condition for consciousness. Since consciousness has already been said to be the condition for sentient body, this has the effect of making consciousness both the cause and the effect of sentient body.[8] And there are versions of the list with only ten links, omitting the first two conditions altogether. These and other problems have led some scholars to suggest that our list of twelve results from the fusion of what were originally two or more separate lists.

But let us put such questions to one side, and look instead at the basic logic underlying the list that we have. The idea seems to be this. One is born into this life because in the last life one acted on the basis of volitions that were formed in ignorance of the facts about our existence. Having been born with a body, senses and mind, one comes in contact with sense objects, and this cognitive contact brings about feelings of pleasure, pain and indifference. These feelings trigger desires, and desires that are conditioned by ignorance lead to the stance known as appropriation: taking certain things (including things that no longer exist or do not yet exist) as 'me', and other things as 'mine' or my possessions. It is this stance that fuels rebirth, and this produces the suffering that is associated with all sentient existence.

How, one might wonder, could the first condition, ignorance, occur without there already being a sentient being (something that is not found until the fourth link in the series)? Doesn't ignorance require someone whose ignorance it is? When we wonder this, we are taking this list as an account of the very beginning of the series of lives. But the list should not be taken this way. What is here treated as the first life in a sequence of three is itself the effect of prior conditions that occurred in some yet earlier life.[9] So it is not saying that ignorance occurred before there were mind and

---

[8]It is this version of the list that will later lead some Abhidharma philosophers to hold that two simultaneously existing things can be both cause and effect of one another. This notion of reciprocal causation will become the center of some Abhidharma controversies.

[9]The Buddha says that we cannot discern the very first life in the series of lives we have lived. In the later tradition this is often taken to mean that the series of lives (and so our ignorance as well) is beginningless. But the Buddha's statement might be interpreted another way: while there might have been a very first life in the series, we could never tell which one that is. For it's always possible that although there were earlier lives, we simply can't remember any. Given this difficulty, it is pointless to speculate about whether there is or is not a first life in the series, and what might explain this. Suffering exists in the present life, and such speculation won't help solve that problem.

body. Ignorance comes first on the list because of its key role in producing suffering. In effect what we have in this theory is an account of how ignorance, by bringing about suffering, reinforces and thus perpetuates itself. When the chain of dependent origination is seen in this way, it is even possible to separate it from the doctrine of karma and rebirth. What it then amounts to is basically just the claim that the ignorance occurring at any one point in one's life causes one to act in certain ways that set the stage for both later suffering and continued ignorance.

The third truth, that there is the cessation of suffering, follows directly from the second truth. Ignorance is a remediable condition. Since it is possible to cure our ignorance, it is possible to put an end to the feedback loop that results in suffering. The fourth truth then spells out a set of eight practices that are designed to bring about this cure. They are: right view, right intention, right speech, right action, right livelihood, right exertion, right self-possession and right concentration. These eight are said to fall into three basic kinds: the first two represent wisdom, the next three are the factors of morality, and the final three are the practices that make up meditation. The factors are listed in a way that might suggest a sequential order: start with right view, follow the rules of right conduct, proceed to concentration, then attain nirvāna. But in actual practice the different factors are said to mutually reinforce one another, so that the mastery of each will involve contributions from the others. For instance, one might begin by acquiring a rudimentary grasp of the basic teachings of the Buddha (right view), on that basis form the (right) intention to seek nirvāna, and then set about trying to obey the moral rules set out for lay followers, such as not lying (right speech), not stealing (right action) and not working as a butcher (right livelihood). But when following these moral rules becomes habitual, this has the effect of clearing the mind of certain passions that can interfere with attaining wisdom. So this can lead to a deeper appreciation of the Buddha's teachings (right view), followed by the (right) intention to become a monk or nun. Entrance into the order of Buddhist monks and nuns (the *saṃgha*) brings with it a new set of moral virtues one must acquire. Practice in accordance with these virtues, along with the newly deepened understanding of the Dharma, helps one then begin to engage in meditation. But meditating also makes it easier to attain the required moral virtues. And meditation likewise produces insights into the nature of the mind that further strengthen one's appreciation of the Dharma. And so on.

For our purposes the reciprocal relation between wisdom and meditation is particularly significant. In the context of the Buddhist path, 'wisdom' means the practice of philosophy: analyzing concepts, investigating arguments, considering objections, and the like. So the content of this 'wisdom' is just the Buddhist philosophy that we are examining here. Now we already know that Buddhists claim ignorance is ultimately responsible for our suffering. And wisdom looks like the antidote to ignorance. So it makes sense that Buddhism should claim doing philosophy is necessary for attaining enlightenment. But will doing philosophy be sufficient? Buddhists generally say no. And it's not too difficult to guess why this is. For we also know something about what this ignorance supposedly consists in: the failure to recognize the three characteristics, the facts of impermanence, suffering and non-self. This failure is exhibited in some fundamental assumptions we make about our lives: that we and the things we want can continue to exist indefinitely, that we can attain happiness by pursuing conventional goals, and that there is a true 'me' for whom this life can have meaning and value. Since almost everything we do is based on these assumptions, we are constantly in the business of reinforcing them. So even if our philosophical practice tells us they are false, it may not be so easy to uproot them. The situation here is like the case of a smoker. They may know perfectly well that smoking shortens their life. But each cigarette smoked reinforces their addiction, making it harder to act on that knowledge. So, the Buddhist says, meditation is needed in order to break the cycle and bring home the knowledge gained through philosophy.

To learn to meditate is to learn to control the mind. That control is then used to examine various mental processes, and to counteract those processes that perpetuate ignorance and suffering. So through meditation one can supposedly confirm that there is no self, by observing how impermanent mental states actually do all the work that we imagine could only be done by an enduring self. We can also see how certain mental states, such as anger and hatred, can reinforce belief in a self and thus perpetuate ignorance. And through meditation we can learn to counteract such states. In the case of anger and hatred, for instance, the adept is taught to cultivate feelings of kindness and sympathetic joy toward ever larger circles of beings, starting with friends and loved ones and eventually extending to those toward whom they feel anger and enmity. So meditation serves as a necessary supplement to philosophy in Buddhist practice. (This is why, even if the Buddhist philosophers are right about things, studying Buddhist philosophy wouldn't bring about liberation by itself.)

At the same time, doing philosophy is said to be necessary if the practice of meditation is to be effective. For one thing, many meditational attainments involve altered states of consciousness. What one is aware of in these states is very different from what goes on in our ordinary experience. This means that we need a conceptual framework to help us sort out our experiences in meditation and figure out their significance. Otherwise we would be confronted with what could only seem like a buzzing, whirring mass of confusion. Doing philosophy is said to help us acquire the conceptual tools we need to make sense of what we encounter in meditation. So, for instance, mastery of the philosophical arguments for the non-existence of a self will make it easier to appreciate the significance of the complex causal connections we find when we closely observe our mental processes. That there are these causal connections will then be seen to confirm that there is no self standing behind the scenes directing our mental lives. And this will bring home the truth of non-self as it applies to our own case. So while meditation is meant to help the practitioner apply the knowledge they acquire through philosophy, philosophy in turn plays an important role in facilitating meditational practice.

Just as there are interesting relationships among the components of the eight-fold path, so it is worthwhile to examine how the three characteristics are related to one another. Suffering is caused, we are told, by ignorance of impermanence, suffering and non-self. And it is overcome by coming to know fully these three facts about the world. We now have some understanding of what Buddhists mean by the truth of suffering. Suppose they are right in their claims about what suffering is and why it is inevitable. They also claim that everything is impermanent, and that sentient beings are devoid of selves. Suppose these claims are also true. What might they have to do with the claim about suffering? It is tempting to think that impermanence is the chief factor here. On this interpretation, it is the fact that everything is impermanent that makes it true both that suffering is inevitable and also that there is no self. On this account, we wrongly believe that the things we desire are permanent, we become attached to them, and then we suffer when they reveal their impermanence by going out of existence. Likewise we base our lives on the assumption that we have permanent selves, and then suffer when our mortality shows this assumption to be false. The solution is then to learn to live with the fact of impermanence. Suffering will cease when we stop clinging to things and learn to live in the moment.

While this interpretation of the three characteristics is tempting, it is wrong. It is the truth of non-self that is said to be key to understanding suffering's genesis and dissolution. And the interpretation just offered does not take sufficiently seriously the fact of non-self. For what it assumes is that I do have a self, just a very impermanent one. This is the assumption behind the advice that we live our lives in the present moment. This advice would make sense only if there were a true 'me' that could derive value and significance from its experiences, but that existed only for a short while, to be replaced by a new self, someone who is not 'me' but someone else. We are advised to live in the present precisely because it is thought that when we plan for the future instead, we are letting the interests of that future self dictate what this present self does. Now while Buddhism is sometimes understood in this way, this is clearly incompatible with the claim that there is no self. Indeed this turns out to be one of the extreme views the Dharma is supposed to be a middle path between.[10] So this cannot be how to understand the three characteristics.

The doctrine of non-self is widely acknowledged to be the most difficult of all the basic teachings of Buddhism. We will examine it in detail in the next chapter. But we can now say this much about its relation to the other two of the three characteristics. Recall that by 'suffering' what Buddhists mean is existential suffering. And existential suffering arises from the assumption that there is a 'me' for whom events can have significance. Such suffering arises out of the suspicion that the kind of meaning we want is not to be had, that our best efforts at attaining happiness will inevitably be frustrated. And we experience suffering because this seems like such an affront to the dignity of the being we take ourselves to be. Now suppose it could be

---

[10]This is what is called 'annihilationism', the view that while I exist now, when the parts that presently make up me cease to exist, I will go utterly out of existence, typically to be replaced by someone else. The other extreme view is called 'eternalism'. It is the view that the true 'me' is eternal. The theory of dependent origination is said to constitute a middle path between these two extremes.

shown that while there are the experiences that make up a lifetime, those experiences have no owner. There is no 'me' whose experiences they are. In that case the conviction that my life should have uniquely special significance to me would turn out to be based on a mistake. For experiences in my life to have meaning, there must be more than just the experiences, there must be something separate from them for which they have good or bad meanings. Without belief in a separate self, existential suffering would no longer arise. Such suffering requires belief in something whose demand for meaning and significance is violated. It requires belief in a self. Impermanence also plays a role here. It is the fact of impermanence that first awakens us to suffering. And the fact that everything is impermanent will play a major role in the arguments for non-self. But it is non-self that plays the central role. And it is our false belief in a self that Buddhists identify as the core of our ignorance.

2.4

What might it be like to be enlightened? The Buddha claims that at the end of his path lies the cessation of suffering. And we've just had a glimpse of how following the path might bring that about. But even if we can make some sense of his path as a cure for suffering, this only tells us what being enlightened is not like. Being enlightened would mean being without existential suffering. Is there anything positive to be said about it? Is it pleasant? Is the enlightened person happy? Or is it just that because it's devoid of suffering, it's the best we can hope for? This would be a reasonable question to ask for someone considering whether or not to follow the Buddha's advice. The 'live for the moment' idea that was just rejected as an interpretation of the three characteristics did at least give an answer to this question. For then the enlightened person would appreciate their present experiences without any concern about what will come in the future. And perhaps this would enhance the enjoyment of any good experiences while diminishing the anxiety that normally accompanies bad experiences. So perhaps on that interpretation being enlightened would be pleasant. But since that is not what Buddhist enlightenment is like, this does not answer our question.

Here is another place where the doctrine of karma and rebirth has a role to play. To become enlightened is to enter into the state of nirvāna. The Sanskrit term *nirvāṇa* literally means 'extinction' or 'going out' (as when a fire is said to go out). What gets extinguished is, of course, suffering. But Buddhists sometimes equate this extinction with another sort, namely the end of the series of rebirths. What would that be like? Well, if there is no self, then to say I won't be reborn is to say I will cease to exist. Is this what nirvāna is, utter and complete annihilation? If so, then our question is answered in the negative: enlightenment would have no positive result, only the purely negative one of escape from all further suffering. And since this escape looks like a state of pure non-being, an utter blank, it also seems singularly unappealing.

That there is something wrong with this understanding of nirvāna is suggested by the fact that one of the extreme views the Buddha rejects is called 'annihilationism'. Moreover, when the Buddha is asked about the fate of the enlightened person after death, he says it would not be correct to say they are utterly non-existent. But the explication of these claims will have to wait until Chapter 4. What we can say at this point is that there is more to nirvāna than what happens after the death of an enlightened person. There is also the state of the person between the time of enlightenment and their death. In discussing the goal of their practice, Buddhists draw a distinction between 'cessation with remainder' and 'cessation without remainder'. By 'cessation' is meant stopping the accumulation of new karma. And the 'remainder' is the residual karma that keeps the present life going. Once that residue is exhausted, this life ends. So they distinguish between nirvāna as the state of a living enlightened person, and nirvāna as the state of the enlightened person after death.[11] If we want to know if there is anything positive to the state of nirvāna, the place to look would seem to be this cessation with remainder.

Unfortunately, there isn't much in the early Buddhist texts about this state. There is a great deal about how to attain cessation, but not much about what it is like to have attained it and remain alive. Artistic depictions of the Buddha and other enlightened persons often portray them with a serene half-smile on their faces, and this suggests that there is a kind of quiet happiness to the state. But this is not stated explicitly in our sources. Buddhists were not, though, the only Indian philosophers to teach the goal of liberation from rebirth. And among the non-Buddhists there is also a debate as to whether or not liberation is pleasant or joyful. Now this debate concerns post-mortem liberation. It is possible for these schools to have such a debate because they all affirm the existence of a self. So unlike the Buddhists, they all claim that the liberated person continues to exist when their last life is over. Some, though, claim that the self enjoys eternal bliss in this state of post-mortem liberation, while others deny this. Indeed some of the latter go so far as to say that the self feels nothing in this state, that its existence forever after is indistinguishable from that of a rock.

Now all the parties to this debate agree that liberation is the supreme goal for humans. They also agree that ignorance about who we truly are is what keeps us in the unliberated state – by making us pursue inappropriate goals like sensual pleasure, wealth and power, and virtue and repute. Since they all seem to mean more or less the same thing by liberation, this makes us wonder why some would deny that the supremely valuable end has any intrinsically desirable features. Why would they expect anyone to seek a state whose only attraction lies in the absence of pain and suffering? If that were all that was being offered, wouldn't most people figure they could beat the odds and stick with the strategy of seeking ordinary happiness?

This is not a question that can be definitively answered by examining the texts of these orthodox schools. But a bit of speculation might throw some light on the situation here, and in so doing suggest an answer to our question about Buddhist

---

[11]This is sometimes referred to as *parinirvāna*, though strictly speaking that term only applies to the death of a Buddha.

nirvāna. Suppose that, as the *Bhagavad Gītā* says, 'desire is here the enemy' (III.37). That is, what keeps us bound to the wheel of *saṃsāra* (the state of perpetual rebirth and consequently suffering) is our desire for things like sensual pleasure, wealth and power, and virtue and repute. Desire for these things is thought problematic because it is based on the false assumption that I am something that could be made better off by having them. Further, suppose that were it not for such desires, and the ignorance about our identity that they both presuppose and reinforce, we would be in a state that is intrinsically valuable. Suppose, that is, that to be liberated from *saṃsāra* is to enjoy true happiness, perhaps even true bliss. There then arises what we could call the paradox of liberation. This paradox involves the following propositions, each of which seems true to the orthodox Indian philosophers:

1   Liberation is inherently desirable.
2   Selfish desires prevent us from attaining liberation.
3   In order to attain liberation one must train oneself to live without selfish desires.
4   One does not engage in deliberate action unless one desires the foreseen result of the action.

Taken together, propositions (3) and (4) tell us that no one will set about trying to attain liberation unless they desire it. And proposition (2) tells us that no one will attain liberation unless they seek it. Liberation isn't something people just fall into through dumb luck: you have to make an effort to overcome ignorance, otherwise it will just perpetuate your bondage in *saṃsāra*. Putting these things together, we get the result that you have to desire liberation to obtain it. And (1) tells us that it's reasonable to desire liberation. The trouble is, (2) also tells us that if we desire liberation we won't get it. So although it's reasonable to want liberation, it's impossible to get it, so it isn't reasonable to want it after all. This is a paradox.

There are different strategies we might use to try to resolve this paradox. We might deny (1), though that would then raise the question why anyone should be interested in attaining liberation. Or we might claim that the desire for liberation is not a selfish desire. But this seems implausible if (1) is true. If liberation is such a good thing, then surely my wanting to attain it would count as a selfish desire – a desire to benefit myself. Perhaps, though, not all such desires are selfish in the sense that's relevant for (2) to apply. Remember that the trouble with desires is that they reinforce the wrong view about who we really are. What if liberation were joyful in a way that didn't conflict with the facts about who we really are? The difficulty is that even if this were true, those of us who have not experienced this bliss would have trouble thinking of it in anything other than conventional terms. When told that liberation is a state of bliss, we would imagine it to be like sensual pleasure, or the thrill that can come from gaining great wealth and power. We would then end up desiring liberation in just the wrong way – the way that (2) says prevents our attaining it. But this suggests a possible strategy: deny (1) not because it is false but because it is misleading for those with conventional views about what is desirable. For such people what should be emphasized is not what is positively good about liberation, but the point that to be liberated is to be forever free of pain and suffering. Then they might attain the bliss of liberation without having aimed at it. Their desire would just have been to rid themselves of pain and suffering.

There are situations where this sort of indirect strategy works. Consider the warm feeling we get when we act benevolently, doing something good for someone else. We get this feeling of gratification when our aim is to help others instead of ourselves. But suppose the only reason I ever helped others were because I wanted to have this warm feeling. Then I would never succeed. If my helping someone else were part of a calculated strategy whose ultimate purpose was to benefit myself, I wouldn't get the warm feeling at all. I can't get the feeling by aiming at it. I only get the feeling when I aim at something else – benefitting another person. Does this mean there is a paradox of benevolence? No, we can and do sometimes act benevolently, and thereby get the warm feeling. The best advice to give someone who wants to feel good in this way is that they should become genuinely concerned about the welfare of others. And this is something we can learn to do. We can get the warm feeling indirectly – not by aiming at it but by aiming at something else. There is no paradox of benevolence.

Could something like this be what's going on in the case of those orthodox Indian schools that denied liberation is pleasant or happy? Perhaps they are simply tailoring their advice to the understanding of their audience. Perhaps because their audience would misunderstand the happiness that comes with liberation, and then want it in a way that would prevent their ever getting it, these schools advise their audience to aim at something else, the cessation of suffering. And perhaps we should understand what early Buddhism says about nirvāna in a similar way. On this interpretation, the fact that nirvāna is depicted primarily negatively, as just the permanent cessation of suffering, and the fact that virtually nothing positive is ever said about cessation with remainder, represent strategic choices. They do not necessarily reflect the nature of nirvāna. Perhaps cessation with remainder is a state of true happiness, though this is importantly different from what is ordinarily taken for happiness.

Something like this interpretation may be necessary if the Buddha's path is going to make sense to those who don't accept the doctrine of karma and rebirth. If there is no rebirth, but the Buddha is right that there is no self, then after I die there won't be any suffering regardless of whether or not I attain enlightenment. So telling me that cessation without remainder is devoid of suffering won't motivate me to try to attain enlightenment. I'll only be motivated by facts about cessation with remainder, the state of being enlightened but still alive. And it isn't clear that being told this state is devoid of all existential suffering would be enough. If that were all I thought I'd get out of enlightenment, I might calculate the odds and decide that I'd do better to pursue conventional happiness. It might be that only a positive portrayal of enlightenment as true happiness would motivate me to seek it. And then there is the question whether my desire for enlightenment would get in the way of my ever attaining it. But this is a question to which we will have to return. For we have not yet considered what it might be like to come to believe that we do not have selves. And coming to believe this is an important component of being enlightened. The Buddhist doctrine of non-self will be the subject of our next chapter. Then in Chapter 4 we will come back to this question of what it might be like to be enlightened.

Further Reading

For more on the details of the Buddha's life and teaching career see Chapters 3 and 4 of A.K.Warder, *Indian Buddhism* (Delhi: Motilal Banarsidass, 1970).

The account of the Buddha's first expounding of his path (S IV.420–4) may be found at *The Connected Discourses of the Buddha,* trans. Bhikkhu Bodhi (Boston, MA: Wisdom Publications, 2000), pp. 1843–47.

For a more detailed account of the reciprocal relationships among the different parts of the eightfold path, see David Burton, *Buddhism, Knowledge and Liberation* (Aldershot, UK: Ashgate, 2004), pp. 62–75.

For a very different account of the nature of cessation with remainder see Paul Griffiths, *On Being Buddha* (Albany, NY: SUNY Press, 1994).

For a discussion of the debate among Hindu schools concerning whether liberation is desirable, see Arindam Chakrabarti, 'Is liberation (*mokṣa*) pleasant?'. *Philosophy East and West*, 33 (1983), pp. 167–82.

The alleged paradox of benevolence, and its resolution, were formulated by the eighteenth-century British philosopher and theologian Joseph Butler. For a discussion of Butler's work see Terence Penelhum, *Butler* (London: Routledge, 1986).

CHAPTER THREE

Non-Self: Empty Persons

The Buddha holds that we experience the suffering of *saṃsāra* because of our ignorance of the three characteristics: impermanence, suffering and non-self. Of these three, it is the characteristic of non-self that plays the central role in his diagnosis. According to early Buddhism, there is no self, and persons are not ultimately real. This may be put somewhat cryptically as: we are empty persons, persons who are empty of selves. In this chapter we will investigate this claim. We will look at some of the arguments found in early Buddhist texts for the claim that there is no self. And we shall try to determine what it means to say that persons are not ultimately real. But before we can do either of these things we need to determine what it would mean to say that there is a self. The word 'self' gets used in several different ways, only one of which is relevant to the philosophical question the Buddha is trying to answer. We can avoid much confusion about what Buddhists mean by their doctrine of non-self if we begin by getting clear concerning what they mean when they speak of a self.

3.1

By 'the self' what Buddhists mean is the essence of a person – the one part whose continued existence is required for that person to continue to exist. This is the definition of 'self' that we will use. But what does it mean? It might be helpful to think of the view that there is a self as one possible answer to the question what it is that the word 'I' refers to. I am a person. And persons are made up of a variety of constituents: parts making up the body, such as limbs and organs, and parts making up the mind, such as feelings and desires. Now persons are things that continue to exist for some time – at least a lifetime, if not longer. But not all the parts of a person must continue to exist in order for that person to continue to exist. I could survive the loss of a finger or toe. And I might lose my desire for coffee without ceasing to exist. So apparently not all the parts of a person are necessary to the continued existence of a person. To say there is a self is to say that there is some one part that is necessary. This one part would then be what the word 'I' really named. The other parts would more properly be called 'mine'; only that one essential part would count as the true 'me'. The alternative to this would be to say that 'I' refers to all the parts collectively. Let us call this alternative the view that 'I' is the name of the person, where by 'person' we mean the whole that consists of all the parts that make up my body and mind over the duration of my existence. So either 'I' is the name of some one essential part of the person or else it refers to the person as a whole. (Of course this applies to the other words we use to refer to persons as well, such as names.)

To say there is a self is to say that there is some one part of the person that accounts for the identity of that person over time. If there were a self, then the person whose self it was would continue to exist as long as that self continued to exist. The self would then be the basis of a person's identity over time. It would be what explained why this present person, me, is the same person as some earlier person. But we need to be careful with the expression 'same person'. For the English word 'same' is ambiguous. When we say 'x and y are the same', there are two things we might mean. We could mean that x and y are qualitatively identical, or we could mean that x and y are numerically identical. To say that x and y are qualitatively identical is to say that they share the same qualities, that they resemble one another or are alike. To say that x and y are numerically identical is to say that they are one and the same thing, that 'x' and 'y' are really just two names for one entity. So there can be cases of qualitative identity but numerical distinctness, as with two t-shirts that come out of the factory looking exactly alike. And there can also be cases of numerical identity but qualitative distinctness, as with a leaf that in summer is green and smooth but in autumn is red and crinkled. We said above that according to the self-theorist, a self is what explains why some person existing now is the same person as someone who existed earlier. The key thing to keep in mind is that here 'same' is meant in the sense of numerical identity.[1]

Like many other things, persons can undergo very significant qualitative changes and yet continue to exist. I can continue to exist as one and the same person, me, even though the properties I now have are quite different from those I used to have. Thanks to the ambiguity of the English word 'same', we can put this as, 'He is the same person but not the same.' When we say this we are not contradicting ourselves. The first 'same' ('the same person') is used in the sense of numerical identity. The second 'same' is used in the sense of qualitative identity; 'not the same' means qualitatively distinct. It is one person, me, who once had the property of liking coffee, but now has the very different property of disliking coffee. A person can undergo qualitative change while retaining numerical identity. Since the self is supposed to be what explains numerical identity over time of persons, perhaps a self could undergo qualitative change. What it could not undergo is numerical change, that is, going out of existence and being replaced by another self.

If there is a self, it is 'what makes me me', 'the true me', that which 'gives me my identity'. These ways of describing what a self is are all open to a common misinterpretation. People often speak of 'discovering their self', of 'finding their true identity'. What they often mean by this is figuring out which characteristics seem

---

[1]The ambiguity of 'same' is often resolved by context. When we say 'x and y are the same P', what is meant is numerical identity. When we say 'x and y are the same', what is often meant is qualitative identity. So I might say that this is *the same leaf* as the one I showed you yesterday, meaning that they are one and the same leaf. Or I might say that this leaf is *the same* as the one that was on this branch last year, meaning that the two leaves are qualitatively identical. Other languages lack this ambiguity. In German, for instance, one says *das selbe* for numerical identity, and *das gleiche* for qualitative identity.

most important or valuable. So someone might say that they have come to realize their identity isn't tied up with physical appearance but with less superficial things like artistic talent or communication skills. Discoveries like this are probably important to personal growth. But they have nothing to do with what the Buddhists mean by a self. We can see this from the fact that even if there is no self, we can still ask which of a person's characteristics are most important to that person's happiness. To speak of a self is to speak of some one part of the person, the part that must always exist as long as the person exists. To speak of an 'identity' that can be 'found' is to speak of characteristics or properties, of what a person is like. There might very well be no single part of the person that must continue to exist in order for that person to continue to exist. (This is exactly what the Buddha is going to argue for.) But it might still be true that some characteristics of a person play a more important role in their life than others. Otherwise it wouldn't make sense to say that a person has 'lost their identity'. Perhaps my life would be less meaningful if I were to lose those traits that now have great importance to me. But it would still be my life. I could survive that qualitative change. I might be a very different kind of person. But I would still be me.

There is another misinterpretation that arises in connection with the idea that the self is what gives me my 'identity'. It is common to think that someone's identity is what sets that person apart from all others. Add to this the idea that one's identity consists in what one is like, one's characteristics or properties. The result is the notion that a self would be what makes one different from everyone else. Now the word 'different' is ambiguous in the same way that 'same' is: there is numerical difference or distinctness, and there is qualitative difference. If it's numerical distinctness that is meant, then it's true that the self would be what makes one different from others. If we have selves, then my self and yours must be two distinct things, not one. But it's not true if what's meant by 'different' is qualitative difference. It is not true that if we had selves, each would have to be unique in the sense of being unlike every other. Two selves could be perfectly alike, like two peas in a pod, and still serve to make one person numerically distinct from another.

The difficulty with the idea that the self must be qualitatively unique is that it once again confuses the notion of the self with the notion of what one is like, one's properties or characteristics. And properties may be shared between two things, whereas numerical identity may not. The leaf on this branch of this tree today might be exactly like the leaf that was here last year – same color, same shape, same pattern of veins, etc. But they are numerically distinct leaves all the same. Perhaps no two persons are ever exactly qualitatively alike. Even twins who share DNA patterns have physical differences, such as different fingerprints. Still there is no contradiction involved in supposing that there might be two persons who are exactly qualitatively alike. Imagine for instance that each of us has lived countless lives in the past. Given the innumerably many beings there may be in the universe, it does not seem unlikely that someone somewhere might once have lived a life just like the one I am now living. Yet that would have been someone else, not me. So if what makes me the person I am is my self, then my self is not what makes me qualitatively unlike other people.

Suppose, moreover, that each person is qualitatively unlike every other. This could be true even if there were no selves. Indeed it could be true if there were selves that were all qualitatively identical. This is actually something that many non-Buddhist Indian philosophers hold. On their view, the self is something that is simple or impartite (lacking parts). The self is just the subject of experiences, the part of us that is aware of the different experiences we have. Your self and mine would then be just like those two peas in a pod. It's common to suppose that what makes different people qualitatively different is that they have different experiences. But on this view of the self, the different experiences that people have would not make their selves qualitatively different. Since the self is simple, it cannot be changed by the experiences it is aware of. It is other parts of the person that are changed by those experiences. The experience of eating changes the shape of my body. The experience of smelling coffee changes a desire in my mind. My self is unaffected by these changes, it is simply aware of them. Someone holding this view of the self who also thought that persons are qualitatively unique could say that their uniqueness is explained by facts about those parts of the person that are not the self. Someone who denied the existence of a self could explain the qualitative uniqueness of persons in the same way.

3.2

In order to show that the self does not exist, we need to know what we are looking for, and where to look. We now know that a self would be that part of the person that 'I' is consistently used to refer to. So we can tell what to look for by seeing how we actually use words like 'I'. For instance, we say things like 'I was born in New York, now live in the Midwest, and will move to Arizona when I retire.' So if 'I' refers to the self, the self would have to be some one numerically identical thing that continues to exist throughout the past, present and future history of the person. There are more clues to be found in the ways we use this word, but this tells us enough for present purposes. Where should we look? Since the self is supposed to be a part of the person, we obviously need to look among the parts that make up persons. It would be helpful if we had a list of the basic categories of person-parts. This is just what the Buddha provides with his doctrine of the five *skandhas*. (The word *skandha* is here used in its sense of 'bundle'.) These are:

- *Rūpa*: anything corporeal or physical;[2]

---

[2]The literal meaning of *rūpa* is 'form' or 'shape', and you will sometimes see the word rendered as 'form' in translations of Buddhist texts. But as the name of the first *skandha*, *rūpa* actually means 'that which has form or shape', that is, anything material or physical. This is one case where it's best to stick with the Sanskrit original rather than try to come up with an acceptable English translation.

- Feeling: sensations of pleasure, pain and indifference;
- Perception: those mental events whereby one grasps the sensible character-istics of a perceptible object; e.g., the seeing of a patch of blue color, the hearing of the sound of thunder;
- Volition: the mental forces responsible for bodily and mental activity, for example, hunger, attentiveness, and
- Consciousness: the awareness of physical and mental states.

A word of caution is necessary concerning these categories. Their names are here being used as technical terms, with precise definitions. Do not confuse these with the ordinary meanings of these words. For instance, the second *skandha*, feeling, refers only to the three kinds of hedonic sensation: pleasure, pain and indifference (neither pleasure nor pain). It does not include most of the things that are often called 'feelings', such as the emotions of anger and jealousy. Those emotions go under the very different *skandha* of volition. Likewise by 'consciousness' is here meant just the awareness itself, and not what it is that one is aware of. So when I am conscious of a pain sensation, there are two *skandhas* involved: the pain, which goes under feeling *skandha*, and the consciousness that is aware of it, which goes under consciousness *skandha*. Again, we sometimes use the word 'perception' to refer to our beliefs about and attitude toward something. So someone might say, 'My perception of the new government is that it is weak and will soon fall.' This is not the sort of thing that would go under perception *skandha*. This is a complex mental state, whereas an instance of perception *skandha* is a simple mental event. A perception in this technical sense is just the occurrence of a sensory content to the mind: the simple thought of a patch of blue or the smell of lemon.

The five *skandhas* are sometimes referred to collectively as *nāma-rāpa* (sometimes translated as 'name and form'). Here *nāma* refers to the four *skandhas* other than *rūpa*. The literal meaning of *nāma* is 'name', but here it means 'that which can only be named'. The idea is that while *rūpa* can be perceived by the external senses, the members of the four other categories cannot be seen or touched. Because they are not publicly observable, we cannot explain what they are by pointing; we can only communicate about them through the names we have learned to use for these private states. What this tells us is that the doctrine of the five *skandhas* expresses a kind of mind-body dualism. The Buddha is claiming that in addition to those parts of the person that we can see and touch – the parts of the body – there are other constituents that are not themselves physical. Some philosophers today hold the view called 'physicalism', according to which all that exists is physical. On this view there is no more to a person than the physical constituents, their body and brain. What we think of as mental events, such as thoughts and emotions, are really just complex brain events. When the Buddha says that in addition to *rūpa skandha* there are the four *nāma skandhas*, he is in effect denying that physicalism is true. On his account, mental events are separate non-physical kinds of things. We will be looking at this claim more carefully later on.

The Buddha uses the doctrine of the five *skandhas* as a tool in his search for a self. He goes through each *skandha* in turn and tries to show that nothing included in that category could count as a self. But this raises a new question: would this really show that there is no self? Isn't it possible that the self exists elsewhere than among the five *skandhas*? In order for the Buddha's strategy to work, he will have to show that the doctrine of the five *skandhas* gives an exhaustive analysis of the parts of the person. We will call this the 'exhaustiveness claim'.

The exhaustiveness claim is this: every constituent of persons is included in one or more of the five *skandhas*.

In the following passage, the later commentator Buddhaghosa argues in support of this claim.

> The basis for the figment of a self or of anything related to a self, is afforded only by these, namely *rūpa* and the rest. For it has been said as follows:
> > When there is *rūpa*, O monks, then through attachment to *rūpa*, through engrossment in *rūpa*, the persuasion arises, 'This is mine; this am I; this is my self.'
> > When there is feeling ... when there is perception ... when there are volitions ... when there is consciousness, O monks, then through attachment to consciousness, through engrossment in consciousness, the persuasion arises, 'This is mine; this am I; this is my self.'
> Accordingly he laid down only five skandhas, because it is only these that can afford a basis for the figment of a self or of anything related to a self.
> As to other groups which he lays down, such as the five of conduct and the rest, these are included, for they are comprised in volition skandha. Accordingly he laid down only five skandhas, because these include all other classifications. After this manner, therefore, is the conclusion reached that there are no less and no more. [VM xiv.218]

This at least makes clear that Buddhists recognize the need to support the exhaustiveness claim. But it is not clear how good an argument this is. The idea seems to be that these are the only things we are aware of when we are aware of persons and so come to believe that persons have selves. Is this true? And if it were true, would it show that the exhaustiveness claim is true? We will return to this question.

3.3

Let us now look at how the Buddha formulates his arguments for non-self. In the following passage the Buddha is addressing his five former companion *śramaṇas*, in the episode we discussed in Chapter 2. It contains two distinct arguments. The first is what we will call the argument from impermanence, since it is based on the claim that all five *skandhas* are impermanent or transitory. But there is also a second argument here.

> Then The Blessed One addressed the band of five *śramanas*:
> '*Rūpa*, O monks, is not a self. For if now, O monks, this *rūpa* were a self, then this *rūpa* would not tend towards destruction, and it would be possible to say of *rūpa*, "Let my *rūpa* be this way; let not my *rūpa* be that way!" But inasmuch, O monks, as *rūpa* is not a self, therefore does *rūpa* tend towards destruction, and it is not possible to say of *rūpa*, "Let my *rūpa* be this way; let not my *rūpaa* be that way!"
> 'Feeling ... perception ... volitions ... consciousness, is not a self. For if now, O monks, this consciousness were a self, then would not this consciousness tend towards destruction, and it would be possible to say of consciousness, "Let my consciousness be this way; let not my consciousness be that way!" But inasmuch, O monks, as consciousness is not a self, therefore does consciousness tend towards destruction, and it is not possible to say of consciousness, "Let my consciousness be this way; let not my consciousness be that way!"
> 'What do you think, O monks? Is *rūpa* permanent, or transitory?'
> 'It is transitory, Reverend Sir.'
> 'And that which is transitory – is it painful, or is it pleasant?'
> 'It is painful, Reverend Sir.'
> 'And that which is transitory, painful, and liable to change – is it possible to say of it: "This is mine; this am I; this is my self"?'
> 'Certainly not, Reverend Sir.'
> 'Is feeling ... perception ... volition ... consciousness, permanent, or transitory?'
> 'It is transitory, Reverend Sir.'
> 'And that which is transitory – is it painful, or is it pleasant? '
> 'It is painful, Reverend Sir.'
> 'And that which is transitory, painful, and liable to change – is it possible to say of it: "This is mine; this am I; this is my self"?'
> 'Certainly not, Reverend Sir.'
> 'Accordingly, O monks, as respects all *rūpa* whatsoever, past, future, or present, be it subjective or existing outside, gross or subtle, mean or exalted, far or near, the correct view in the light of the highest knowledge is as follows: "This is not mine; this am I not; this is not my self."
> 'As respects all feeling whatsoever ... as respects all perception whatsoever . . . as respects all volitions whatsoever ... as respects all consciousness whatsoever, past, future, or present, be it subjective or existing outside, gross or subtle, mean or exalted, far or near, the correct view in the light of the highest knowledge is as follows: "This is not mine; this am I not; this is not my self."
> 'Perceiving this, O monks, the learned and noble disciple conceives an aversion for *rūpa*, conceives an aversion for feeling, conceives an aversion for perception, conceives an aversion for volitions, conceives an aversion for consciousness. And in conceiving this aversion he becomes divested of passion, and by the absence of passion he becomes free, and when he is free he becomes aware

that he is free; and he knows that rebirth is exhausted, that he has lived the holy life, that he has done what it behooved him to do, and that he is no more for this world.'

Thus spoke The Blessed One, and the delighted band of five *śramanas* applauded the speech of The Blessed One. Now while this exposition was being delivered, the minds of the five *śramanas* became free from attachment and delivered from the depravities. [S III.66–68]

Here the Buddha cites two different sorts of reasons why the *skandhas* are not the self: they are impermanent ('subject to destruction', 'transitory'), and they are not under one's control ('painful', 'it is not possible to say of x, "Let my x be this way…"'). To separate out the argument from impermanence from the second argument, let's ignore the claims about the five *skandhas* not being under one's control (we'll discuss this in §4), and focus on the claims about their being subject to destruction and transitory. If we add the exhaustiveness claim as an implicit premise,[3] the argument is then:

1   *Rūpa* is impermanent.
2   Sensation is impermanent.
3   Perception is impermanent.
4   Volition is impermanent.
5   Consciousness is impermanent.
6   If there were a self it would be permanent.
IP [There is no more to the person than the five *skandhas*.]
C   Therefore there is no self.

This argument is valid or logically good. That is, if the premises are all true, then the conclusion will also be true. So our job now will be to determine if the premises really are all true. But before we can do that, there is one major point that needs clarifying: just what do 'permanent' and 'impermanent' mean here? Once again the doctrine of karma and rebirth becomes relevant. For those like the Buddha and his audience who accepted the doctrine, 'permanent' would mean eternal, and 'impermanent' would mean anything less than eternal. This is because if we believe it is the self that undergoes rebirth, and we also believe that liberation from rebirth is possible, then we will hold as well that the self is something that continues to exist over many lives, and can even exist independently of any form of corporeal life. This is probably what the Buddha had in mind with premise (6). And in that case, all that would be needed to show that something is not a self is to establish that it does not last forever – even if it did last a long time. So if, for instance, the *rūpa* that is my body does not last forever,

---

[3] An implicit premise is an unstated premise that must be supplied for an argument to work, and that the author of the argument did not state because they thought it would be redundant – typically because it seemed to the author to be common knowledge that the author and the audience shared. We will follow the practice of putting implicit premises in square brackets.

then it is not my self. And of course my body does go out of existence when I die, so this would be sufficient to show that it is not my self.

What about those of us who do not accept the doctrine of karma and rebirth? To believe in rebirth is to believe that the person exists both before and after this life. If we do not believe in rebirth, then we may believe that the person exists only a single lifetime. In that case, a self would not have to exist any longer than a lifetime in order to serve as the basis of a person's numerical identity over time. So all that 'permanent' in premise (6) could mean is 'existing at least a whole lifetime'. It could not mean 'eternal'. Likewise, to show that a *skandha* is impermanent in the relevant sense, we would have to show that it does not exist for the entire duration of a person's life. Does this mean that the argument won't work without the assumption of karma and rebirth? After all, isn't it true that our bodies last for our entire lives?

Not necessarily. First, we need to remember that the self is supposed to be the essential part of the person, and the body is a whole made of parts. Which of these parts – the organs that make up the body – is the essential one? There doesn't seem to be any single organ that I could not live without. Granted I could not survive without a heart. But as heart replacement surgery shows, I don't need *this* heart in order to continue to exist. If my heart were my self, then when I got a replacement heart I would cease to exist and someone else would then be living in my body. That replacement heart came from someone else, so it would be that person's self. But surely if I chose to have heart replacement surgery I would not be committing suicide! What about the brain? Not only can I not live without a brain; there is no such thing as brain replacement surgery, so I cannot live without this brain. But here the problem seems to be entirely practical, not an 'in-principle' difficulty. If we knew how to reprogram an entire brain, then we might be able to replace a diseased brain with a healthy one while preserving all of a person's psychology. This would be like copying the contents of the failing hard drive of your computer, replacing the hard drive, then reinstalling everything onto the new hard drive.

This brain-replacement scenario might seem too science-fictional to support premiss (1). But there's a second reason someone might give for denying that the body is permanent in the relevant way. This is that all the parts of the body are constantly being replaced – at the level of the molecules that make up our cells. We've all heard it said that none of the atoms that made up our body seven years ago is among those making up our body now. Life processes such as metabolism and meiosis involve the constant, piecemeal replacement of the parts that make up a life-form. After these processes have gone on long enough, all the matter making up a given organ is new: the atoms now making up that organ are numerically distinct from the atoms that made it up earlier. Given this, it could be said that the body and brain I have now are not numerically identical with the body and brain I had seven years ago. *Rūpa* would then be impermanent in the relevant sense.

We have been discussing how to interpret premise (6), the premise that a self would have to be permanent, and how premise (1), which says that *rūpa* is impermanent, might be true in light of our interpretation of (6). Our general practice in examining arguments will be to first look at what reason there might be to think that the premises are true, and then to evaluate the argument overall. How might someone defend the remaining premises, (2)–(5)? These are not affected by the question of karma and rebirth in the way that premise (1) is. For regardless of whether we interpret 'permanent' to mean eternal, or just to mean lasting a single lifetime, the four *nāma skandhas* will all count as impermanent. This is the point the Buddha makes in the following passage:

> It would be better, O monks, if the uninstructed worldling regarded the body which is composed of the four elements as a self, rather than the mind. And why do I say so? Because it is evident, O monks, that this body which is composed of the four elements lasts one year, lasts two years, lasts three years, lasts four years, lasts five years, lasts ten years, lasts twenty years, lasts thirty years, lasts forty years, lasts fifty years, lasts a hundred years, and even more. But that, O monks, which is called mind, intellect, consciousness, keeps up an incessant round by day and by night of perishing as one thing and springing up as another.
>
> Here the learned and noble disciple, O monks, attentively considers dependent origination: 'this exists when that exists, this originates from the origination of that; this does not exist when that does not exist, this ceases from the cessation of that'. O monks, a pleasant feeling originates in dependence on contact with pleasant objects; but when that contact with pleasant objects ceases, the feeling sprung from that contact, the pleasant feeling that originated in dependence on contact with pleasant objects ceases and comes to an end. O monks, an unpleasant feeling … an indifferent feeling originates in dependence on contact with indifferent objects; but when that contact with indifferent objects ceases, the feeling sprung from that contact, the indifferent feeling that originated in dependence on contact with indifferent objects ceases and comes to an end.
>
> Just as, O monks, heat comes into existence and flame into being from the friction and concussion of two sticks of wood, but on the separation and parting of these two sticks of wood the heat sprung from those two sticks of wood ceases and comes to an end; in exactly the same way, O monks, a pleasant feeling originates in dependence on contact with pleasant objects; but when that contact with pleasant objects ceases, the feeling sprung from that contact, the pleasant feeling that originated in dependence on contact with pleasant objects, ceases and comes to an end. An unpleasant feeling … an indifferent feeling originates in dependence on contact with indifferent objects; but when that contact with indifferent objects ceases, the feeling sprung from that contact, the indifferent feeling that originated in dependence on contact with indifferent objects ceases and comes to an end. [S II.96f]

Of course the Buddha knows that reflective people are more likely to consider the mind the self than the body. In the Western philosophical tradition this is just what Descartes did. He concluded that the true 'I' is not the body but the mind – a substance that thinks (that is, is conscious), endures at least a lifetime, and is immaterial in nature. Many Indian philosophers reached somewhat similar conclusions. The Buddha's point is that the conclusion that the mind endures at least a lifetime rests on an illusion. For what we call the mind is really a continuous series of distinct events, each lasting just a moment, but each immediately followed by others. There is no such thing as the mind that has these different events, there are just the events themselves. But because they succeed one another in unbroken succession, the illusion is created of an enduring thing in which they are all taking place.

The eighteenth-century British philosopher David Hume said something similar in response to Descartes. Descartes claimed to be aware of the mind as something that is aware, that cognizes, perceives, wills, believes, doubts – that is the subject of all one's mental activities. Hume responded that when he looked within, all he ever found were particular mental contents, each of them fleeting, and never an enduring substance that has them. He concluded that it is just the relations among those mental events that make us invent the fiction of the self as an enduring subject of experience. The Buddha claims something similar. And like Hume, he uses the relation of causation to support his claim.

In the last chapter we saw how the doctrine of dependent origination is used to explain the origin of suffering. In the passage we are looking at, that doctrine gets put to a different use. Dependent origination is the relation between an effect and its causes and conditions. Where this relation holds, the effect will arise when the causes and conditions obtain, and the effect will not occur when the causes and conditions do not. The Buddha asserts that all the *nāma skandhas* are dependently originated. He uses the example of feeling, but this example generalizes to the other kinds of mental events as well. Consider the feeling of pleasure I derive from eating my favorite kind of ice cream. This feeling originates in dependence on contact between my sense of taste (located in the taste buds on my tongue) and the ice cream. Before that contact there was no feeling of pleasure, and when the contact ceases so does the feeling. I may have a feeling of pleasure in the next moment, but that occurs in dependence on a new event of sense-object contact – say, when I take my next bite of ice cream. So that feeling is numerically distinct from the first, for it has a different cause. One feeling has gone out of existence and been replaced by another. Now the senses are by nature restless, always making contact with new objects. This means that there will be an unbroken stream of feelings and other mental events. It is easy to mistake this stream for a single enduring thing. But the Buddha claims that if we attend to the individual events making up this stream, then seeing how they are dependently originated will help us overcome the illusion of a persisting subject of experience.

The appeal to dependent origination is meant to show two things: that there is no such thing as the mind over and above the mental events making up the mental stream; and that each of those events is very short-lived. Suppose we agreed with the Buddha on the first point. How successful is this appeal with regard to the second point? It is relatively easy to agree that feelings of pleasure and pain are transitory. We don't really need to use dependent origination to prove this. And since they are transitory, they could not be the self. Likewise for perceptions. But what about volitions? Granted my desire for some new soft drink may last only as long as the effects of the commercial I just saw. But we also seem to have volitions that endure, such as my desire for coffee. To this it could be replied that this is an acquired volition, one that I did not always have and might very well get rid of. So the opponent must look for volitions that seem to endure a whole lifetime. They might suggest what are sometimes called 'instinctual desires', such as the desire to escape life-threatening situations. Might this not be a volition that is permanent in the relevant sense? The Buddha will reply that what we are then describing is not one enduring volition, but rather a pattern of recurring volitions, each lasting only a brief while before ceasing. This is shown by the fact that I am only aware of a desire to escape danger when I perceive a threatening situation. The desire thus originates in dependence on a specific sense-object contact event, and ceases to exist when that event ceases. The opponent will then want to know what explains the pattern of recurring volitions. What the opponent suspects is that this pattern can only be explained by supposing that there is one enduring volition, a permanent desire to escape life-threatening situations, that is always present in me. My perception of a life-threatening situation brings the volition out into the part of my mind that is illuminated by consciousness, but it persists even when I am not aware of it.

Since we have no evidence that the Buddha was ever presented with this line of objection, we don't know how he would have responded. But later Buddhist philosophers do show us how it might be answered. What we have here is a certain phenomenon – a pattern of recurring desires over the course of a person's lifetime – and two competing theories as to how to explain the phenomenon. Call the opponent's theory the 'in-the-closet' theory, since it claims that some desires continue to exist hidden away in a dark corner of the mind when not observed. It explains the phenomenon by claiming that it is a single continuously existing volition that manifests itself at different times as the desire to duck a falling safe, the desire to dodge a runaway car, etc. The Buddhist dependent origination theory, by contrast, claims that these are many numerically distinct desires. It explains the pattern by appealing to the ways in which the parts of a person's body are arranged. Consider the thermostat that controls the heat in a house. It is because of the way in which the parts of the thermostat are put together that whenever the temperature goes below a certain threshold, the thermostat signals the furnace to go on. It is not as if the signal for the furnace to go on waits in the thermostat's closet until the room gets too cold. By the same token, the Buddhist would say, it is because of the way that the human body is organized that a danger stimulus causes a danger-escaping volition.[4] Now this seems like a plausible explanation. It makes sense to suppose that, for instance, it is because of the way in which certain neurons in the brain are arranged that we have this desire to escape whenever we sense danger. But the in-the-closet theory also seems plausible to many people, so which should we choose?

---

[4]No Buddhist text actually says this. This represents an extrapolation from what members of the Sautrāntika school of Abhidharma say about continuity of karmic seeds during meditational states in which there is no consciousness. Their approach to that problem is dictated by their overall aversion to talk of dispositions or powers as real things.

There is a principle that governs cases like this. It is known in the West as Ockham's Razor, but Indian philosophers call it the Principle of Lightness, for it dictates that we choose the 'lighter' of two competing theories. The Principle of Lightness may be stated as follows: given two competing theories, each of which is equally good at explaining and predicting the relevant phenomena, choose the lighter theory, that is, the theory that posits the least number of unobservable entities.

To posit an unobservable entity is to say that something exists even though we never directly observe that thing. Now you might think that positing an unobservable entity is always a bad idea. Why believe something exists when no one can see or feel it? But modern physics tells us that there are subatomic particles like electrons and protons, and no one has ever seen or felt such things. Does that make modern physics an irrational theory? No. What the Principle of Lightness tells us is that we should only posit unobservable entities when we have to, when there is no other way to explain what we observe. We accept the theory that says there are subatomic particles because no other theory does as good a job of explaining the phenomena. In the case of the phenomenon of recurring desires, though, things are different. We said that the in-the-closet theory and the Buddhist dependent origination theory give equally good explanations of this phenomenon. But the in-the-closet theory posits an unobservable entity that the dependent origination theory does not. The former theory says that volitions continue to exist in our minds even when we are not aware of them. The latter theory speaks instead of patterns of neurons in the brain – something that can be observed. This makes the latter theory lighter, and so it is the theory that we ought to choose.

The Principle of Lightness would help the Buddhist answer the objection about seemingly permanent volitions. It can also be used in defense of premise (5), the premise that says consciousness is impermanent. In the following passage the Buddha claims that consciousness also originates in dependence on sense-object contact:

> Just as, O monks, fire is named from that in dependence on which it burns. The fire which burns in dependence on logs of wood is called a log-fire. The fire which burns in dependence on chips is called a chip-fire. The fire which burns in dependence on grass is called a grass-fire. The fire which burns in dependence on cow-dung is called a cow-dung fire. The fire which burns in dependence on husks is called a husk-fire. The fire which burns in dependence on rubbish is called a rubbish-fire. In exactly the same way, O monks, consciousness is named from that in dependence on which it comes into being. The consciousness which comes into being in respect of color-and-shape in dependence on the eye is called eye-consciousness. The consciousness which comes into being in respect of sounds in dependence on the ear is called ear -consciousness. The consciousness which comes into being in respect of odors in dependence on the nose is called nose-consciousness. The consciousness which comes into being in respect of tastes in dependence on the tongue is called tongue-consciousness. The consciousness which comes into being in respect of things tangible in dependence on the body is called body-consciousness. The consciousness which comes into

being in respect of *dharmas* in dependence on the mind is called mind-consciousness. [M I.259–60)]

To this someone might object that we experience consciousness as some one thing that endures. That when I first see and then take a bite of ice cream, it is one and the same consciousness that is first aware of the color of the ice cream and is then aware of the taste of the ice cream. The Buddhist would respond by pointing out that there are periods in a person's life when there seems to be no consciousness at all occurring. If the opponent were to claim that consciousness continues to exist even then – only in the closet – the Buddhist could reply that their theory of dependent origination gives a lighter explanation of the apparent continuity of consciousness.[5]

But the Principle of Lightness would also help the Buddhist defend their claim that the mind is an invented fiction. As both the Buddha and Hume point out, we are never actually aware of the mind as something standing behind such mental events as feeling, perceiving and willing. We are just aware of the feelings, perceptions and volitions themselves. So the mind is unobservable. And it is the causal relations among these mental events that the Buddha says explain all the facts about our mental lives. So the mind becomes an unnecessary, unobservable posit.[6]

Why, though, should we accept the Principle of Lightness? The idea behind this principle is that what makes some statement true has to be objective: the truth of a statement is not determined by such subjective factors as our interests, or limitations in our cognitive capacities, but rather just by facts that are independent of our interests and limitations. The thought is that when it comes to finding out what the facts are, we should let the world outside our mind dictate what it is that we believe. To think that factors in my mind could determine what the facts are would be to indulge in magical thinking. By the same token, we could say that positing unobservable entities is inherently suspect. Why believe that something exists when no one could possibly observe it? Because saying so makes it easier for us to explain what we do observe? This is letting what seems to us like a good explanation determine what we say the mind-independent facts are. This is letting our cognitive limitations determine what statements we believe are true. Magical thinking. The Principle of Lightness says we should resort to positing unobservable entities only when the world tells us we have no alternative.

---

[5]The Buddha's argument in the passage we just looked at is slightly different. It depends on the claim that there are six distinct kinds of consciousness, corresponding to the six senses and their respective objects. These twelve items (vision and the visible, hearing and the audible, etc.) are collectively referred to as the *āyatanas*.

[6]Remember, though, that early Buddhism is dualist. One can deny the existence of the mind and still be a dualist. The most familiar form of dualism is substance dualism, the view that there are two kinds of substance, physical substance and mental substance. Descartes was a substance dualist. Buddhists deny the existence of the mind. But they affirm the existence of mental events, such as feeling and perception, as things that are distinct from the physical (*rūpa*). While early Buddhism denies substance dualism, it affirms what could be called event dualism.

We are now done with our review of the explicit premises in the argument from impermanence. There still remains the one implicit premise, the exhaustiveness claim. If we accept this, then it seems we must say the argument from impermanence succeeds in establishing that there is no self. There is one important objection to the exhaustiveness claim. Many find this claim unacceptable because it leaves unexplained the sense we have that there is an 'I' that has a body and various mental states. If the exhaustiveness claim were true, then while there would be a body and various mental states such as feelings and desires, these would not be the body and mental states of anyone or anything. They would be ownerless states without a subject. And this strikes many as absurd. Is this a valid objection to the exhaustiveness claim, and so to the argument from impermanence? We will defer this question. We turn instead to the second argument contained in the passage we have been investigating, the argument from control. This argument also relies on the exhaustiveness claim. Examining this argument will help us better frame the important objection to the exhaustiveness claim. We will then be better positioned to determine whether we should accept this claim, and with it the arguments that turn on it.

3.4

The argument from impermanence starts from one way in which we use the word 'I'. The argument from control starts from another. We often say things like, 'I felt okay about my hair today, but my nails look pretty ratty; I need to do something about them.' This tells us that we think of the 'I' as something that evaluates the states of the person and seeks to change those it finds unsatisfactory. Let us call this the executive function. Then if there is a self, the self would be that part of the person that performs the executive function. Recall that in the passage we looked at earlier, the Buddha says of each *skandha* that it cannot be the self because it is sometimes other than we want it to be. This makes it sound as if he is assuming that we would have complete control over the self, so it would always be perfect in our own eyes. And why would this be? If the self performs the executive function then it tries to control the other parts of the person. But why must it have complete control over anything? And isn't there something odd about supposing that it exercises control over itself? Isn't the point of the executive function to exert control over other things? So far the argument does not look very promising.

But there is a different way of understanding the argument. Consider the Anti-Reflexivity Principle: an entity cannot operate on itself. This principle is widely accepted among Indian philosophers. As supporting evidence they point to the knife that can cut other things but not itself, the finger that can point at other things but not at itself, etc. Are there counter-examples to this principle, cases that show it not to be universally valid? What about a doctor who treats herself? The difficulty with this case is that when the doctor removes her ingrown toenail, it is not the ingrown toenail that does the treating, it is other parts of the doctor. Those who support the principle claim that all seeming counter-examples will turn out to involve one part of a complex system operating on another part. So there are no counter-examples, and the principle is valid.

Suppose this is right. Then if the self performed the executive function, it could perform that function on other parts of the person, but not on itself. This means I could never find myself dissatisfied with and wanting to change my self. And this in turn means that any part of me that I can find myself disliking and seeking to change could not be my self.[7] Suppose, for instance, that I thought my nose might be my self. My nose would then be the part of me that performs the executive function. When I evaluate the different parts of my body and mind, it would be my nose that did this. When I decided I didn't like something about my hair, or tried to rid myself of some habit I disliked, this would be the nose's doing. The one thing the nose could never do is dislike and try to change itself. So if I ever found myself wanting to change something about my nose, that would show that my nose is not my self. And of course I do dislike it when my nose itches; I try to make it stop by scratching it. Therefore my nose is not my self. The argument as a whole will then go like this:

1   I sometimes dislike and seek to change *rūpa*.
2   I sometimes dislike and seek to change feeling.
3   I sometimes dislike and seek to change perception.
4   I sometimes dislike and seek to change volition.
5   I sometimes dislike and seek to change consciousness.
6   If the self existed it would be the part of the person that performs the executive function.
IP [There is no more to the person than the five *skandhas*.]
C   Therefore there is no self.

Does this argument work? The first five premises seem to be true. There doesn't seem to be any observable part of the person that I could not find myself dissatisfied with and wanting to change. (Whether I succeed in changing it is another matter, but that's not relevant here.) We've seen how the anti-reflexivity principle comes in: if the self is the one part of me that's at work when I evaluate my states and try to change those I find unsatisfactory, then it is the one thing I could never evaluate and seek to change. So it looks like the argument does prove its conclusion provided the one implicit premise is true – that there is no more to me than the five *skandhas*.

At this point it may strike you that there is something very peculiar going on here. On the one hand we have an argument designed to show that there is no part of the person that is the controller – no part that performs the executive function. Yet in this

---

[7]This way of interpreting the argument is suggested by the fact that the Sāṃkhya school of orthodox Indian philosophy gives an argument for the existence of the self that uses the same basic ideas (though put to very different ends). See *Tattvakaumadī* on *Sāṃkhya-kārikā* XVII.

very argument we have premises stating 'I sometimes dislike and seek to change ...'
To say that I dislike and seek to change something is to say that I perform the
executive function. Yet according to the conclusion of the argument, there is nothing
that performs the executive function. If there really were no one in charge, then
wouldn't the evidence that is being used to show that no one is in charge really be
bogus? Doesn't the evidence presented in the premises actually require that the
conclusion be false?

This suspicion can be developed into a very powerful challenge to the
exhaustiveness claim. Here is how it goes. Suppose that the five *skandhas* contain all
the parts of the person that we ever observe. We agree that we sometimes dislike and
seek to change each of the *skandhas*. And we also agree that whatever is performing
this executive function cannot perform it on itself. The conclusion then seems
inescapable that there must be more to the person than just the observable parts, the
five *skandhas*. And this 'something else' must be the self, the part that performs the
executive function. This would explain how it is possible to exercise control over all
the observable parts of the person without violating the anti-reflexivity principle. The
controller is itself unobservable. This would also explain why Hume and the Buddha
were unable to find a self when they 'looked within'. The self is the observer, and by
the anti-reflexivity principle, it cannot observe itself. It can only observe the other
parts of the person, the five *skandhas*. The exhaustiveness claim is false: there is more
to the person than the five *skandhas*. Not only do the Buddha's two arguments not
succeed in proving there is no self. The evidence they present actually turns out to
support the view that there is a self.

This is by far the most serious objection we have encountered to the Buddhist
arguments for non-self. Can the Buddhists mount a successful response? They will
begin by pointing out an error in the opponent's characterization of the situation. In
spelling out their objection to the controller argument, the opponent said that the
argument's conclusion is that there is nothing that performs the executive function.
But this is not what the conclusion of the argument says. It says there is no self that
performs the executive function. This leaves it open that there might be something
else performing that function. Or rather, that there might be several somethings
performing that function. What the Buddhist has in mind is that on one occasion one
part of the person might perform the executive function, on another occasion another
part might do so. This would make it possible for every part to be subject to control
without there being any part that always fills the role of controller (and so is the self).
On some occasions a given part might fall on the controller side, while on other
occasions it might fall on the side of the controlled. This would explain how it's
possible for us to seek to change any of the *skandhas* while there is nothing more to us
than just those *skandhas*.

Consider this analogy. In a monarchy, there is the monarch, and there are his or her
subjects. A monarch is not their own subject; a ruler rules over others, not
themselves. Now in the case of Great Britain, it is true that every living British citizen
has been the subject of a British monarch. But it is also true that Queen Elizabeth II is

a British citizen. How is this possible? If she is a British citizen, that means she has been the subject of a British monarch. But she is the British monarch, and by the anti-reflexivity principle she is not her own subject. Does this mean that there is some unobservable meta-monarch presiding over the UK? Of course not. Queen Elizabeth was the subject of her father, King George, when she was still Princess Elizabeth before her father's death.

This shows how it is possible for the following propositions all to be true:

1   There is no more to the person than the five *skandhas* (the exhaustiveness claim).
2   I can perform the executive function on each of the *skandhas*.
3   An entity cannot operate on itself (the anti-reflexivity principle).

They can all be true because it need not be the same part of the person that performs the executive function on every occasion. So on one occasion my nose might form a coalition with other parts of me and perform the executive function on my hair. On another occasion a coalition with different members might perform the same function on my nose. We will call this the 'shifting coalitions' strategy; it will prove useful to the Buddhist in other contexts as well. In effect, the Buddhist is claiming the opponent has forgotten the second possible meaning of 'I'. The opponent saw this word in premises (1)–(5) of the argument from control, and assumed it meant a self, some one thing that exists as long as the person does. They assumed that when we say I can dislike and seek to change all the *skandhas*, it must be one and the same thing that evaluates and seeks to change all of them. But 'I' might also refer to all the parts of the person taken together. It might refer not to a self but to the person.

The Buddhist is not yet out of the woods though. For one thing, we already know that the Buddha says the person is not ultimately real. We don't yet know just what that means, but it certainly doesn't sound like good news for the shifting coalitions strategy as a way around the objection. What's more, if 'I' refers to the person, then the person should be one thing, not many. 'I' is the first-person singular pronoun; 'we' is the first-person plural. Yet the shifting coalitions strategy requires that it be different things that perform the executive function at different times. How is it that these distinct things all get called by a single name for one thing?

The Buddhist has an answer to this question. It is that 'I' is what they call a 'convenient designator', a word that refers to something that is just a useful fiction. The person is that useful fiction. The person is a whole made of parts. And wholes are not themselves real things, only the parts are. I think that 'I' must refer to one and the same thing every time I use it because I have forgotten that the person is a useful fiction. I have forgotten that 'I' is just a useful way to talk about all the parts taken together.

This is the basic strategy the Buddhist will use to answer the challenge to the exhaustiveness claim. But we need to investigate that strategy in much greater detail. Before we begin that task it would be good to summarize the state of play to this point. The Buddha gave two arguments for non-self, the argument from impermanence and the argument from control. Both arguments relied on the exhaustiveness claim, which says there is no more to the person than just the five *skandhas*. This claim was crucial to both arguments, since they both proceed by showing that there is some property of a self that all the *skandhas* lack. Showing this would not show there is no self if there could be more to the person than just these *skandhas*. The opponent objects that the exhaustiveness claim cannot be true if it is true that we can exercise some degree of control over all five *skandhas*. Indeed the opponent takes this fact to show that there must be more to the person than the five *skandhas*. The first Buddhist response is to point out that if the *skandhas* took turns performing the executive function, then all five could be subject to control without violating the anti-reflexivity principle. To this the opponent objects that in that case there would be not one controller but many. The second Buddhist response will be that there is a single controller, the person, but the person is only conventionally real. We now turn to an examination of just what this might mean.

3.5

The text we are about to examine comes from a work called *Milindapañha* or *The Questions of King Milinda*. It is a dialogue between a king, Milinda, and a Buddhist monk named Nāgasena. Milinda is an historical figure. He lived in the second century BCE, was of Greek ancestry (his Greek name was Menandros), and was a ruler in Bactria (in present-day Pakistan) after its conquest by Alexander the Great. Milinda probably did discuss Buddhist teachings with Buddhist monks, but we don't know if there was a Nāgasena among them. The work was composed early in the first century CE, and it is probably not the transcription of an actual conversation. More importantly, it is not an early Buddhist work; it does not record the teachings of the Buddha and his immediate disciples. It is still useful for our purposes, though. For it is recognized as authoritative by a number of different Abhidharma schools. So its views represent a consensus position among a wide variety of commentarial traditions on the teachings of the Buddha.

The passage we are going to look at represents the first meeting of Nāgasena and Milinda. Notice how the conventional practice of exchanging names leads right to a substantive philosophical dispute.

> Then King Milinda drew near to where the venerable Nāgasena was; and having drawn near, he greeted the venerable Nāgasena; and having passed the compliments of friendship and civility, he sat down respectfully at one side. And the venerable Nāgasena returned the greeting; by which, verily, he won the heart of King Milinda.
>
> And King Milinda spoke to the venerable Nāgasena as follows: 'How is your reverence called? Sir, what is your name?'
>
> 'Your majesty, I am called Nāgasena; my fellow-monks, your majesty, address me as Nāgasena: but whether parents give one the name Nāgasena, or

Sūrasena, or Vīrasena, or Sīhasena, it is, nevertheless, your majesty, just a counter, an expression, a convenient designator, a mere name, this Nāgasena; for there is no person here to be found.'

Notice that his point here is not that his parents could have given him any of those other names instead. While this is true, it's not philosophically significant. His point is rather that whatever name he was given is just a useful way of labeling something that is not actually a person:

> Then said King Milinda, 'Listen to me, my lords, you five hundred Yonakas, and you eighty thousand monks! Nāgasena here says thus: 'There is no person here to be found.' Is it possible, pray, for me to assent to what he says?'
> And King Milinda spoke to the venerable Nāgasena as follows: 'Nāgasena, if there is no person to be found, who is it then that furnishes you monks with the priestly requisites – robes, food, bedding, and medicine, the needs of the sick? who is it that makes use of the same? who is it that keeps the precepts? who is it that applies himself to meditation? who is it that realizes the Paths, the Fruits, and nirvāna? who is it that destroys life? who is it that takes what is not given him? who is it that commits immorality? who is it that tells lies? who is it that drinks intoxicating liquor? who is it that commits the five crimes that constitute "proximate karma"? In that case, there is no merit; there is no demerit; there is no one who does or has done meritorious or demeritorious deeds; neither good nor evil deeds can have any fruit or result. Nāgasena, neither is he a murderer who kills a monk, nor can you monks, Nāgasena, have any teacher, preceptor, or ordination.'

If there are no persons, there can be no one who gives alms to monks, nor can there be monks who embark on the path to nirvāna. Likewise there can be none who commit evil deeds. These and other absurdities are what Milinda thinks follow from Nāgasena's claim:

> When you say, 'My fellow-monks, your majesty, address me as Nāgasena,' what then is this Nāgasena? Pray, sir, is the hair of the head Nāgasena?'
>   'Indeed not, your majesty.'
>   'Is the hair of the body Nāgasena?'
>   'Indeed not, your majesty.'
>   'Are nails ... teeth ... skin ... flesh ... sinews ... bones ... marrow of the bones ... kidneys ... heart ... liver ... pleura ... spleen ... lungs ... intestines ... mesentery ... stomach ... faeces ... bile ... phlegm ... pus ... blood ... sweat ... fat ... tears ... lymph ... saliva ... snot ... synovial fluid ... urine ... brain of the head Nāgasena?'
>   'Indeed not, your majesty.'
>   'Is now, sir, *rūpa* Nāgasena?'
>   'Indeed not, your majesty.'
>   'Is feeling Nāgasena?'
>   'Indeed not, your majesty.'

'Is perception Nāgasena?'
'Indeed not, your majesty.'
'Is volition Nāgasena?'
'Indeed not, your majesty.'
'Is consciousness Nāgasena?'
'Indeed not, your majesty.'
'Are, then, sir, *rūpa*, feeling, perception, volition, and consciousness unit-
edly Nāgasena?'
'Indeed not, your majesty.'
'Is it, then, sir, something besides *rūpa*, feeling, perception, volition, and
consciousness, which is Nāgasena?'
'Indeed not, your majesty.
'Sir, although I question you very closely, I fail to discover any Nāgasena.
Verily, now, sir, Nāgasena is a mere empty sound. What Nāgasena is there here?
Sir you speak a falsehood, a lie: there is no Nāgasena.'

Notice that Milinda goes through each of the different parts of the body first, before
coming to *rūpa*, or the body as a whole; in each case he asks if this is what 'Nāgasena'
is the name of. He next asks about the four *nāma skandhas*. Nāgasena says 'no' in
each case, though he doesn't say why. We can imagine that he has the same reasons
as those the Buddha gave in his two arguments for non-self. The next possibility
Milinda suggests is the five *skandhas* taken collectively. It is noteworthy that
Nāgasena denies this as well. The last possibility is that it is something distinct from
all five *skandhas*. Nāgasena's denial is tantamount to the exhaustiveness claim: there
isn't anything else. Finally, note that Milinda takes this all to mean that 'Nāgasena' is
a 'mere empty sound', a meaningless bit of nonsense. This is not what Nāgasena said
the name is. He called it a 'convenient designator'. These two views about what the
name is have very different consequences. If Milinda is right that 'Nāgasena' is a
mere empty sound, then all the absurd consequences Milinda mentioned will follow.
As we'll see in a bit, though, they don't follow if Nāgasena is right and the name is a
convenient designator.

Nāgasena now tries to get Milinda to see the difference between a name's being a
mere empty sound and its being a convenient designator. He does this by turning
Milinda's own reasoning back on him, applying it to the word 'chariot'. This
reasoning leads Milinda into absurdities. Milinda will then realize that the way out of
those absurdities involves distinguishing between a word's being a mere empty
sound, and its being a convenient designator. The absurdities don't follow if we think
of the word as a convenient designator:

> Then the venerable Nāgasena spoke to King Milinda as follows: 'Your majesty,
> you are a delicate prince, an exceedingly delicate prince; and if, your majesty,
> you walk in the middle of the day on hot sandy ground, and you tread on rough
> grit, gravel, and sand, your feet become sore, your body tired, the mind is
> oppressed, and the body-consciousness suffers. Pray, did you come on foot, or
> riding?'

'Sir, I do not go on foot. I came in a chariot.'

'Your majesty, if you came in a chariot, tell me what the chariot is. Pray, your majesty, is the pole the chariot?'

'Indeed not, sir.'

'Is the axle the chariot?'

'Indeed not, sir.'

'Are the wheels the chariot?'

'Indeed not, sir.'

'Is the chariot-body the chariot?'

'Indeed not, sir.'

'Is the banner-staff the chariot?'

'Indeed not, sir.'

'Is the yoke the chariot?'

'Indeed not, sir.'

'Are the reins the chariot ?'

'Indeed not, sir.'

'Is the goading-stick the chariot ?'

'Indeed not, sir.'

'Pray, your majesty, are pole, axle, wheels, chariot-body, banner-staff, yoke, reins, and goad unitedly the chariot?'

'Indeed not, sir.'

'Is it, then, your majesty, something else besides pole, axle, wheels, chariot-- body, bannerstaff, yoke, reins, and goad which is the chariot?'

'Indeed not, sir.'

'Your majesty, although I question you very closely, I fail to discover any chariot. Verily now, your majesty, the word chariot is a mere empty sound. What chariot is there here? Your majesty, you speak a falsehood, a lie: there is no chariot. Your majesty, you are the chief king in all the continent of India; of whom are you afraid that you speak a lie? Listen to me, my lords, you five hundred Yonakas, and you eighty thousand monks! King Milinda here says thus: "I came in a chariot;"' and being requested, "Your majesty, if you came in a chariot, tell me what the chariot is," he fails to produce any chariot. Is it possible, pray, for me to assent to what he says ?'

When Nāgasena accuses Milinda of telling a lie, he is just driving home to Milinda the consequences of following Milinda's reasoning about the name 'Nāgasena' when that reasoning is applied to the case of the word 'chariot'. Nāgasena is being a skillful teacher. He wants Milinda himself to come up with the resolution of the difficulty. This is just what happens next:

> When he had thus spoken, the five hundred Yonakas applauded the venerable Nāgasena and spoke to King Milinda as follows: 'Now, your majesty, answer, if you can.'
>
> Then King Milinda spoke to the venerable Nāgasena as follows: 'Nāgasena, I speak no lie: the word "chariot" functions as just a counter, an expression, a convenient designator, a mere name for pole, axle, wheels, chariot-body, and banner-staff.'

'Thoroughly well, your majesty, do you understand a chariot. In exactly the same way, your majesty, in respect of me, "Nāgasena" functions as just a counter, an expression, convenient designation, mere name for the hair of my head, hair of my body ... brain of the head, *rūpa*, feeling, perception, volition, and consciousness. But ultimately there is no person to be found. And the nun Vajira, your majesty, said this before the Blessed One:

'Just as there is the word "chariot" for a set of parts,
So when there are *skandhas* it is the convention to say, "There is a living being".'

'It is wonderful, Nāgasena! It is marvelous, Nāgasena! Brilliant and prompt is the wit of your replies.' [MP 25–28]

Notice how Milinda agrees that 'chariot' is not a mere empty sound, but a convenient designator, a useful way of referring to the parts when they are put together in a certain way. So when Milinda said he came in a chariot, what he said was true, he was referring to something real – just not a chariot. But why is this? Why not simply say that 'chariot' is the name of a chariot? The answer is that a chariot is actually not a real thing. The parts are real, but the whole that is made up of those parts is not. The whole can be reduced to the parts, it isn't anything over and above the parts. This is the view known as 'mereological reductionism'.[8]

This was the view of early Buddhism. This view was systematically developed and argued for in Abhidharma. We will examine the argument when we investigate Abhidharma (in Chapter 6). In early Buddhism we just have what looks like a kind of ontological bias against wholes:[9] wholes are not really real, only the parts are. There is a way of making sense of that bias though. Consider a set of all the parts needed to make a chariot. Suppose those parts are arranged in what we would call the 'assembled-chariot' way: rim attached to spokes, spokes connected to felly, felly connected to axle, axle to body, etc. In this case we have one word that we apply to the set, 'chariot'. Now suppose those parts are arranged in a different way, the 'strewn-across-the-battlefield' way: rim partly submerged in the mud, one spoke wrapped around a tree root, another spoke lying on the ground three meters north-east of the first, etc. In this case we do not have a single name for the set. The best we can do is 'all the parts that used to make up the chariot'. This difference is reflected in another difference. In the first case we think of the parts as one thing; in the second case we think of the parts as many things. Why this difference in attitude? Is it just because in the first case the parts are all in immediate proximity to one another? But if the parts were all jumbled together in a heap, we still wouldn't think of them as one

---

[8]Mereology is that part of metaphysics concerned with the relation between the whole and the parts. So mereological reductionism is the view that whole and parts are related by way of the whole being reducible to the parts.

[9]Ontology is that part of metaphysics concerned with determining the basic kinds of existing things. When philosophers speak of 'an ontology', they mean a list of the basic categories of existents. So for instance the doctrine of the five *skandhas* represents an ontology if the exhaustiveness claim is true.

thing, we'd think what we had then was just a bunch of parts in a pile. No, the difference in our ontological attitude (thinking of them as one thing in the one case but as many things in the other) stems from the fact that we have a single word for the parts in the first case but not in the second. And why do we have this single word in the one case? Because we have an interest in the parts when they are arranged in that way. When the set of parts is arranged in the assembled-chariot way, they serve our need for a means of transportation 'across the hot sandy ground'.

At this point you might be thinking, 'Well, of course. We only have a single word for the parts when they are put together in a way that serves our interests. This is no doubt why Nāgasena calls the word "chariot" a convenient designator. Because it's convenient for us to have a way to designate the parts when they're assembled in that way. That configuration is one we're likely to encounter frequently (if we live in a society that uses chariots). And it's one we're likely to want to be able to refer to. It's much easier to tell your servant to fetch a chariot than to ask that they bring a rim attached to some spokes attached to a felly attached to … By contrast it's much less likely that we'll ever need to refer to the set of parts when it's arranged in the strewn-across-the-battlefield way. And there are only so many words we can learn to use before our brains begin to clog up. If we had to learn a different word for every possible arrangement of those parts our minds would melt. So we only have a single word in the case that serves our convenience. This all makes good sense. But why is it supposed to show that the chariot isn't really real?'

The answer is that our ontological attitude should not be dictated by our interests. Common sense says that the chariot is a real thing. Suppose we simply followed common sense. We would then be thinking of the chariot as one thing, but the same parts arranged in some different way as many things, because it was more convenient for us to think that way. We would be letting our interests dictate what we take reality to be like, and we know where that can lead. Assessing your finances that way can lead to disaster. This is why strictly speaking the chariot is not a real thing. It is just what Abhidharma will call a 'conceptual fiction': something not ultimately real that is nonetheless accepted as real by common sense because of our use of a convenient designator. Here are some other examples of conceptual fictions: a house, a lute, an army, a city, a tree, a forest and a column of ants. The list could be extended indefinitely. Our common-sense ontology is full of things that we think are real, but are also wholes made of parts. The early Buddhist view is that strictly speaking none of these things is really real.

Notice, though, that the word 'chariot' is not a 'mere empty sound'. Nāgasena sees a difference between that status and a word's being a convenient designator. To call a word a mere empty sound is to say it has no meaning. And in this context that would mean that there is nothing that it refers to. So if chariots are not really real, why isn't the word 'chariot' a mere empty sound? We already gave the answer, but it is worth repeating and elaborating on. 'Chariot' does refer to something, but not to what it appears to refer to. Its reference is misleading, for it seems to be the name of a single thing, a chariot, and there really is no such thing. It is, though, a useful way of talking about a set of parts when they are arranged in a certain way. So when we use the word correctly, there is something in the world that we are talking about. This is different from the case of a word that refers to nothing whatever, such as 'sky-flower' or 'son of a barren woman'. (The Sanskrit equivalents of these expressions are both single words.) Since a barren woman has no children, there is no such thing as the son of a barren woman. So there is nothing that the word is the name of. Using the word 'chariot' might help us get what we want, but using 'son of a barren woman' never will. The chariot might be a fiction, but it isn't an utter fiction, like the son of a barren woman. Instead it's a useful fiction.

In this respect the chariot is like the average college student. Just looking at the form of the expression 'the average college student', we might be misled into thinking that it refers to a flesh-and-blood person. It does not. There is no such person as the average college student. So it doesn't make sense to ask what school they go to, what their major is, or who their parents are. But this does not make the concept useless. For there are real facts that back up what is said about the average college student, facts about all the flesh-and-blood college students. Those facts are very complex, for they involve details about the lives of many people. So for certain purposes it is useful to be able to express them in simplified form. This is just what happens when statisticians come up with the facts about the average college student. The average college student is a fiction, but a useful one. The concept helps fulfill certain interests, like those of college loan officers and credit card companies. And the same goes for the chariot, but not for the son of a barren woman.

3.6

There is one last point to make about the passage we have been looking at. Toward the very end Nāgasena says, 'Ultimately there is no person to be found'. We can now see that he means to call the person a mere conceptual fiction, something we believe to exist only because of our use of a convenient designator. We will have more to say about this in the next section. But we might ask what the force of this 'ultimately' is. The answer is that it involves a distinction between two ways in which a statement may be true: ultimately and conventionally. What Nāgasena is saying is that it is not ultimately true that there are persons. He would, however, say that it is conventionally true that there are persons. The distinction may be characterized as follows:

- A statement is **conventionally true** if and only if it is acceptable to common sense and consistently leads to successful practice.
- A statement is **ultimately true** if and only if it corresponds to the facts and neither asserts nor presupposes the existence of any conceptual fictions.

Suppose there is a soft-drink machine in the lobby of the building, and consider the statement, 'There's a soft-drink machine in the lobby.' You might think that what the statement says corresponds to the facts. But even if there is a sense in which that is correct, still it asserts the existence of a conceptual fiction, the soft-drink machine. Does that mean the statement is ultimately false? No. To call it ultimately false is to be committed to the ultimate truth of the statement that is its negation, 'There is no soft-drink machine in the lobby.' And for that statement to be true it would have to be true that there are or at least could be such things as soft-drink machines. It presupposes the existence of a conceptual fiction. No statement that uses the concept of a soft-drink machine could be ultimately true. Our statement is conventionally true though. Any speaker of English who was informed about the building would agree to it, so it is acceptable to common sense. And its acceptance consistently leads to satisfaction of our desires, such as my craving for a diet soda.

So any statement that uses convenient designators can only be conventionally true. It cannot be ultimately true, or ultimately false either. From the ultimate perspective such a statement is simply without meaning, and so not the sort of thing that could be either true or false. The Sanskrit word (*saṃvṛti*) that we are translating as 'conventional' literally means 'concealing'. And Buddhist commentators explain their use of this term by saying that convenient designators conceal the nature of reality. Words like 'chariot' are misleading because they seem to refer to a single thing when they actually refer to a plurality. If we want a complete description of how things actually objectively are, we should avoid using them. Of course that objectivity would come at a steep price. If we could never use convenient designators in describing the world, then when we wanted to ride over the hot sandy ground we would have to list all the parts that make up the chariot and describe how each is related to the others. That would take a long time. So inevitably we lapse back into using conventional truth.

This is not necessarily a problem though. After all, not just any statement using convenient designators will be conventionally true. The definition said such statements must consistently lead to successful practice.[10] The statement about the soft-drink machine might, but no statement about there being a teletransportation machine in the lobby will. There is no such thing as a teletransportation machine. Isn't it also true that there really aren't any soft-drink machines either? Why should the belief in those non-existent things lead to successful practice? The answer, of course, is that there are all the suitably arranged parts that make up what we call a

---

[10]The definition also mentioned being acceptable to common sense. And some statements that were once acceptable to common sense no longer are. People once believed that the world is flat, but no one does now. But the statement that the world is flat was never conventionally true. Remember that a statement must also consistently lead to successful practice to be conventionally true. The belief that the world is flat leads to the belief that if you sail far enough in the same direction you will reach the edge. But since the world is round, you can never succeed in reaching the edge of the world. Most (though not all) statements that are acceptable to common sense are so because they consistently lead to successful practice.

soft-drink machine. It's because of their interactions that my desire for a cold dose of artificially sweetened carbonated flavored water gets satisfied. And if we wanted to we could probably spell this all out. Usually, though, we don't want to. We just use our shorthand description of the situation: 'There's a soft-drink machine in the lobby.' It's worth remembering, though, that standing behind every conventionally true statement is some (much longer) ultimately true statement that explains why accepting the conventionally true statement leads to successful practice. This connection between conventional truth and ultimate truth plays an important role in what follows.

3.7

The distinction between conventional truth and ultimate truth was developed by commentators on the early Buddhist texts in order to solve an exegetical problem. The problem is that the Buddha's teachings seem inconsistent. On some occasions he teaches that there is no self and that what we think of as a person is really just a causal series of impermanent, impersonal states. On other occasions he says nothing of this and instead teaches a morality based on the doctrine of karma and rebirth. The inconsistency stems from the fact that the latter teaching appears to involve the idea that it is one and the same person who performs a deed in this life and reaps the karmic fruit in the next life. So the Buddha seems to affirm in those teachings what he elsewhere denies when he teaches the unreality of the person. Of course we could simply agree that the Buddha contradicted himself and leave it at that. But the commentators saw a way around attributing such a major error to the founder of their tradition: the first sort of teaching represents the full and final truth, whereas the second represents what ordinary people need to know in order to progress toward being able to grasp the full and final truth.[11] Using this distinction, commentators came to say that some sūtras have meanings that are 'fully drawn out' (*nītārtha*), while others have meanings requiring explication (*neyārtha*). The former came to be considered statements of the ultimate truth, the latter were said to be couched in terms of conventional truth.

The original point of the distinction between the two truths was, then, to clarify the early Buddhist view on the person. It was not to help us see that chariots are not ultimately real. It isn't too hard to see that chariots don't belong in our final ontology,

---

[11]This is said to be a manifestation of the Buddha's pedagogical skill (*upāyakauśala*), his ability to fashion his teaching to the capacities of his audience. Presumably the second sort of teaching is given to an audience that has not yet fully grasped the consequences of rebirth. They thus engage in immoral conduct, which only binds them more firmly to the cycle of rebirth. By teaching them a karmically based morality the Buddha hopes to make them less prone to conduct that reinforces their ignorance. Then they will be better able to appreciate the full and final truth about persons. It is an interesting question whether this practice represents deception on the Buddha's part.

and that we think they are fully real only because of the way in which we talk.[12] It is much more difficult to believe these things about persons. As the following passage from *Milindapañha* makes clear, much work is needed before we can see how this might be true. Nāgasena and Milinda have now been discussing the Buddha's teachings for a while:

> 'Nāgasena,' said the king, 'is the one who is born that very person, or is it someone else?'
> 'He is neither that person,' said the elder, 'nor is he someone else.'
> 'Give an illustration.'
> 'What do you say to this, your majesty? When you were a young, tender, weakly infant lying on your back, was that you, the person who is now king?'
> 'Indeed not, sir. The young, tender, weakly infant lying on its back was one person, and the grownup me is another person.'

Milinda's question is whether it is one and the same person who is born and then goes on to become an adult. Two things are worth noting. First, Nāgasena's answer is decidedly odd. How can the adult me and the infant me be neither the same person nor distinct persons?[13] Doesn't one or the other of these two possibilities have to be the case? Second, Milinda's answer is not what we would expect from someone whose views are supposed to represent common sense. Common sense says that adult and infant are the same person. Milinda says they are distinct persons. Here it's useful to bear in mind that Milinda has now been talking to Nāgasena for some time. One thing Milinda has learned is that all the *skandhas* are impermanent and that there is no self. He has concluded that a Buddhist should thus say adult and infant are distinct persons. Nāgasena will now show him why this common misinterpretation of non-self is wrong:

> 'If that is the case, your majesty, there can be no such thing as a mother, or a father, or a teacher, or an educated man, or a righteous man, or a wise man. Pray, your majesty, is the mother of the zygote one person, the mother of the embryo another person, the mother of the fetus another person, the mother of the newborn another person, the mother of the little child another person, and the mother of the grownup man another person? Is it one person who is a student, and another

---

[12]A 'final ontology' is an ontology that makes no concessions to our interests and limitations, and accurately reflects the objective nature of reality. In early Buddhist terms it would be an ontology that contains no mere conceptual fictions.

[13]It would not be odd if what Nāgasena said was that while adult and infant are not the same qualitatively, neither are they numerically different persons. In fact, most people would say that's true. That baby and I are one and the same (numerically identical) person; but the baby had qualities I now lack, such as cuteness, so we are qualitatively different. This interpretation of 'neither the same nor different' is only possible, though, if we translate what Nāgasena says using the ambiguous English 'same' and 'different'. That ambiguity is not present in the original. It is numerical identity and numerical distinctness that he is denying.

person who has finished his education? Is it one person who commits a crime, and another person whose hands and feet are cut off [in punishment]?'

'Indeed not, sir. But what, sir, would you reply to these questions?'

Said the elder, 'It was I, your majesty, who was a young, tender, weakly infant lying on my back, and it is I who am now grown up. In dependence on this very body all these different elements are collected together.'

'Give an illustration.'

'It is as if, your majesty, someone were to light a lamp; would it shine all night?'

'Certainly, sir, it would shine all night.'

'But now, your majesty, is the flame of the first watch the same flame as the flame of the middle watch?'

'Indeed not, sir.'

'Is the flame of the middle watch the same flame as the flame of the last watch?'

'Indeed not, sir.'

'But then, your majesty, was there one light in the first watch, another light in the middle watch, and a third light in the last watch?'

'Indeed not, sir. In dependence on that first flame there was one light that shone all night.'

'In exactly the same way, your majesty, is the series of psychophysical elements (*dharmas*) connected together: one element perishes, another arises, seamlessly united as though without before and after. Therefore neither as the same nor as a distinct person does this latest aggregation of consciousness connect up with earlier consciousness.'

'Give another illustration.'

'It is as if, your majesty, new milk were to change in process of time into sour cream, and from sour cream into fresh butter, and from fresh butter into clarified butter. And if anyone, your majesty, were to say that the sour cream, the fresh butter, and the clarified butter were each of them the very milk itself – now would he say well, if he were to say so?'

'Indeed not, sir. They came into being in dependence on that milk.'

'In exactly the same way, your majesty, is the series of psychophysical elements (*dharmas*) connected together: one element perishes, another arises, seamlessly united as though without before and after. Therefore neither as the same nor as a distinct person does this latest aggregation of consciousness connect up with earlier consciousness.' [MP 41f]

The overall point of the passage is clear enough: the ultimate truth about what are conventionally called persons is just that there is a causal series of impermanent *skandhas*. But there are a number of puzzling features that require close attention. First there is Nāgasena's examples of the mother, the student and the criminal. What point is he trying to make with these? Remember that Milinda thought the infant and the adult must be distinct persons. He thought this because he realized that the *skandhas* making up the infant are numerically distinct from those making up the adult. So he reasoned that in the absence of a self existing over and above the *skandhas*, adult and infant have to be two different persons. He is thus implicitly accepting a principle we might name: **Milinda's Principle** – that is, numerically distinct *skandhas* make for numerically distinct persons.

What Nāgasena is doing is showing that we must reject this principle by showing that absurd consequences would follow if we accepted it.[14] It would for instance follow that there is no such thing as a mother. A mother is a woman who conceives and then bears a child and typically raises it to adulthood. So for there to be mothers there must be persons who continue to exist from the time they conceive until the time their offspring is grown. But the *skandhas* making up a person are constantly going out of existence and getting replaced. For instance, the *skandhas* that make up the woman with an embryo in her uterus (second week of pregnancy) are numerically distinct from the *skandhas* that make up the woman carrying a fetus of six months. So by Milinda's Principle, these are distinct persons, and neither one is a mother. Likewise the *skandhas* that make up the person taking exams and the *skandhas* making up the person who receives a diploma are numerically distinct. So by Milinda's Principle the person who gets the degree is not the same person as the one who took the exams for that degree. The one who receives the diploma didn't do the work for it. Similarly the *skandhas* that make up the convicted robber now sitting in prison are numerically distinct from the *skandhas* that held up the flower shop last year. So the prisoner is not the person who committed the crime; they don't deserve to be punished.

Milinda is quick to agree that these are all absurd consequences. But it is important to stop and consider why. When we think of ourselves and others as persons, we are thinking of a person as something that endures at least a whole lifetime. We are, in other words, gathering together all the *skandhas* from birth until death under one convenient designator, 'person'. Why would this practice be useful? The examples of mother, student and criminal show why. If the pregnant woman didn't follow our practice, but followed Milinda's Principle instead, she would not identify with the woman who will later give birth. So she would see no reason to follow her doctor's prenatal healthcare advice. If the student didn't identify with the graduate, she would see no reason to study for an exam that will only benefit the degree-holder. If the criminal didn't identify with the person who robbed the flower shop, he would see no reason to refrain from robbing again after getting out of prison.

Our concept of a person has it that persons endure at least a lifetime. If we followed Milinda's Principle we would have to replace that concept with the concept of something that lasted nowhere near as long – perhaps for a day, maybe for just a minute. (It depends on how long individual *skandhas* last, and how many must be

---

[14]This strategy is called *reductio ad absurdum* or reducing to absurdity. The idea is to show that some statement is false by first assuming that it is true and then deducing absurd consequences from that assumption. Since these absurd consequences are presumably unacceptable to everyone, this is supposed to show that we should deny the statement in question. Indian philosophers call this strategy *tarka* or *prasaṅga*.

replaced before we say we have a new whole.) To think of ourselves in that way would not be to think of ourselves as persons as we understand that concept. Let's call the resulting view 'Punctualism', and the new concept of what we are 'P-persons'. What the examples show is that it would be a disaster if we thought of ourselves as P-persons rather than as persons. Our convenient designator 'person' is convenient because it helps us avert this disaster. Why is this, though, if there really are no such things as persons? To think of yourself as a person is to think of yourself as a whole that is made up of all the *skandhas* that occur over a lifetime. And wholes like chariots and persons are mere conceptual fictions, not ultimately real things. So why should it work better to think of ourselves in this way?

The answer to this question lies in the point made in the preceding section. Statements that are conventionally true are ones that work. And for every statement that is conventionally true, there is some (much longer) ultimately true statement that explains why it works. Nāgasena is making this point when he tells Milinda that adult and infant are the same person, and then goes on to say that past and present *skandhas* are united through their bodily causal connections. He is speaking first of what is conventionally true and then of what ultimate truth stands behind that conventional truth. But there was something else Nāgasena said about adult and infant, so let's look at all three of his statements.

1   Adult and infant are neither the same person nor distinct persons.
2   Adult and infant are the same person.
3   There is a causal series running from the 'infant' *skandhas* to the 'adult' *skandhas*.

We noted earlier that (1) seems odd. We can now add that (1) and (2) seem to contradict each other. (1) says that adult and infant are not the same person, while (2) says that they are. But perhaps we can now see a way out of both difficulties. Suppose we were to say that (2) represents the conventional truth, while (1) (and (3) as well) are supposed to be ultimately true. What (1) is meant to remind us of is that at the level of ultimate truth no statement about persons could be true; all such statements are simply meaningless. To ask whether these are the same person or distinct persons is to assume that there are such things as persons. Since this presupposition is false, the question has no answer. Questions of personal identity simply can't arise at the ultimate level.

At the conventional level, though, we can say that I was that infant, that we are the same person. The examples of mother, student and criminal are meant to show why (2) is conventionally true: because it works. And why does it work? As (3) tells us, the ultimate truth is that when the infant *skandhas* went out of existence, they caused child *skandhas* to come into existence, and so on in an unbroken chain until we arrive at the present adult *skandhas*. There are thus many causal connections between the *skandhas* existing at one time in the series and those existing later in the series. This in turn means that what happens to the earlier *skandhas* can influence how things are for the later *skandhas* in that series. Good eating habits early on make for well-functioning *rūpa skandhas* later. Excessive beer consumption tonight makes for pain sensations tomorrow. The desire to study now can bring about diploma-receiving for later *skandhas* in the series. And so on. So when present *skandhas* identify with past and future *skandhas* in the series – when they think of those other *skandhas* as 'me' – they are more likely to behave in ways that make it better for the later *skandhas*. To think of oneself as a person is to have the habit of identifying with the past and future *skandhas* in the series. This is why it is useful that we think of ourselves as persons.

Finally, Nāgasena gives two examples of causal series. The point of the first is clear enough. This is a case where an unbroken chain of closely resembling particulars leads to a conceptual fiction, the one light that shone all night. When we look more closely at what we ordinarily think of as one light that endures an entire night, we see that it is really a series of short-lived flames. Each flame only lasts a moment, for it is composed of incandescent gas molecules produced by the burning of the oil. But when those molecules dissipate, they cause new ones to take their place. For the heat of the first flame causes more oil to burn, producing a new replacement flame. So while each flame only lasts a moment, it causes another to take its place immediately upon its ceasing to exist. The result is what looks like a single thing that endures from dusk till dawn. And so it is conventionally true that there was one light that shone all night. The reality, though, is that there are just the many numerically distinct flames, not the one light that has them. The ultimate truth is that there is just the unbroken succession of flames, each causing the next.

The point of the second example is less apparent. What it illustrates, though, is a case that is in one respect like that of the light, but in other respects is different. Like the series of flames, the series of dairy products is unbroken: there is no gap between the time when there is milk and the time when there is ghee. Unlike the flames, though, the members of this series do not all resemble one another. Milk is white, butter yellow; milk is liquid, ghee is semi-solid. And we use each in different ways. We drink milk, put butter on our toast, and use ghee for frying. By contrast, each flame serves the same purpose for us, to light the room. For this reason we are not tempted to think of the dairy series as just one enduring thing. Instead we think of it as a succession of distinct products. Our ordinary way of thinking about this series is closer to the ultimate truth about causal series than is the common-sense view of the series of flames. But it too is dictated by our interests – the fact that we have different uses for different parts of the series. The point is to learn to look behind our wants and needs and see what is really there, the ultimate truth.

When it comes to the causal series of psychophysical elements,[15] Nāgasena gives an interesting description of the ultimate truth. The conventional truth is that I am a person who has existed for some time. I experience this existence as involving there

---

[15]The *dharmas*: these are the particular entities that get classified under the headings of the five *skandhas*. We will have much more to say about what these are when we come to our investigation of Abhidharma in Chapter 6.

being a 'me' who is aware of the different experiences that this 'I' has. Right now I am aware of reading these words and thinking about these ideas. Earlier this same 'I' was aware of other experiences – eating dinner, listening to music, conversing with friends. The objects that this conscious thing is aware of vary over time, but it is always the same 'I' that is aware of them. There is one thing, the 'I', holding together a plurality, the experiences. This is how things seem to us when we use the convenient designator 'person'. The ultimate truth, though, is that there is a causal series of psychophysical elements. Each exists for a while, then goes out of existence, but causes a replacement element to come into existence. In some cases the replacement resembles what was there a moment ago, as with the flames. Consciousness elements are like this. At each moment there is a new consciousness, but each is qualitatively identical with its predecessor. In other cases what follows an element does not resemble it. A feeling of pleasure gives rise to a desire, and that desire may in turn lead to other kinds of experiences. This is the reality behind the appearance of a person living a life. There is no enduring 'I' who has the different experiences. But neither does this mean that each experience is had by a distinct person, in the way that each stage in the dairy series is a distinct thing. There are just the psychophysical elements and their causal connections. This is the reality that makes it useful to think of the series as a person living a life.

We are now in a position to return to the dispute over the exhaustiveness claim and the Buddha's two arguments for non-self. Both arguments relied on there being no more to the person than the five *skandhas*. The opponent objected to the argument from control on the grounds that our ability to exercise some degree of control over all the *skandhas* shows that there must be more to us than the five *skandhas*. The response was that there could be control over all the *skandhas* if it were a shifting coalition of *skandhas* that performed the executive function. But the opponent challenged this response on the grounds that there would then be many distinct I's, not the one we have in mind when we say that I can dislike and seek to change all the *skandhas*. We can now see how the Buddhist will respond. They will say that ultimately there is neither one controller nor many, but conventionally it is one and the same person who exercises control over first one *skandha* and then another. This is so because the controller is a conceptual fiction. It is useful for a causal series of *skandhas* to think of itself as a person, as something that exercises some control over its constituents. Because it is useful, it is conventionally true. This is how we have learned to think of ourselves. But because this person, this controller, is a conceptual fiction, it is not ultimately true that there is one thing exercising control over different *skandhas* at different times. Nor is it ultimately true that it is different controllers exercising control over them. The ultimate truth is just that there are psychophysical elements in causal interaction. This is the reality that makes it useful for us to think of ourselves as persons who exercise control. Our sense of being something that exists over and above the *skandhas* is an illusion. But it is a useful one.

3.8

Does this strategy succeed in defending the exhaustiveness claim against the opponent's attack? I shall leave this question unanswered. Let us move on to a different objection to the arguments for non-self. Perhaps you have long been wondering how the Buddha could have argued for the non-existence of a self given his belief in rebirth. How is rebirth possible if there is no self that gets reborn, that goes from one life to the next?

Notice that this is a very different sort of objection than the one against the exhaustiveness claim. That objection tried to show that a key premise in the two arguments for non-self is false. This one doesn't do that. Instead it tries to show that the conclusion of the arguments (that there is no self) is incompatible with something else that the Buddha believes (that there is rebirth). If these two things really are incompatible, then the Buddhist could respond in either of two ways: by accepting a self, or by abandoning belief in rebirth. Given the centrality of non-self to the Buddha's teachings, the latter might seem the better choice. But the Buddhist will say that we don't need to choose. For there is no incompatibility between non-self and rebirth. This is the point Nāgasena makes in the following:

> Said the king: 'Nāgasena, does rebirth take place without anything transmi-grating [passing over]?'
> 'Yes, your majesty. Rebirth takes place without anything transmigrating.'
> 'How, Nāgasena, does rebirth take place without anything transmigrating? Give an illustration.'
> 'Suppose, your majesty, a man were to light a light from another light; pray, would the one light have passed over [transmigrated] to the other light?'
> 'Indeed not, sir.'
> 'In exactly the same way, your majesty, does rebirth take place without anything transmigrating.'
> 'Give another illustration.'
> 'Do you remember, your majesty, having learnt, when you were a boy, some verse or other from your poetry teacher?'
> 'Yes, sir.'
> 'Pray, your majesty, did the verse pass over [transmigrate] to you from your teacher?'
> 'Indeed not, sir.'
> 'In exactly the same way, your majesty, does rebirth take place without anything transmigrating.'
> 'You are an able man, Nāgasena.' [MP 71]

In both examples we have a causal process whereby one thing brings about the arising of some distinct but similar thing: a lit candle serves as cause of there being a lit oil lamp, and the teacher's knowledge of the poem serves as cause of the student's knowing the poem. The idea, then, is that rebirth occurs when one set of *skandas*, those making up the person in this life, causes a new set of *skandhas* to come into existence in a new life. This is not different in kind from the sort of thing that regularly occurs during a single lifetime. The cells in our bodies constantly wear out and die, but give rise to similar replacement cells. Desires, in getting satisfied and so being exhausted, set the stage for similar future desires. The continued existence of a person over the course of a lifetime is just the occurrence of a causal series of impermanent *skandhas*.

There are, of course, important differences between the case of a single lifetime and the case of rebirth. While qualitative changes occur during a life, they are gradual. I might wake up with a few more grey hairs than I had yesterday, but I never wake up to find I've become a cow; it is, though, thought possible to die as a human and be reborn as a cow. Unless I'm riding in a train or flying, I don't go to sleep in one place and wake up in another; typically, though, one is said to be reborn somewhere other than where one died. I can usually remember what I did yesterday, but one doesn't typically remember the events from one's past lives. Still the process of rebirth is governed by causal laws, namely the laws of karma. It is because I did these things out of these desires that I am reborn into this kind of life. In the case of a single lifetime, it is because the distinct psychophysical elements are causally connected that it is useful to collect them all together under the convenient designator 'person'. The same goes for the *skandhas* in distinct lives.

There may be another worry here. Rebirth is supposed to be governed by karmic causal laws. And karma is supposed to represent a kind of natural justice: people get what they deserve, good rebirth for virtuous actions, bad rebirth for vicious actions. And how can it be just if it isn't one and the same thing that performs the action and then gets the reward or punishment? This is something that bothers Milinda:

> 'Nāgasena,' said the king, 'what is it that is born into the next existence?'
> 'Your majesty,' said the elder, 'it is *nāma* and *rūpa* that is born into the next existence.'
> 'Is it this same *nāma* and *rūpa* that is born into the next existence?'
> 'Your majesty, it is not this same *nāma* and *rūpa* that is born into the next existence; but with this *nāma* and *rūpa*, your majesty, one does a deed – it may be good, or it may be evil – and by reason of this deed another *nāma* and *rūpa* is born into the next existence.'
> 'Sir, if it is not this same *nāma* and *rūpa* that is born into the next existence, is one not freed from one's deeds?'
> 'If one were not born into another existence,' said the elder, 'one would be freed from one's evil deeds; but, your majesty, inasmuch as one is born into another existence, therefore is one not freed from one's evil deeds.'
> 'Give an illustration.'
> 'Your majesty, it is as if a man were to light a fire in the winter-time and warm himself, and were to go off without putting it out. And then the fire were to burn another man's field, and the owner of the field were to seize him, and show him to the king, and say, 'Sir, this man has burnt up my field;' and the other were to say, 'Sir I did not set this man's field on fire. The fire which I failed to put out was a different one from the one which burnt up this man's field. I am not liable to

punishment.' Pray, your majesty, would the man be liable to punishment?'

'Assuredly, sir, he would be liable to punishment.'

'For what reason?'

'Because, in spite of what he might say, the man would be liable to punishment for the reason that the last fire derived from the first fire.'

'In exactly the same way, your majesty, with this *nāma* and *rūpa* one does a deed – it may be good, or it may be wicked – and by reason of this deed another *nāma* and *rūpa* is born into the next existence. Therefore is one not freed from one's evil deed.' [MP 46]

In the case of the fire, strictly speaking the wood-fire that the man lit to warm himself is not the grass-fire that consumed the other man's field. A fire that depends on one kind of fuel cannot be numerically identical with a fire that depends on another kind of fuel. But since the one fire caused the other, it is conventionally true that the first man burnt the second man's field. Likewise the *skandhas* involved in doing an evil deed are ultimately distinct from the *skandhas* born into the painful circumstances of a *preta*. Suppose I'm the one who did the evil deed. If I die without ever being punished, does the fact that nothing transmigrates mean that I escape getting what I deserve? No. Since these human *skandhas* caused those *preta skandhas*, it is conventionally true that that *preta* will be me, the one who did the deed. I will get what I deserve.[16]

This is how the Buddhist defends the doctrine of karma and rebirth against the charge that it is incompatible with non-self. Of course you might think that karma and rebirth are implausible beliefs that a reasonable Buddhism would abandon. The point here is just that the theory of two truths and the claim that persons are conventionally real may be used to show that rebirth and non-self are not incompatible. If Buddhists ought to stop believing in rebirth, it is not because that belief is inconsistent with their central tenet that there is no self.

There are still some questions that the Buddhist needs to answer. The most important of these is the following. The early Buddhist defense of non-self makes crucial use of the claim that wholes are unreal. This was the basis for their claim that persons are mere conceptual fictions that are only conventionally real. When we discussed the case of the chariot, perhaps it occurred to you that a spoke is also a whole made of parts. A spoke consists of many particles of metal or wood. So if wholes are only conceptual fictions, the spoke can't be ultimately real either. The only things that could be ultimately real would have to be impartite things. And just what are they like? Behind this question may lurk the suspicion that nothing that is genuinely impartite. That would represent a major difficulty for the Buddhist

---

[16]Notice that this case is not different in kind from the case of the convicted criminal that Milinda asked about earlier. That was a case of human justice, while this is a case of natural justice. And in that case justice gets carried out in a single lifetime, while this requires two lives. But the principle is the same: where there are the right kinds of causal connections, it is conventionally true that punishment is deserved even when ultimately distinct *skandhas* are involved.

approach. The Abhidharma movement in Buddhist philosophy represents an attempt to solve this difficulty. In Chapter 6 we will look at some Abhdiharma attempts to work out what the ultimately real impartite entities are like.

Before we do that, though, we will look at the ethical consequences of the doctrine of non-self. In the last chapter we wondered what it might be like to achieve the Buddhist goal of enlightenment. We now know more about what it would be like. To be enlightened is to know that strictly speaking there is no 'me' but only impersonal impermanent psychophysical elements in a causal series. It is to know that the 'I' is just a conceptual fiction. What might it be like to live with that knowledge? Would it be liberating, or would it be depressing? And how might it affect my behavior toward others? Would it make me more concerned about their welfare? Or would I figure that since there are no persons, I needn't worry about infringing on their rights? Would I conclude that anything goes? These are some of the questions we will address in the next chapter.

Further Reading

The complete debate between Nāgasena and King Milinda may be found in *The Questions of King Milinda*, trans. T.W. Rhys Davids (originally published by Oxford University Press, 1890; reprinted at Delhi: Motilal Banarsidass, 1965).

A recent formulation of reductionism about persons that is like that of early Buddhism is that of the British philosopher Derek Parfit. For exposition of the position and arguments in support, see his *Reasons and Persons* (Oxford: Oxford University Press, 1984), Chapters 11–13.

CHAPTER FOUR

Buddhist Ethics

The view of persons that we discussed in the last chapter is a form of reductionism. To be a reductionist about a certain kind of thing is to hold that things of that kind do not exist in the strict sense, that their existence just consists in the existence of other kinds of things. The Buddhist view of non-self, for instance, says that the existence of a person just consists in the occurrence of a complex causal series of impermanent, impersonal *skandhas*. But Buddhists are not the only ones to hold a reductionist view of persons. On some interpretations both Locke and Hume held such a view. More recently, Derek Parfit has given a sophisticated defense of reductionism about persons, which he explains as the denial that the continued existence of a person involves any 'further fact' over and above the facts about a causal series of psychophysical elements. Here is what he says about the effects of coming to believe that the reductionist view is true of oneself:

> Is the truth depressing? Some may find it so. But I find it liberating, and consoling. When I believed that my existence was such a further fact, I seemed imprisoned in myself. My life seemed like a glass tunnel, through which I was moving faster every year, and at the end of which there was darkness. When I changed my view, the walls of my glass tunnel disappeared. I now live in the open air. There is still a difference between my life and the lives of other people. But the difference is less. Other people are closer. I am less concerned about the rest of my life, and more concerned about the lives of other people. [1984: 281]

Buddhists say something similar. They say that becoming enlightened, coming to know the truth of reductionism, relieves existential suffering. They also claim that it makes us more concerned about the welfare of others. In this chapter we will explore how that might be. Ethics is concerned with questions concerning how we should live our lives, and how we should act toward others. Buddhists are reductionists about persons: they claim there is no self, and the person is only conventionally real. We will be investigating the ethical consequences of this claim.

4.1

The Buddha claims that the supreme goal for humans is nirvāna. We saw in Chapter 2 that this claim is based on the notion that only by becoming enlightened can we hope to permanently escape existential suffering. But it was unclear at that point whether there is anything more to being enlightened than just being without suffering. Is nirvāna pleasant? Is it a state of happiness? The early Buddhist texts are silent on this point. We saw, though, that this might be part of a strategy to get around the paradox of liberation. Now that we have a better understanding of the Buddhist doctrine of non-self, we might be able to resolve some of these issues.

You will sometimes encounter the claim that Buddhist nirvāna is ineffable, that it simply cannot be described or understood, it can only be experienced. If this were right, then there would be no point in our asking what nirvāna is like. If we were trying to decide whether to seek it ourselves or not, we would be stuck. We would have to simply take the word of those who have attained it that it is supremely valuable. We would have to embark on the path without knowing where it went. But this claim is based on a misunderstanding of certain early Buddhist texts, such as the following:

> Thus have I heard.
> ... Vaccha the *śramana* spoke to the Blessed One as follows:
> 'How is it, Gotama? Does Gotama hold that the arhat exists after death, and that this view alone is true, and every other false?'
> 'No, Vaccha. I do not hold that the arhat exists after death, and that this view alone is true, and every other false.'
> 'How is it, Gotama? Does Gotama hold that the arhat does not exist after death, and that this view alone is true, and every other false?'
> 'No, Vaccha. I do not hold that the arhat does not exist after death, and that this view alone is true, and every other false.'
> 'How is it, Gotama? Does Gotama hold that the arhat both exists and does not exist after death, and that this view alone is true, and every other false?'
> 'No, Vaccha. I do not hold that the arhat both exists and does not exist after death, and that this view alone is true, and every other false.'
> 'But how is it, Gotama? Does Gotama hold that the arhat, neither exists nor does not exist after death, and that this view alone is true, and every other false?'
> 'No, Vaccha, I do not hold that the arhat neither exists nor does not exist after death, and that this view alone is true, and every other false.'
> 'Vaccha, the theory that the arhat exists after death is a jungle, a wilderness, a puppet-show, a writhing, and a fetter, and is coupled with misery, ruin, despair, and agony, and does not tend to aversion, absence of passion, cessation, quiescence, knowledge, supreme wisdom, and nirvāna ...
> 'Vaccha, the theory that the arhat neither exists nor does not exist after death is a wilderness, a puppet-show, a writhing, and a fetter, and is coupled with misery, ruin, despair, and agony, and does not tend to aversion, absence of passion, cessation, quiescence, knowledge, supreme wisdom, and nirvāna.
> 'This is the objection I perceive to these theories, so that I have not adopted any one of them.'
> 'But has Gotama any theory of his own?'
> 'The Tathāgata, O Vaccha, is free from all theories; but this, Vaccha, the Tathāgata does know: the nature of rūpa, and how rūpa arises, and how rūpa perishes; the nature of sensation, and how sensation arises, and how sensation perishes; the nature of perception, and how perception arises, and how perception perishes; the nature of the predispositions, and how volition arises, and how

volition perishes; the nature of consciousness, and how consciousness arises, and how consciousness perishes. Therefore say I that the Tathāgata has attained deliverance and is free from attachment, inasmuch as all imaginings, or agitations, or false notions concerning a self or anything pertaining to a self have perished, have faded away, have ceased, have been given up and relinquished.'

'But, Gotama, where is the monk reborn who has attained to this deliverance for his mind?'

'Vaccha, to say that he is reborn would not fit the case.'

'Then, Gotama, he is not reborn.'

'Vaccha, to say that he is not reborn would not fit the case.'

'Then, Gotama, he is both reborn and is not reborn.'

'Vaccha, to say that he is both reborn and not reborn would not fit the case.'

'Then, Gotama, he is neither reborn nor not reborn.'

'Vaccha, to say that he is neither reborn nor not reborn would not fit the case ...'

'Gotama, I am at a loss what to think in this matter, and I have become greatly confused, and the faith in Gotama inspired by an earlier conversation has now disappeared.'

'Enough, O Vaccha! Be not at a loss what to think in this matter, and be not greatly confused. Profound, O Vaccha, is this doctrine, recondite, and difficult of comprehension, good, excellent, and not to be reached by mere reasoning, subtle, and intelligible only to the wise; and it is a hard doctrine for you to learn, who belong to another sect, to another faith, to another persuasion, to another discipline, and sit at the feet of another teacher. Therefore, Vaccha, I will now question you, and answer as you think right. What do you think, Vaccha? Suppose a fire were to burn in front of you; would you be aware that the fire was burning in front of you?'

'Gotama, if a fire were to burn in front of me, I should be aware that a fire was burning in front of me.'

'But suppose, Vaccha, someone were to ask you, "On what does this fire that is burning in front of you depend?" What would you answer, Vaccha?'

'Gotama, if someone were to ask me, 'On what does this fire that is burning in front of you depend?' I would answer, Gotama, "It is on fuel of grass and wood that this fire that is burning in front of me depends."'

'But, Vaccha, if the fire in front of you were to become extinct, would you be aware that the fire in front of you had become extinct?'

'Gotama, if the fire in front of me were to become extinct, I should be aware that the fire in front of me had become extinct.'

'But, Vaccha, if someone were to ask you, "In which direction has that fire gone: east, or west, or north, or south?" what would you say, O Vaccha?'

'The question would not fit the case, Gotama. For the fire which depended on fuel of grass and wood, when that fuel has all gone, and it can get no other, being thus without nutriment, is said to be extinct.'

'In exactly the same way, Vaccha, all rūpa by which one could predicate the existence of the arhat, all that rūpa has been abandoned, uprooted, pulled out of the ground like a palmyra-tree, and become non-existent and not liable to spring up again in the future. The arhat, O Vaccha, who has been released from what is styled rūpa, is deep, immeasurable, unfathomable, like the mighty ocean. To say

that he is reborn would not fit the case. To say that he is not reborn would not fit the case. To say that he is both reborn and not reborn would not fit the case. To say that he is neither reborn nor not reborn would not fit the case.
'All sensation …
'All perception …
'All volition … All consciousness by which one could predicate the existence of the arhat, all that consciousness has been abandoned, uprooted, pulled out of the ground like a palmyra-tree, and become non-existent and not liable to spring up again in the future. The arhat, O Vaccha, who has been released from what is styled consciousness, is deep, immeasurable, unfathomable, like the mighty ocean. To say that he is reborn would not fit the case. To say that he is not reborn would not fit the case. To say that he is both reborn and not reborn would not fit the case. To say that he is neither reborn nor not reborn would not fit the case.' [M I.483–88]

It should be clear how passages like this might lead some to think that the state of nirvāna is ineffable. First we find the Buddha denying that any of the four possibilities listed by Vaccha correctly describes the situation of the arhat after death. Then he says that this situation is 'deep' and 'immeasurable'. Since logic suggests that one of the four possibilities would have to be true,[1] the conclusion seems inescapable that the Buddha is calling nirvāna something that transcends all rational discourse. But now that we understand the distinction between the two truths we can see why this would be a mistake. As the example of the fire makes clear, the Buddha's four denials all have to do with the fact that any statement about the enlightened person lacks meaning at the level of ultimate truth.

When a fire has exhausted its fuel, we say that it's gone. Where has it gone? The question makes no sense. For the extinguished fire to have gone somewhere, it would have to continue to exist. The question presupposes that the fire continues to exist. Yet the question still seems to be meaningful. Since we are saying something about the fire – that it is extinguished – must there not be a real fire that we are talking about? How can you talk about something that is utterly unreal? And since this real fire is not here in front of us, must it not be somewhere else? When we encounter this sort of paradoxical situation, it is useful to stop and ask about the nature of the words we are using. How does the word 'fire' actually function? Consider the situation

---

[1]Logic actually seems to suggest that there are only two possibilities, not four. There are a number of so-called disputed questions where the Buddha considers four possible answers: P, not P, both P and not P, and neither P nor not P. This general form or scheme is called the tetralemma (*catuṣkoṭi*). But logic seems to limit us to just a dilemma: either 'P' is true, or else it is false, in which case 'not P' is true. Scholars have disputed whether the presence of the third and fourth possibilities in this scheme indicate that Buddhists use some kind of alternative logic. One plausible answer is that the logic is standard. The third possibility (both P and not P) is meant to cover cases where 'P' is ambiguous, so that it could be said to be true in one sense but false in another. And the fourth possibility is meant to cover cases where there genuinely exists some third possibility besides those of 'P' and 'not P'.

where we say we kept the fire burning by adding more fuel. Here we are talking as if there is one enduring thing, the fire, that first consists of flames from kindling, then later consists of flames from logs, then still later consists of flames from new logs. This should tell us that 'fire' is a convenient designator for a causal series of flames (just as 'the one light that shone all night' was really a causal series of lamp flames). And this in turn means that no statement using the word 'fire' can be ultimately true (or ultimately false). Any such statement lacks meaning at the ultimate level of truth. All that can be talked about at the ultimate level are individual flames, not the series of flames as a whole. This is why no answer to the question where the fire has gone is true. For a statement to be true (or false) it has to be meaningful. And statements about mere conceptual fictions are not ultimately meaningful.

When we apply this analysis to the case of the arhat after death, it becomes clear why the Buddha can reject all four possibilities without implying that nirvāna is an ineffable state. The word 'arhat' is a convenient designator, just like 'fire'. So nothing we say about the arhat can be ultimately true. The only ultimately true statement about the situation will be one that describes the *skandhas* in the causal series. It is, for instance, true that at a certain point (which we conventionally call 'the death of the arhat') the *nāma skandhas* existing at that moment do not give rise to successor *nāma skandhas*. Does this mean that the arhat is annihilated – that nirvāna means the utter extinction of the enlightened person? No. There is no such thing as the arhat, so it lacks meaning to say that the arhat is annihilated. And for exactly the same reason, it lacks meaning to say that the arhat attains an ineffable state after death.

4.2

So it is possible to say meaningful things about nirvāna. What, then, would it be like? In particular, what would it be like to know that 'I' is just a convenient designator, that strictly speaking there is no such thing as the enduring person?[2] Parfit said that coming to believe a reductionist view of persons made him less concerned about the rest of his life. This suggests that the enlightened person takes no care for what tomorrow will bring. Perhaps this is because they know that whatever it does bring, it will be someone else who receives it. Is this what cessation with remainder, being enlightened but still alive, is like? Is the arhat someone who lives wholly in the present moment? This is a popular interpretation of Buddhist nirvāna. But it is also a mistake. As we saw earlier (in Chapter 2), this Punctualist view is a form of annihilationism. And annihilationism, we know, is one of the two extreme views

---

[2]More specifically, what would it be like to be an arhat, someone who has become enlightened by following the path laid out by a Buddha? The Buddhist tradition holds that becoming a Buddha takes an immense amount of effort expended over very many lives. So it would be natural to hold that conceiving of what it would be like to be a Buddha would be very difficult for most people. But this need not be so with the life of an arhat.

about our existence that the Buddha says should be rejected in favor of his middle path.

At this point, though, you might have begun to wonder whether this can be right. Suppose it's true that there is no enduring self to make me the same person from one stage in my life to the next (or from one life to the next). When I get ready for bed tonight, should I brush my teeth and floss? Brushing my teeth is tedious, and sometimes flossing hurts. So why should I do it? Certainly not for any benefit that these present *skandhas* get out of it. If there's any benefit in doing it, that benefit accrues to the future *skandhas* that avoid the pain of tooth decay and gum disease. And we now know that those future *skandhas* are distinct from these present *skandhas*. So why should these present ones make this sacrifice on behalf of those future ones? Why shouldn't they just appreciate the present for what it is and not worry about the future? Why isn't Punctualism the right conclusion to draw from the reductionist view of persons?

Punctualism is the view that since there is no self, and the parts of the person are all impermanent, the true 'I' doesn't last very long: perhaps a day or a week, but maybe just an instant. Since they think this is the truth about us, Punctualists hold we should stop putting so much effort into planning for and worrying about the future. Once we do this, they think we will learn to truly appreciate the here and now for what it is. We'll learn to live in the present, and our lives will be fuller and richer for it. But let's think about what the Punctualist says is the truth about us.

The Punctualist says that the 'I' is something that exists only as long as a particular set of *skandhas* lasts. Now each of us has a special concern for themselves. We all take a special interest in our own welfare. And the 'I' represents what it is that we identify with. To say that something is part of the 'I' is to say that it is one of the things whose welfare I should be concerned about. This is why **P** has the consequence that we should only be concerned about the present moment. But now in what way is **P** supposed to be true? Is it ultimately true? No. What the Punctualist says we should identify with is the collection of *skandhas* that exist together at present: these present body parts, and these present thoughts and feelings. This 'I' of theirs is a whole. It is not the same whole as the whole that we call a 'person'. That whole is a causal series of sets of *skandhas*. The whole that the Punctualist says we should identify with is just one set of *skandhas* – the ones existing right now – and not the series made up of such sets. Still it is a whole. And wholes are mere conceptual fictions. Since **P** contains a reference to a whole, it could not be ultimately true. (Nor could it be ultimately false either.)

So could **P** be conventionally true? Remember that for a statement to be conventionally true it must consistently lead to successful practice. Which way of thinking of ourselves leads to greater success: as things that last for just a very short while, or as persons, things that last at least a lifetime? To answer this question we need to decide what counts as success in practice. And of course different people have different ideas as to what constitutes success. But this is only because of individual differences in how people obtain pleasure and happiness. Surely everyone could agree that successful practice is practice that brings about more pleasure and happiness, and less pain and suffering.[3] That makes it quite clear which statement is conventionally true. There is greater overall pleasure and happiness, and less overall pain and suffering, when we think of ourselves as persons than when we think of ourselves in the Punctualist way. When these present *skandhas* identify with future *skandhas* in the causal series, they brush and floss. And that means less tooth decay and gum disease. If we were to follow the Punctualist's advice there would be more of this sort of pain and suffering. There would also be less pleasure and happiness. So **P** is conventionally false. As Nāgasena said, the conventional truth is that we are persons. This is conventionally true because it is ultimately true that these present *skandhas* are the cause of the future *skandhas* in this series. So what these *skandhas* do will affect the welfare of those future *skandhas*. This is why thinking of ourselves as persons results in greater overall welfare.

Punctualism is not the right way to understand Buddhist nirvāna. Still someone might try to defend Punctualism against the argument we have just looked at. They might say that this argument wrongly defines success as achieving more pleasure and less pain now and in the future. Instead success should be defined as achieving more present pleasure and less present pain. Future pleasure and pain should not be included in our calculations. The Punctualist would say this is because future pleasure and pain mean nothing to the present 'I'. Only present pleasure and pain should be counted, since those are the only feelings that this 'I' ever has. Future pleasure and pain are felt by another 'I'. And when we define success in this way, **P** turns out to be conventionally true. If we think of ourselves as persons, then we will brush and floss. At best these result in present feelings of indifference. There are much better ways to maximize present pleasure and minimize present pain.

Does this objection to the argument succeed? Here are some things to consider. The argument was for the conclusion that **P** is conventionally false. The Punctualist objection is that this begs the question by assuming that future pleasure and pain should count in determining whether a theory is conventionally true or false.[4] But the Buddhist could respond that it would be question-begging for the Punctualist to

---

[3]It's sometimes objected that there are times when we aim at more rather than less pain, as when someone goes through a hard workout. But the point of working out is not to experience the pain that comes from strenuous exercise. The point is to enjoy the benefits that the workout produces. These may include good health, which amounts to less pain in the long run. They may also include the pleasure that comes with the sense that one has overcome a difficult obstacle. If strenuous exercise only produced pain and no benefits, then no one would ever bother to work out.

[4]The fallacy of begging the question is committed when an argument smuggles its conclusion in among its premises. Here is a stock example: 'Of course God exists. It says so in the sacred texts. And everything in the sacred texts is true, since it is the word of God.' This argument begs the question by including a premise, 'the sacred texts are the word of God', that presupposes the truth of the conclusion, 'God exists'. It is fallacious because you can't prove that the conclusion 'God exists' is true by using evidence that already assumes it is true.

assume that only present pleasure and pain should count. Is there a neutral standpoint to be found here?

4.3

We have now ruled out two views about what nirvāna might be like: the view that it is ineffable, and the Punctualist view that it means living wholly in the present. Is there anything positive we can say? By now it should be clear why enlightenment brings about the cessation of existential suffering. In effect the Buddhist is saying we experience such suffering because we take too seriously the useful fiction of the person. We experience existential suffering when the fact of our transitoriness undermines the belief that our lives can have meaning. But how did I come to think that my life might have meaning? This seems to be part of what it means to think of oneself as a person. And a person is just a useful fiction, like the average college student. We wouldn't make the mistake of searching for the meaning of the life of the average college student. So when we feel despair over the seeming pointlessness of our own lives, this is because of a fundamental error in our view of what we are.

To see the Buddhist's point here it might be useful to consider how we go about socializing small children. As adults we automatically think of ourselves as persons, so we naturally assume that we always did. But the experience of child-rearing tells us differently. Much of the work of raising a child involves getting the child to think of itself as a person. That is, the child must learn to identify with the past and future stages in the causal series of psychophysical elements. Take food issues, for instance. Eating healthy foods does not always bring immediate pleasure. But telling the recalcitrant child that eating these foods will promote long-term health has little effect. This isn't necessarily because the child doesn't believe what they are told. It's because the child doesn't identify with the healthy adult it will become if it eats the right food. Its basic attitude is, 'Why eat something now that doesn't taste good for the sake of someone who doesn't even exist? Why should I care about what happens to them?' Likewise when the child is punished for a past misdeed. Until the child has learned to identify with those past psychophysical elements, it will seem quite unfair: 'Why make me suffer for something somebody else did?' Coming to see itself as a person is not an easy lesson for the child to learn. We try to make it easier, though, by getting the child to think of their life as a story they get to write. To become a person involves learning to make present sacrifices for the sake of future welfare. The child learns to do this by learning to think of its present choices as having meaning for the future. It learns to think of its life as a kind of narrative. And it learns to think of itself as the central figure in that narrative. Because we learned those lessons well, we expect our lives to have significance.

Notice that the Buddhist is not recommending that we become like that small child. The lesson the child learns is important. It leads to there being less overall pain and suffering in the world. It is conventionally true that we are persons. The difficulty the

Buddhist is pointing out comes from the way in which we learned that lesson. We learned it by coming to think of ourselves as characters in a drama, figures whose actions have meaning for the future of the story. And this bit of useful myth-making is what sets the stage for existential suffering. What we need to do is unlearn the myth but continue the practice. I should continue to identify with the past and future stages of this causal series. But I should not do so because I think of myself as the hero of the story that is my life. I should do so because this is a way of bringing about more pleasure and less pain in the world. Because I feel special concern for the future elements in the series, I brush and floss. And so there is less pain. Because I take responsibility for the past elements in the series, I acknowledge past mistakes and avoid repeating them. And so there is less pain. In one respect the enlightened person's life is just like ours. We all identify with the past and future stages of the causal series. And we try to brush and floss. The difference is that the enlightened person does so without leaning on the crutch of a self that confers significance on the events of a life. The enlightened person avoids the pain of tooth decay, just like the rest of us. But the enlightened person also avoids existential suffering.

One common reaction to this account of nirvāna is to find it hugely depressing. This often stems from the sense that the Buddhist account robs life of all meaning. If the events in my life don't fit into some larger scheme, then what's the point? It's little consolation to be told that the sense that our lives each have their own unique purpose was always just an illusion. But according to the Buddhist, this reaction rests on a still deeper mistake. For there to be depression over the lack of ultimate meaning, there must be a subject for whom meaninglessness is a source of despair. When the Buddhist denies that our lives have meaning, it is not because they hold that our lives are inherently meaningless. It is rather because they hold that meaning requires something that does not ultimately exist, the subject for whom events in a life can have meaning. If there is no such subject – if there is no self – then there is equally no subject whose life can lack all meaning. There is no one whose life either has or lacks meaning. There is just the life.

This last point helps us see how there might be some truth to the claim that being enlightened means living in the here and now. We saw that being enlightened does not mean having no concern for the future consequences of my present actions. But it is one thing to consider tomorrow's hangover when deciding how much beer to drink tonight. It is another to see that decision as defining who I am. It can be burdensome to see each event in my life as having meaning for my identity. This can detract from our appreciation of the present. And it can make bad experiences worse. Being sick or injured is painful. But in addition to the pain itself, there is the anxiety that comes from wondering what this pain says about who I am and where I am going. When the enlightened person is sick or injured they will seek the appropriate medical help to relieve their pain. But they will not experience the suffering we ordinarily feel in those circumstances. They are liberated from the burdens that come with the sense of a self. Perhaps this is why, in Buddhist art, enlightened persons are often depicted with a serene half-smile on their faces.

4.4

Let us move on to the second part of our investigation of Buddhist ethics. We have been looking at the consequences of non-self for the part of ethics concerned with how we should live our own lives. We will now examine how the doctrine of non-self affects our obligations toward others. What moral consequences might follow from the person's being a mere conceptual fiction? If the enlightened person is someone who knows this to be true, how would this affect their moral conduct? In the passage we quoted earlier, Parfit said that coming to accept the reductionist view of persons led him to be less concerned about the rest of his life, and more concerned about the lives of others. We have seen how Buddhists could agree with the first part of this statement. Do they also agree with the second? Does enlightenment lead to moral improvement?

If we think of Buddhism as a religion, we will certainly expect Buddhists to have much to say about morality. Religions are widely seen as a major source of moral training for their adherents. This expectation will not be disappointed. Buddhist literature is rife with lists of virtues that should be cultivated and vices that should be abandoned, uplifting stories of moral exemplars, cautionary tales about the sad fates of people who went astray, and the like. But many people see a much tighter connection between religion and morality. They think of religion as belief in a transcendent power, and morality as a set of rules specifying acceptable treatment of others. The connection they see is that the rules are commands of the higher power. On this view, religious faith is actually required if one is to be moral. Only belief in God, it is thought, will move one to obey the moral law when temptation urges otherwise. But no Buddhist would accept this picture. Since Buddhism is atheist (in the sense discussed in Chapter 1), Buddhists will not think of moral rules as divine commandments. What makes it wrong to take another's property, for instance, cannot be that the Buddha forbids it. So can Buddhism actually provide a foundation for morality? Can it give a satisfactory answer to the question, 'Why should I be moral?'.

Consider the way Plato posed this question in his dialogue *Republic*. Suppose there were a ring that made one invisible. Would someone with such a ring not use it to their own advantage even when doing so meant violating the commonly accepted moral rules? If you could steal from a bank in a way that was guaranteed to be undetectable, would you? The problem here is not one of moral ignorance. We know that stealing is wrong. The problem is one of moral motivation: why should I be moral? A theist has a ready answer to this question. While a magic ring might make us invisible to other humans, God would see us, and punish us for our sin. A Buddhist cannot say this. Nor can they say we should be moral out of love of our creator. Buddhists do not believe there is a being who created us. So what can the Buddhist say? Why, according to the Buddhist, should we be moral?

The Buddhist answer has three layers. Each layer answers the question of moral motivation in a way that is responsive to the abilities of people at a certain stage on the path to nirvāna. The first answer is that we should obey the moral rules because they reflect the karmic causal laws. Stealing, for instance, is motivated by a desire that causes bad karmic fruit, such as rebirth as a *preta*. Acts of benevolence toward strangers, on the other hand, are motivated by desires that cause good karmic fruit, such as rebirth as a god or a high-caste human. Since I would much rather be reborn as a high-caste human than as a *preta*, it is to my advantage to refrain from stealing and to practice benevolence toward strangers. This answer will obviously satisfy only those who accept the doctrine of karma and rebirth. More importantly, though, it works only for those whose primary aim in life is to attain pleasure and happiness. These are not people who are actively seeking nirvāna. We said above that each layer represents a teaching designed for those who have reached a certain point on the path to nirvāna. How can such people be said to be on the path? Does this teaching contribute to anyone's progress toward nirvāna?

The answer to this question takes us into the second layer. The Buddha speaks of three poisons (*kleśas*), factors that account for our staying bound in *saṃsāra*. The three are greed, hatred and delusion. These factors have the interesting property of being self-perpetuating. This is because the three poisons tend to motivate certain sorts of actions, and these actions in turn tend to reinforce the three poisons. Here delusion is ignorance of the three characteristics (impermanence, suffering and non-self). Greed and hatred clearly presuppose such ignorance, particularly ignorance of non-self. Greed and hatred also lead us to act in ways that reinforce our ignorance, thus setting the stage for further bouts of greed and hatred. When my greed leads me to take something that is not mine, for instance, I am reinforcing the belief that there is an 'I' that can be made better off through what it possesses. The result is a kind of feedback loop that is supposed to explain why the cycle of rebirths has gone on for so long. The eight-fold path that the Buddha taught (see Chapter 2) is meant to help us break out of this loop. Recall that three of the eight factors in this path – right speech, right conduct and right livelihood – represent the basic moral virtues that lay followers of the Buddha are to cultivate. Right conduct, for instance, includes such things as habitually refraining from stealing, while right speech includes the virtue of honesty. Why are these included in the path to nirvāna? Not because they generate pleasant karmic fruits. Rather because such virtues help counteract the three poisons. A certain kind of moral training is a necessary prerequisite for attaining the kind of insight that leads to nirvāna.

The answer of the first layer said we should be moral because doing so will lead to a pleasant rebirth. The answer of the second layer says we should be moral because doing so is part of the training necessary for attaining nirvāna. In order to counteract the three poisons, we must develop habits that serve as antidotes to greed, hatred and delusion. The virtue of honesty, for instance, will make us more likely to accept the truth about ourselves. And the virtue of habitually refraining from taking what is not ours will help diminish our desire for possessions. Of course the three poisons still have ample scope in the life of the conventionally virtuous person. I might never steal and yet covet those things I can rightfully attain. I might feel righteous anger at those not as morally upstanding as myself. But the conventional morality that is inculcated through belief in karma and rebirth is just an early stage of the path. The point of these moral practices is to counteract the three poisons just enough to make it possible to renounce the householder's existence and become a monk or nun. With entry into the Buddhist monastic order comes a whole new set of moral practices designed to help extinguish the three poisons. One is, for instance, required to be celibate, and the only possessions traditionally allowed the monk or nun are robes and an alms bowl. There are meditation exercises designed to counteract sensual desire, which is an especially powerful form of greed. There are exercises designed to help one cultivate equanimity and loving-kindness toward all, thereby curbing our tendency toward anger. The claim is that by following this regime of retraining our emotional habits, we will ultimately become able to fully grasp the truth about ourselves – that there is no self – and thus attain nirvāna.

Suppose this is right. Then the person who seeks nirvāna will know not to engage in immoral conduct. This is not because nirvāna is a reward for those who are morally pure. It is rather because immoral conduct stems from motives that interfere with the liberating insight of non-self. But what about the person who has attained nirvāna? Why should they be moral? Not because doing so will help them attain nirvāna. They have already attained it. Is there anything about enlightenment that could constitute a source of moral motivation? We have reached the third layer. What we will find here is an argument for the obligation to be benevolent: whenever we are able to prevent others from experiencing pain or suffering we must do so. So to the extent that morality consists in giving equal consideration to the welfare of others, this can be seen as an argument for an obligation to be moral. The immorality of stealing, for instance, can be explained by the fact that the thief intends to benefit while causing others pain. To be moral is to give others' welfare no less weight than one gives one's own welfare. Benevolence could be said to be the soul of morality. So an argument for the obligation to be benevolent would answer the question, 'Why should I be moral?'.

This argument will not claim that being moral is a means to some other end we might want, such as good rebirth or nirvāna. Instead it will claim that if we properly understand what it is that we say we want, we will see that we must want to promote the welfare of others. The key to this proper understanding is, of course, becoming enlightened. What the argument will claim is that once we grasp the truth of non-self, we will see that there is no reason to prefer our own welfare over that of others. And since everyone already acknowledges that they ought to promote their own welfare, it follows that anyone who is enlightened must acknowledge an obligation to promote the welfare of others as well. But the obligation that it argues for does not apply just to the enlightened. It applies to all of us, if it is true that there is no self.

The argument begins by comparing our usual attitude toward the suffering of others with our attitude toward our own possible future suffering. It uses the assumption of karma and rebirth, and describes the attitude one might take toward one's next life:

If I do not prevent the suffering of others because it does not hurt me,
What is the point of preventing the suffering of a future body that likewise does
    not hurt me?
'That will also be me then', this is an imagined error,
For it is one thing that dies and quite another that is reborn.
If it is thought that it is just for the one whose pain it is to prevent it,
A pain in the foot is not the hand's, so why should the hand prevent it?
If it is said that, while wrong, still this behavior stems from the sense of 'I',
That is unwise. Suffering, both one's own and that of others, is to be prevented to
    the best of one's ability.
The continuant and the collective are unreal, like the row, the army, etc.
There exists no one whose suffering this is, hence who will there be to say 'This
    is mine'?
Ownerless sufferings are all devoid of distinction between 'mine' and 'other'.
It is just because they are suffering that they are to be prevented; how can this be
    limited?
If it were asked why suffering is to be prevented, everyone without exception
    agrees that it is.
Thus if it is to be prevented, then all of it is to be prevented; if not, then one's own
    case is also like that of other persons. [BCA 8.97–103]

The first two verses are discussing the fact that someone who believes in karma and
rebirth would do what they could to prevent being reborn with a very painful body.
We think this is perfectly sensible, since if you believe in rebirth then you think the
person with that painful body will be you. The point being made in the verses is that
the *skandhas* constituting the future person with the painful body are not the
skandhas that make up me now. Of course not everyone believes in rebirth. But as we
saw in the last chapter, we could say the same thing about the *skandhas* making up a
person at one stage of life and the *skandhas* constituting that person later in life. So
we could say the same thing about the person brushing their teeth and the person
whose cavities are thereby prevented. Consequently we could change the second half
of the second verse to 'It is one set of teeth that are brushed and quite another whose
cavities are prevented.'

The third verse considers the case where my hand removes a splinter from my foot.
We think this is equally sensible, since hand and foot are both parts of me, so I am
acting to stop my own suffering. The verse makes the point that hand and foot are
nonetheless distinct things. So we now have two cases where we think it is sensible to
prevent pain, yet strictly speaking it is one thing that experiences the pain and
something else that acts to prevent it. Yet we also think it is perfectly reasonable for
each of us to take a special interest in our own welfare. If someone else's suffering
won't affect me in any way, then I have no obligation to do anything about it. While
we may think it would be very nice to help others, we believe it would not be
irrational to attend to only my own pain and not that of others. The rest of the passage
discusses the apparent conflict between this common attitude and the two cases
discussed in the first three verses. We could put all of this as follows:

1   Suppose that we are each obligated to prevent only our own suffering.
2   In the case of one's own future suffering, it is one set of *skandhas* that does the preventing for another set that has the suffering.
3   In the case of one's own present suffering, it is one part that does the preventing for another part that has the suffering.
4   The sense of 'I' that leads one to call future *skandhas* and distinct present parts 'me' is a conceptual fiction.
5   Hence it cannot be ultimately true that some suffering is one's own and some suffering is that of others.
6   Hence the claim that we are obligated to prevent only our own suffering lacks ultimate grounding
7   Hence either there is an obligation to prevent suffering regardless of where it occurs, or else there is no obligation to prevent any suffering.
8   But everyone agrees that at least some suffering should be prevented (namely one's own).
C   Therefore there is an obligation to prevent suffering regardless of where it occurs.

What this argument in effect does is accuse us of irrationality if we think it's justifiable to be concerned about our own pain and not be equally concerned about the pain of other people. The crucial premise is (4). This is where non-self gets brought in. It claims that there is no ultimate fact that could back up our discriminating between our own pain and that of others. Suppose there is no self. If wholes are also unreal, then hand and foot cannot be parts of one whole, my body. This is likened to the case of an army. When the helicopter pilot evacuates the wounded soldier, it is one thing that acts on another. If wholes are unreal, then the present body and the future body cannot be stages of one thing, me. This is likened to the case of a row. The line for a movie is made up of different people at 9:00 and 9:15. The army and the movie line are just useful fictions. There are really just the parts making them up. So, as (6) concludes, there are no ultimate facts that could explain on the one hand why I should take that splinter out of my foot and I should brush and floss, but on the other hand why I need not have the same concern for preventing the suffering of others. Premise (7) then points out that there are two remaining options: that suffering should be prevented regardless of 'whose' it is, or that absolutely nothing matters. It would be consistent of me to do nothing to prevent any pain anywhere – my own or that of others. But that would be insane. So the obligation that I already acknowledge to prevent my own pain extends equally to the suffering of others. Once I overcome the illusion of a self, I will see that my desire to prevent my own pain is really just a desire to prevent pain, period.

We know that Buddhists deny the existence of a self. It is also widely known that Buddhists claim an enlightened person will be benevolent (or compassionate). It might be tempting to see these two things as connected in the following way: 'If I have no self, then you and I aren't really distinct people, we are really one, so I should be just as concerned about your welfare as I am about my own.' But this is not what the Buddhist is saying. The trouble comes with the 'we are really one'. There are Indian philosophers who actually say something like this. But they are not Buddhists; they belong to the orthodox school called Advaita Vedānta. Unlike the Buddhists, they hold that there is a self. Moreover, they hold that there really is just one self. So they would say that what we think of as distinct persons really aren't distinct. The Buddhist argument we just looked at agrees that we are not really distinct persons. But what Buddhists deny is not the distinctness. They deny that there are persons. They deny that there are those things that could be either many or else really one. The Advaitin and the Buddhist can both argue for the same conclusion – that we should show equal concern for the welfare of all. But they argue for it in very different ways.

Does the Buddhist argument work? Here is one question to consider. In (6) it is concluded from (4) and (5) that there is no ultimate ground for the claim that we are obligated to prevent only our own suffering. Is this right? We saw (in Chapter 3) how the Buddhist defends (4). And if (4) is true, then (5) must be as well. Ultimately there is just suffering, not the person who has it. But suffering only occurs together with other *skandhas*, as part of a causal series of *skandhas*. Remember that while persons are not ultimately real, it is conventionally true that we are persons. And this conventional truth is grounded in the ultimate existence of a causal series of *skandhas*. Because these *skandhas* were caused by those earlier ones, it is conventionally true that it's my own fault if I have cavities – I am the same person as the one who didn't brush regularly. All of this we already knew. But here is another point that has not yet come up: there are many distinct causal series. These can be distinguished by virtue of where the effects show up. The refusal to brush in this series will not cause cavities in another causal series, only in this one. Might this not explain why we conveniently designate the one series as 'me' and the other as 'you'? Might this not be the ultimate truth that makes it conventionally true that we are distinct persons? In this case perhaps there is some ultimate ground for the claim that we are obligated to prevent only our own suffering. Perhaps (6) does not follow from (4) and (5). Perhaps (6) is false. Perhaps the argument does not work.

In philosophy we often come across arguments that look convincing but make claims that seem too strong to be plausible. The Buddhist argument for benevolence is an example. If we have understood and accepted the doctrine of non-self, the argument seems perfectly simple and straightforward. But when we reflect on what it purports to prove, it starts to seem too good to be true. Philosophers in the Western tradition have long sought to establish a rational obligation to be moral, with little success to show for their efforts. Could it really be this easy? The study of philosophy will make us skeptical. This is why, when we encounter a plausible-seeming argument for a surprising conclusion, we need to be careful. We need to test the argument by looking for hidden flaws: false premises, or holes in the reasoning. We need to adopt the stance of someone raising objections to the argument, looking for ways to show that the argument does not really prove its conclusion. But our work is not over once we've found an objection – sometimes objections are also not as good as they initially seem. So we need to lay out the objection clearly and carefully. And then we need to adopt the stance of someone defending the argument against that objection. Is there anything they can say that shows the argument does not really have the problem the opponent alleges it has? In the case of the Buddhist argument for benevolence, we sketched a strategy for raising an objection in the preceding paragraph. But this was just a sketch. Now the details need to be filled in more carefully. Once this is done, you should ask yourself what the Buddhist could say in response. If you have spelled out the objection with sufficient care, you may find there are still moves the Buddhist can make. Or perhaps not. What is important is that the effort be made. Philosophical arguments can be very persuasive. But we want to be sure we are not persuaded for the wrong reasons. This is why, when we encounter such an argument, we put it to the test. First we try to understand it, then we put ourselves in the position of an opponent and look for objections, then we see how those objections might be replied to. If you do this with the Buddhist argument for benevolence, you may end up more confident that the final conclusion you reach is based on good reasons.

Further Reading

For a rather different view of the overall character of Buddhist ethics, as well as a survey of Buddhist views on a variety of specific ethical questions, see Peter Harvey. *An Introduction to Buddhist Ethics: Foundations, Values and Issues* (New York: Cambridge University Press, 2000).

For a very different reading of the argument for benevolence, see Paul Williams, *Altruism and Reality: Studies in the Philosophy of the* Bodhicāryāvatāra (Richmond, Surrey: Curzon Press, 1998).

For a discussion of the nature of altruism and its treatment in Buddhist ethics and in utilitarianism, see the chapter entitled 'The Emotions of Altruism, East and West' in Joel Kupperman's *Learning from Asian Philosophy* (New York: Oxford University Press, 1999), pp. 145–55.

Derek Parfit's discussion of the ethical consequences of reductionism about persons is contained in Chapters 14 and 15 of his book *Reasons and Persons* (Oxford: Oxford University Press, 1984). There is now a substantial critical literature on his position. Some of the best essays are collected in Jonathan Dancy (ed.), *Reading Parfit* (Oxford: Basil Blackwell, 1997).

CHAPTER FIVE

A Nyāya Interlude

In this chapter we will examine the Nyāya school of orthodox Indian philosophy. Nyāya agrees with Buddhism that life as ordinarily lived is suffering, and that the ultimate cause of suffering is our ignorance about our identity. But as an orthodox ('Brahmanical') school, Nyāya accepts the existence of a self. It also holds that there are things that exist eternally. So it disputes two of the three Buddhist claims about the characteristics of existence. Moreover, the foundational literature of this school was composed perhaps as much as five centuries after the death of the Buddha, in the second century CE. Even if this literature reflects an older oral tradition, the Buddha himself probably knew nothing of Nyāya. Why, then, should we study Nyāya? There are two reasons. First, the debate between Buddhism and Nyāya over the existence of the self had a profound effect on the development of Buddhist philosophy from the second century CE on. Second, some of the key tools and concepts of Indian philosophy originated with Nyāya. So a brief examination of the Nyāya system will help us better understand that debate. And the better our understanding of the debate, the better position we will be in to decide who was right about the self and the nature of the world.

What we will examine are Nyāya metaphysics and epistemology. Strictly speaking, the metaphysics we will look at comes from another school, Vaiśeṣika. It was this school that first developed a doctrine of seven categories of reals, which Nyāya subsequently borrowed. We won't worry about this, though. We will simply use the name 'Nyāya' to refer to the combined views of Nyāya and Vaiśeṣika. First we will examine the metaphysical theory of the seven categories. Then we will look at Nyāya epistemology, which takes the form of a theory of the means of knowledge. Finally, we will look at a Nyāya argument for the existence of the self. Here is where the hard work of trying to understand Nyāya metaphysics and epistemology will be repaid. For here it will start to become clear how answers to the abstract questions of metaphysics and epistemology affect our view of what we are.

5.1

A doctrine of categories represents an attempt to lay out the basic constituents of reality. We have already encountered one such doctrine. The Buddha's list of the five *skandhas* represents his view as to what are the fundamental kinds of things making up the world we experience. Nyāya claims that there are not five but seven factors that need to be distinguished in any complete ontology. But their list also reflects a fundamentally different approach to the matter. The Buddha's doctrine of the *skandhas* seems to be an attempt to find the basic kinds of things that serve as the parts of persons and other common-sense objects. Hairs and bones (*rūpa skandha*) are things that are parts of the body, while pains (feeling *skandha*) and hunger (volition *skandha*) can be thought of as things that are parts of the mind. Not all the Nyāya categories fit comfortably under the label 'thing' however. The white color of this piece of paper, for instance, is a quality, and qualities are one of the Nyāya categories. Likewise the downward movement of a falling raindrop is a motion, and motion is another category in the Nyāya scheme. We wouldn't ordinarily call these 'things'. This suggests that Nyāya arrived at its list of categories by starting with a different question. If the question is not 'What are the most basic kinds of things in reality?', what might the question be?

The Nyāya categories are: substance, quality, motion, universal, inherence, individuator, and absence. Suppose you see a white cow standing alone in a field swishing its tail:

1   The cow is a substance.
2   Its white color is a quality.
3   The swishing of its tail is a motion.
4   So far so good. But what is it about this thing that makes it a cow? Why does it get called by the same name as all those other animals in other places? There would seem to be something common to all that makes it correct to call them all by the same name. Nyāya calls this a universal, in this case *cowness*.
5   We say of the cow that it is white, it is swishing its tail, and it is a cow. When we say these things we are connecting the substance (the 'it') with a quality, a motion and a universal. But what is the connection that is expressed by the 'is'? It is the relation of inherence. Inherence is the relation of 'being in' that we are talking about when we say that white color, swishing and *cowness* occur in the cow.
6   We also say that this is one particular cow. The cow in the barn that looks just like this one is a distinct cow. For certain kinds of substances, what makes two qualitatively identical substances numerically distinct is the inherence in each of an individuator. For reasons that we will discuss later, an individual cow is not made distinct by an individuator of its own. But its being the particular cow it is, still is explained by individuators indirectly.
7   We might also notice that a goat that was in the field earlier is not there now. The cow is standing alone in the field. In this case what we are aware of is the absence of the goat.

What our example suggests is that the Nyāya categories represent those aspects of reality that correspond to the different elements in our judgments about what we perceive. Suppose when asked what we see we say, 'It is a white cow standing alone in the field swishing its tail.' And suppose we are right. What Nyāya is claiming is that there must be these seven distinct kinds of aspects of reality in order to explain how what we said is true. There must be substances, qualities, motions, etc. There must be 'things' (that is, substances) in order for there to be anything for us to talk about. But then there are all the parts of our statement that constitute the 'saying something about it' side of the judgment. Those parts of the judgment must also hook up somehow with reality. So there must also be qualities, motions and universals. And then there is the fact that whatever is expressed by words like 'white', 'swishing' and 'cow' must also be related somehow to the substance that is expressed by 'it'. So we'll need a relation like that of inherence; otherwise what we'd have is just a list of unconnected names. And so on. The Nyāya list of categories is generated by reflecting on what the most fundamental aspects of reality must be in order for our cognitions to capture adequately facts in the world.[1]

Let's look a bit more closely at some of the Nyāya categories. The obvious place to begin is with substance, for in a sense the whole system revolves around this category. Substances are concrete particulars, such as a cow, a pot, or a tree. It's important to be clear about how the word 'substance' is being used here. We sometimes use the word 'substance' to mean a stuff, something that can occur spread out over different locations, such as iron, mud, or water. But in philosophy the word is almost never used that way. A substance is always a particular thing, something that occurs in a single discrete spatial location.[2] The stuff called 'mud' is in many different places in the world, but a substance such as a cow can only be at one place at a time.

We can get clearer about what substances are by looking at how this category is related to the other categories. Substances are inhered in by qualities, motions, universals and individuators. That is, items in these four categories can occur in substances. White color, swishing motion and *cowness* all inhere in our cow. Qualities, motions and individuators only inhere in substances; there would be no qualities, motions, or individuators if there were no substances for them to reside in. And every substance has some qualities and at least one universal inhering in it.

There are two different basic types of substance: eternal and non-eternal. The non-eternal substances are compounded out of eternal substances, which are themselves

---

[1] The Nyāya approach to ontology is thus more sophisticated than the approach we find reflected in the doctrine of the five *skandhas*. Buddhist philosophers respond by developing new ontologies, culminating in the single category of the *svalakṣaṇa* (discussed in Chapter 10). While the doctrine of the five *skandhas* is never completely abandoned, it later becomes a purely classificatory device with little ontological significance.

[2] There are three exceptions to this in the Nyāya category of substance. Space is considered a substance, and space cannot be said to have a spatial location, for that would lead to an infinite regress: its location would have to be in another space, which would itself need its own spatial location, etc. Another exception is time, which seems to be all-pervading: it is one and the same 'now' in which events here and on the other side of the world are currently happening. The third exception is the self. For Nyāya, the self is the subject of experience. Since it's possible for us to be aware of feelings in different parts of the body, the self can't be located in just one part. But if the self were the size of the whole body it would be compounded and so not eternal. Nyāya thus concludes that the self is ubiquitous or omnipresent.

simple or partless. A pot, for instance, is non-eternal: its existence had a beginning (when a potter made it) and will have an end (when it breaks). Now the pot is made from bits of clay, but these are themselves made up of still smaller things. At the end of this process are atoms, things so small that they are literally without parts.[3] And because they are without parts, it was concluded that they must be eternal. The reasoning is that creation and destruction of substances only occur through rearrangement of parts. The potter makes the pot by putting bits of clay together and firing them. The cat destroys the pot by knocking it onto the floor and smashing it into bits. Anything simple – that is, not made of parts – could be neither created nor destroyed. So if anything exists that is like that, it must be eternal: it could never have come into existence, and can never cease to exist. Nyāya thus concluded that in addition to the non-eternal physical substances we can perceive, such as cows, pots and trees, there must be the eternal physical atoms out of which the former are made. These were thought to come in four varieties, corresponding to the four elements of earth, water, fire and air. But there are non-physical eternal substances as well: space, time, ether, the inner sense and the self.

Substances have qualities and motions. The cow is white, the stone falls, etc. Nyāya would put these facts as: the cow is inhered in by white color, the stone is inhered in by downward motion. The relation of inherence is defined as a kind of necessary connection between that which inheres and what it inheres in. This means that the white color and the downward motion cannot occur apart from the cow and the stone. But the reverse is not true. The cow can continue to exist if it loses its white color and becomes brown instead. Likewise the stone continues to exist when it ceases falling and comes to rest. Substances are the substrata of qualities and motions – they are what stand beneath and support items in these categories. As such, substances can endure changes in the qualities and motions inhering in them. This is not true, though, of the universals that inhere in substances. A cow cannot continue to exist without being inhered in by *cowness*. When that relation no longer holds, the cow ceases to exist. The universal does continue to exist though. It still inheres in other cows.

No simple substances inhere in anything else. But non-eternal substances – the ones that have simple substances as their parts – do inhere in other things. They inhere in each of their parts. A tree, for instance, is equally present in each of its leaves, branches, its trunk and roots. If you think about this claim, it may seem odd. How can one thing be equally present in many different places at the same time? The tree as a whole, you might think, could not be in the leaf; it's only a part of the tree

---

[3]The original meaning of the word 'atom' is 'partless'. Of course the things that are today called atoms have parts: the electron, proton, etc. But this is because when physicists first discovered these things, they were under the mistaken impression that they were partless. When Indian philosophers talk about atoms, what they mean are the truly partless material particles. Perhaps what are now called 'quarks' will turn out to be the atoms that the Indian philosophers had in mind. In any event, we will use the word 'atom' to mean a partless physical particle.

that is located where the leaf is. After all, the tree is big but the leaf is small. (Buddhists, who do not think wholes are real, will exploit this feature of the Nyāya theory in attacking it.) But the claim might not be as odd as it sounds. Most people accept something similar with respect to time. Suppose we agreed with Nyāya that a substance like a cow can endure through time. Flossie the cow existed yesterday, she exists today, and she will exist tomorrow. Suppose we thought of yesterday's Flossie as one stage or part of Flossie, today's as another, and tomorrow's as yet a third. Should we say that Flossie is equally present in each of these temporal parts? The alternative is to say that it is only one part of Flossie that is present today, another part that was present yesterday, etc. But in that case, when does Flossie exist? It seems that then you could only say that Flossie exists at the end of her life, after all the time-slices have occurred. And remember that Flossie is supposed to be something that endures through different times. Most people would find it very odd to say that Flossie didn't actually exist until she died. They would say instead that Flossie is equally present in all her different temporal parts.[4] Nyāya says the same thing about her spatial parts. Just as most people think Flossie is equally present yesterday, today and tomorrow, so Nyāya says Flossie is equally present in her head, her left foreleg and her tail.

We said earlier that two substances might be qualitatively identical but numerically distinct. Flossie might exactly resemble her twin sister Bossie, yet they are two distinct cows. What explains the fact that each is a distinct individual? Nyāya answers that Flossie is individuated by the atoms in which she inheres. It is one set of atoms that makes up Flossie, and another set that makes up Bossie. But suppose (as seems likely) these atoms are all qualitatively identical. What makes them numerically distinct? This is where individuators come in. Inhering in each atom is an individuator that makes that atom be the distinct individual it is. The same is true of selves. Here we have a good example of Nyāya using lightness or parsimony in building its system. Flossie and other compound substances do not have their own individuators. They are individuated by virtue of the parts in which they inhere. It is only the ultimate parts of compound substances – the eternal substances – that have individuators. Nyāya is trying to get by with less. It is trying to avoid positing entities unnecessarily.

The category of quality seems fairly straightforward. But it does have one surprising feature. Qualities are just as individual as the substances they inhere in. The white color that is in Flossie is one quality, and the white color that is in Bossie is another. The two white colors may be indistinguishable, but they are still two. One is here in Flossie, the other is over there in Bossie. True, we do say that Flossie and Bossie are the same color. But Nyāya would say what we really mean is that both colors are inhered in by the same universal: *whiteness*. The universal exists in

---

[4]There are philosophers today who deny that a substance is equally present in each of its stages. Among these, the best-known is David Lewis. See his 'Survival and Identity', in Amelia Rorty (ed.), *The Identities of Persons* (Berkeley: University of California Press, 1976).

everything that is white. The color that inheres in Flossie is inhered in by *whiteness*. But the white color in Flossie can only exist in Flossie. If she turned brown, that white color would go out of existence. Likewise if Flossie died and her body were cremated, that white color would go out of existence. This is what it means to say that qualities are dependent on the substances in which they inhere. Notice too that while qualities are said to be individual, they do not have their own individuators. Instead they are individuated by the substances they inhere in. This white color is the distinct individual it is because it inheres in Flossie.

Universals are Nyāya's response to what philosophers call the problem of One over Many. Flossie and Bossie and the rest of the herd are many distinct things, yet we call them all by one name, 'cow'. Likewise for the color of Flossie, the color of milk, and the color of this piece of paper, all of which get called 'white'. Why is this? We might say that we perceive, respectively, their being cows, and their being white. We look at Flossie and see that she is a cow. But how do we do that? What do we see that makes us say that? Suppose we were to say that in each case it is because the many things all resemble one another. In that case we wouldn't need to posit a One over the Many. We would just have Flossie and the way she looks, and Bossie and the way she looks; then, based on that, there would be our judgment that they resemble each other. Would this allow us to avoid saying there is one thing, *cowness*, that is in both of them? The problem with this approach is that there are many different ways in which two things might resemble one another. My brother and I resemble one another in some ways (same hairline) but not in others (he's taller). There would then have to be some special way in which Flossie and Bossie resembled one another, that differed from the way that the color in Bossie and the color in this piece of paper resembled one another. But now we have another One over Many problem: the many different kinds of resemblance all get called by one name, 'resemblance'. So it looks like this strategy won't help us get around positing some one thing that is common to all the many instances. It looks like we have to suppose there are universals.

In the case of Flossie and Bossie this one thing that is common is *cowness*, the property of being a cow. It is because of the inherence of *cowness* in each of these particular substances that we see them both as cows. Where does *cowness* exist? The usual answer is that it is everywhere; we perceive it only in cows because it requires inherence in a substance in order to be made manifest. But this view has the difficulty that then something else would be needed to explain why it inheres in Flossie and Bossie. Perhaps the better way to interpret the claim that universals are omnipresent is that this is a way of saying they really have no spatial location of their own. As for when they exist, they are timeless or eternal. Granted there was a time when there were no cows. So this apparently commits Nyāya to the view that a universal can exist apart from the instances it inheres in. And this view creates difficulties. But the alternative is to say that *cowness* came into existence when the first cow did. And that seems like an odd thing to say. How could the first cow have been a cow if there weren't already such a thing as being a cow?

Universals strike many people as odd things to posit. Nyāya thinks we must posit them in order to solve the One over Many problem. But it shows restraint in the number of universals it is willing to posit (just as it did with individuators). So far we have seen them posit *cowness* on the grounds that we have one word 'cow' for many distinct individuals like Flossie and Bossie, and *whiteness* on similar grounds concerning 'white'. Suppose we had a single word that applied to all the white cows. Would that mean there is a *white-cowness* universal? Not according to Nyāya. We would not need such a universal to explain our ability to apply this word, since we could already explain it using the two universals *cowness* and *whiteness*. For the most part, Nyāya restricts its recognition of universals to what are nowadays called 'natural kind' terms, such as 'cow', 'tree', 'white', 'yellow', 'earth', 'air', 'fire', 'water', etc. Nyāya is also quite explicit about there being no universal in the case where there is just one thing of that kind. Since there is just one space, there is no *spaceness*. This helps explain why Nyāya also makes the rather odd claim that there is just one inherence. It would be natural to suppose that the inherence that relates *cowness* to Flossie is one relation, and the inherence that relates *whiteness* to the color of this paper is another relation. Nyāya says they are not distinct relations, though. There is just one inherence that does the work of relating in every case of inseparable connection. Suppose we disagreed. Suppose we said that there are many inherences, but they all get called by one name. Then we would need to posit a universal, *inherenceness*. But now how is this universal related to each of the many inherences? Well, in general a universal is related to its instances through inherence. So *inherenceness* would have to have inherence relations to all those inherences. We now have a new One over Many problem. We have the many inherence relations that connect *inherenceness* with all the inherences there are between *cowness* and cows, *whiteness* and colors, etc. If we solve this One over Many problem the same way we solved the others, we will get a second *inherenceness*. And this won't stop the problem. We are on our way to an infinite regress. Better to say that there is just one inherence. Then the Nyāya view of universals will not require us to posit *inherenceness*.

The last category we need to discuss is absence, which will also play an important role in the debate between Nyāya and Buddhism. Absences might seem like odd things to include in our list of aspects of reality. Isn't an absence, such as the absence of a drill press from this room, just the sort of thing we would say is unreal? Naiyāyikas would answer that absences are non-existent but not unreal. By this they mean that while absences are fundamentally different from the other categories (all of which we can say exist), they must still be acknowledged as an aspect of reality. For otherwise how would we account for the truth of the judgment that there is no drill press in the room? Someone might say that we don't need to posit absences to explain what makes this judgment true. All we need, they would claim, is to point to the bare floor; that's what makes it true. But Nyāya would respond by asking what it means to say the floor is bare. Is its being bare something positive or something negative? If it's positive, it isn't clear why it would make true the negative judgment, 'There's no drill press in the room'. What could a positive property of the floor have to do with the negative word 'no'? If it is negative, then we do need negative facts after all, and absences must be accorded a place in our ontology.

5.2

We now have enough Nyāya metaphysical theory to get by with. Let's have a brief look at Nyāya epistemology. In general, epistemology is concerned with understanding what it is to have knowledge. But there is an ambiguity in the word 'knowledge' that needs to be brought out if we're to avoid confusion about what it is we are analyzing. When we say that someone knows something, we might mean 'know' in a dispositional sense, or we might mean 'know' in the sense of an episode. When we use 'know' in the dispositional sense, we can say that someone knows something even when they are asleep. I might not now be thinking about New Zealand, but I can still be said to know that Wellington is the capital, for if anyone were to ask me, this is what I would say. I have the power or ability to give the right answer, hence I know in the dispositional sense. But for me to know this in the episodic sense, there must be going on within me a cognition that represents Wellington as the capital of New Zealand. So when we use 'know' this way, we can't say I know this even in my sleep. Now if an epistemological theory gives us an analysis of knowledge in one of these two senses, we can then work out what to say about knowledge in the other sense. So it doesn't make much difference which sense we start with. What is important is that we be clear about where we are starting. For the most part Western epistemologists have been concerned with knowledge in the dispositional sense. Indian theories of knowledge have always been theories of knowledge in the episodic sense. When Indian epistemologists seek a definition of knowledge, what they are after is the best way to characterize those cognitive occurrences that correctly represent the facts.

Nyāya approaches this task by looking for the means of knowledge. A means of knowledge is a set of conditions that causes true cognitions. To call something a means of knowledge is to say that any cognition it produces will correctly represent how things are. A means of knowledge is a reliable cause of veridical cognition. Other Indian schools (including the Buddhists) follow Nyāya in this approach to epistemology. Their debates are primarily about how many distinct means of knowledge there are, and how each should be defined. But a word should be said here about another difference with Western epistemology. In the West, not only has epistemology been concerned with knowledge in the dispositional sense; there has also been wide agreement that knowledge should be analyzed as justified true belief. According to this analysis, for me to know something I must believe it, what I believe must be true, and I must have good reasons for believing it. The key point here is that on the Indian means-of-knowledge approach to epistemology, the concept of justification has no significant role to play in the analysis of knowledge. At least not when the justification condition on knowledge is understood as requiring that a knower be able to give justification. Suppose that my vision is working properly, the lighting conditions are adequate, and I visually cognize a red flower. Then my cognition counts for Nyāya as a case of knowledge even if I haven't checked to make sure my vision is working properly, there's enough light, there aren't any holographic projectors operating in the room, I am not asleep and dreaming, etc. Of course if I were asleep and dreaming then my belief wouldn't be knowledge (even if there were a red flower in the room). But that's because dreaming I see something is not a reliable cause of veridical cognitions. In the present case I do know, because I have a veridical cognition resulting from a reliable process. It's enough that the cause of my cognition is of the right sort. I don't need to be able to show that the cause of my cognition is of the right sort.[5]

Nyāya claims there are four means of knowledge: perception, inference, testimony and comparison. Buddhists disagree, and claim that only perception and inference are means of knowledge. This disagreement is not about whether a process like the testimony of a qualified expert is a reliable source of veridical beliefs. What is controversial is whether this is a separate means of knowledge. Buddhists claim, for instance, that testimony is just a case of inference. But this dispute is not important for our purposes.

Perception is defined as sense-object contact that is non-wandering and definite. Like Buddhists, Naiyāyikas recognize six senses: the five external senses and the inner sense. When one of these faculties comes in contact with an object of the appropriate sort, it produces a cognition. Nyāya recognizes two main ways in which the resulting cognition can fail to be veridical. The first is that the senses 'wander'. By this is meant that the senses produce a cognition that attributes to the object a character that is not in the object but somewhere else. If jaundice makes me see the white cow as yellow, that is a case of wandering. Likewise if the straight branch sticking into the water looks bent, that is a case of wandering. The yellow color and the bent shape are characters that I have perceived with my senses, but somewhere else, not here. Perceptual error results when the senses present as connected two things that are not in fact connected. The other way in which perceptual cognitions can fail to be veridical is when they are not definite, as for instance when the object is too far for me to tell whether it is a person or a post.

Perceptual cognitions come in two varieties, non-conceptual and conceptual. What we would ordinarily consider a perceptual cognition is always conceptual: it is something that may be expressed as a judgment, something of the form '*x* is ___'. To see or feel something is to perceive it *as* being of a certain character. We don't just see or feel the object, we see or feel it as being some particular way. To see a cow is to see the object *as* a cow. To feel a warm wall is to feel it *as* warm. We need not say it or

---

[5]Recently the idea that knowledge should be understood not as justified true belief, but as true belief caused in a reliable way, has found favor among some Western epistemologists. For a classic statement of this alternative approach that sounds remarkably like Nyāya, see Alvin I. Goldman, 'A Causal Theory of Knowing', *Journal of Philosophy* 22: 357–72.

think it in so many words, but our perceptual cognitions can always be expressed in this way. They are attributive in nature: they attribute some character to the object we are perceiving. Now Nyāya says that for this sort of conceptual cognition to occur, there must first occur a non-conceptual perception, one that is not attributive in character. In this sort of cognition what we perceive are the individual constituents of the conceptual cognition by themselves, separately. So in order to have the conceptual perception of Flossie as a cow, I must first non-conceptually perceive Flossie just as such, *cowness* just as such, and the inherence that connects Flossie and *cowness* just as such. Of course we are never aware that we are doing this. We couldn't be, since the contents of non-conceptual cognitions can never be expressed. To express something requires making a judgment, attributing a character to the object. But, Nyāya argues, there must be this non-conceptual perception before every conceptual perception, since otherwise we would be unable to connect the object and the character we attribute to it. The argument for this last claim is simple. We cannot connect two things unless we are first aware of each of them separately. Likewise we cannot be aware that two things are connected unless we are first aware of the connection separately. So we must posit the occurrence of a non-conceptual perceptual cognition immediately prior to our conceptual perceptions. Of course the object and its character do not exist separately. Flossie never exists apart from *cowness*. But, Nyāya claims, to see Flossie as a cow we must first see Flossie, and see *cowness*, and see the inherence that connects them. We do this in non-conceptual perception.

Notice that Nyāya says we perceive universals like *cowness* and *whiteness*. Just as many people (including Buddhists) find the very idea of real universals difficult to accept, so many people find this claim hard to believe. Universals strike many as a perfect example of something abstract. And the things that we think of as abstract, such as numbers, we tend to think of as things that cannot be perceived but can only be cognized by the mind. Still Nyāya insists that universals are part of our perceptual experience. When we see the cow Flossie, we see not only the individual substance but also her *cowness*. If this were not true, then how would it be possible for us to learn to call Flossie a cow? To learn to use the word 'cow', there must be some feature that we can observe to be common to Flossie and Bossie. And if *cowness* were something we could not perceive, then our awareness of something common would be dependent on our having learned to use the word. We would be stuck in a circle of mutual dependency.

Saying that universals are perceived will also help Nyāya solve some other epistemological problems. It will explain how we can know causation, and how we know when what they call 'pervasion' obtains. Like many other philosophers, Naiyāyikas hold that causation is a relation between universals. Take the case of fire being the cause of smoke. Nyāya would say that this amounts to there being a certain relation between the two universals *fireness* and *smokeness*. If we did not think universals were real, we would have to reject this analysis. Then we would have to say that fire's causing smoke amounts to this: every occurrence of fire, in all times, is preceded by an occurrence of smoke. But we know that fire is the cause of smoke, and how could we know this, when we can only perceive a limited number of all the cases of smoke that will ever exist? If causation is a relation between universals, and we can perceive universals, then we will not need to perceive all the instances of smoke that ever occur. We will be able to cognize the causal connection just by observing that the two universals are related in the right way. And we can do this by observing how they are connected in particular cases. Likewise for pervasion, which is the relation at the heart of inferences. If this relation is understood as one that holds between universals, and not just between particular instances, then we can explain how we could come to know that it holds.

To explain this last point, we need to examine the nature of inference as a means of knowledge. We can begin to explain what inference is by contrasting it with perception. By means of perception we come to directly cognize states of affairs in the world. By means of inference we indirectly cognize them. Thus we can know that someone has walked down the beach either by seeing them walk by, or else by inferring this from footprints in the sand. Notice that it is here assumed to be the same state of affairs that we cognize in these two different ways. It is the walking of one and the same person that we know either directly through perception or indirectly through inference. This is an instance of the Nyāya doctrine that the means of knowledge 'intermingle'. By this they mean that a given object may be cognized by more than one means of knowledge.[6] From down in the valley I cognize the fire on the mountain by inferring it from the smoke that I see, but I could perceive that fire through vision or touch if I were up on the mountain where the fire is.

The basic structure of an inference can be explained using the stock example of inferring fire from smoke. The inference that produces the resulting cognition of fire on the mountain has the following structure (simplifying somewhat):

- There is fire on the mountain.
- Because there is smoke on the mountain.
- Whatever has smoke has fire, like the kitchen and unlike the lake.

If we think of this as an argument, like the arguments that are studied in Western logic, then the first member would represent the conclusion of the argument, and the second and third would represent the premises or evidence put forward to support the conclusion. But Indian logicians analyze the inference differently. They think of it as made up of five terms: the subject (the mountain), the property to be proved (fire), the reason (smoke), a positive example (the kitchen) and a negative example (the lake).

---

[6]The Buddhists of the Yogācāra-Sautrāntika school will disagree. They will claim that each means of knowledge has its own distinctive type of object. We will discuss their reasons in Chapter 10. But at this point we can perhaps see how doubts could be raised about the Nyāya claim. When I see someone walking on the beach, it is that very person that I'm aware of. When I infer a walker from footprints, does that make me aware of the very person who made the footprints? Or am I aware of just 'someone or other'?

We will call the property to be proved by its Sanskrit name, *sādhya*. So in an inference we find, first, the assertion that the subject is characterized by the *sādhya*. This is supported by the grounds that the subject is characterized by the reason, and that the reason is pervaded by the *sādhya*. The claim of pervasion, in turn, is supported by a positive example and a negative example.

The relation of pervasion is a universal relation. The claim that is being made is that wherever there is smoke there is fire. This is why it is significant that this can be understood as a relation between universals: *smokeness* is pervaded by *fireness*. (Notice that smoke is said to be pervaded by fire and not the other way around; there can be smokeless fires, just no smoke without fire.) We said earlier that the Nyāya doctrine that we perceive universals will help them solve an epistemological problem with respect to pervasion. The problem was that we cannot cognize every possible instance of smoke to see if fire also occurs there. Nyāya tries to resolve this problem by pointing out that we can perceive the universals *smokeness* and *fireness*. Presumably we can then perceive the relation of pervasion that holds between them. What then is the epistemic role of the examples? They represent the way in which we come to be aware of the relation of pervasion. When we perceive smoke and fire together in the kitchen, we perceive the universals *smokeness* and *fireness* together. This makes us aware of the relation of pervasion that actually holds between these two universals. But sometimes it's only a coincidence that two things occur together. To assure ourselves of the pervasion we look for counter-examples: cases where the reason occurs without the *sādhya*. If we can find one then we'll know this is not a case of pervasion. For instance we know that there is no fire in the lake, yet isn't that smoke that rises off it in the early morning? No, it isn't smoke but mist. The negative example of the lake is evidence that our search for counter-examples has come up empty. The positive example is supportive evidence, while the negative example shows we've put the alleged pervasion to the test by looking for evidence against it.

This Nyāya view about how we apprehend pervasion may seem complex, but it really reflects our common-sense practice. Pervasion claims assert general principles: they claim that all instances of the reason are instances of the *sādhya*. So think about what happens when someone introduces another general principle, such as the anti-reflexivity principle. First they are likely to give supporting examples: the knife can't cut itself, the finger can't point at itself, etc. But if we are at all critical we'll want to scrutinize this claim more carefully for ourselves. We'll look for possible counter-examples, such as the doctor who performs minor surgery on herself, or the light that illuminates itself. The anti-reflexivity principle states that no entity ever occurs without the absence of performing its activity on itself. The doctor and the light look like they might be cases of entities without that absence. So they look like possible counter-examples. But perhaps not. Perhaps in the doctor case what we have is not one entity, but many, some of which perform the surgery on others. If so, and if the case of the light can also be dealt with satisfactorily, we will have good reason to accept the anti-reflexivity principle. The principle will have survived our efforts to show it is false. It's always possible that the principle is still false. There might still be a killer counter-example out there somewhere. But then in the game of knowledge nothing is ever guaranteed. We are fallible. All we can do is make a good-faith effort to find the truth.

One final point needs to be made. We just saw that for all we know, what we take to be a good inference may not be. There are a number of ways in which we can go wrong in forming beliefs indirectly. Nyāya develops a catalogue of some of the more common mistakes that people make in inferring. This then becomes a kind of check-list for use in philosophical investigations: if an inference does not commit any of these common errors, then it is reasonable to accept it as establishing a veridical belief. But it is instructive to think about their name for these errors in inferring, *viz.* 'pseudo-inferences'. What this name tells us is that these are not really inferences at all, they just appear to be inferences. They are not inferences because they are not reliable causes of veridical belief. And an inference, being a means of knowledge, is by definition a reliable cause of veridical beliefs. So nothing that is really an inference can ever lead us to believe something that is false. And there are cases of real inference. We may not always know whether what we have is a genuine case of indirect knowledge. But it would be a mistake to conclude from this that we can never really know anything. That sort of skepticism – the sort that was ushered into modern Western philosophy by Descartes – is simply not warranted under the Nyāya approach to epistemology.

5.3

It is now time to look at the Nyāya side of the Nyāya-Buddhist controversy over the existence of the self. We begin with the comments of Vātsyayana (fifth century CE) on the argument for the self in the foundational text the *Nyāya Sūtra*. Vātsyayana begins by explaining that while the self is not perceived, it is known not just by testimony, by the fact that the *Vedas* speak of it (a reason that no Buddhist would accept), but by inference as well. He then quotes the relevant *sūtra*, and explains the inferences in his commentary:[7]

> Among the substances the self is not grasped by direct acquaintance. Is it then only established by testimony? No, for it is established by inference. How?
>
> 'Desire and aversion, effort, pleasure, pain and cognition are the marks of the self.' [NS I.1.10]

---

[7]This passage and the passage from Uddyotakara's commentary that follows were originally translated by Matthew Kapstein in his 1987 PhD dissertation, 'Self and Personal Identity in Indian Buddhist Scholasticism: A Philosophical Investigation', and later reprinted in his *Reason's Traces: Identity and Interpretation in Indian and Tibetan Buddhist Thought* (New York: Columbia University Press, 2001). I have for the most part followed Kapstein's translation, but have amended it where it seemed to me that he missed the sense of the original.

The self, having acquired pleasure due to contact with an object of a certain type, desires to possess an object of that very type when it perceives it. It is the mark of the self that this desire to possess occurs, because a single seer unites the [distinct acts of] seeing. For even with respect to a persistent object, that cannot be based on distinct mental events, for example, those connected with distinct bodies. Likewise because the seeings are united by one seer of many objects, there is aversion toward a [previously perceived] cause of suffering; and when for instance its object is an established cause of pleasure, perceiving an object of that kind it seeks to possess it, and this would not be the case were there not one seer uniting the [distinct] seeings. And it would not be possible if there were only [distinct] mental events with their own determinate objects, just as with mental events associated with different bodies. In the same way, effort with respect to the cause of pain is explained. Recalling pleasure or pain, one sets about striving to achieve that, realizes pleasure or pain, and thus experiences pleasure or pain. The reason is as was stated before. Moreover, desiring to know, one reflects, 'What is....?' Having reflected, one knows, 'This is....' It is the mark of the self that this is grasped as being of a single agent of both the desire to know and the act of reflecting. The reason is as was stated earlier.

Here 'connected with distinct bodies' is to be analyzed thus: according to those who hold the thesis of non-self, just as distinct mental events with their own objects that occur in different bodies (that is, occur to different persons) are not united, so too a single body's objects ought not be united, for the distinctive feature is absent. It is generally acknowledged that one only remembers what one has oneself perceived, not what was perceived by another. It is generally acknowledged that what one has perceived is not remembered by another. Neither of these two things can be accounted for by the non-self theorist. Thus it is proven: the self exists (NB on NS I.1.10).

The inferences should be fairly clear. Take the case of desire. Why is it that when I see mangoes displayed at the greengrocer I have a desire to buy one and eat it? Obviously because I remember the pleasure I felt when I ate a mango in the past. But the ability to remember a past experience requires that it was I who had that past experience. We never remember the experiences of other persons. So there must be something that unifies the present desirous person and the past person who enjoyed eating a mango. And that something must be a self. The same thing follows from the fact that I feel aversion when I smell a food that gave me indigestion in the past. And so on.

But while the argument is clear, we can also anticipate the Buddhist response. You should be able to see how they would use their notion of the person as a causal series to answer this objection. What we need is a formulation of the inferences that takes this into account. The comments of Uddyotakara (*ca.* sixth–seventh century CE) on the above passage of Vātsyayana's *Bhāṣya* do that. Notice the point in the first paragraph, that this illustrates the fact that the means of knowledge 'intermingle' – that the same object may be cognized by more than one means of knowledge.

'Desire...' is the verse whose purpose is to distinguish the self from things belonging to its class as well as things that do not. Or its purpose is to connect testimony with inference, i.e., to link the self, which is known by means of testimony, with inference [by also stating an inference that there is a self]. Alternatively its purpose is to illustrate the mingling of means of knowledge, for when I said earlier that the means of knowledge intermingle it was with this object in mind.

It says in the *Bhāṣya* 'due to contact with an object of a certain type'. There it is the unification of desire etc. that establishes the existence of the self. The question to be examined is this: how is it that desire etc. cause there to be cognition of a self that is not perceived? It is because of sharing a single object with memory; for it is because desire etc. arise having the very same object as memory that they establish the oneness of agency. There is no unification, in the case of diverse agents, of diverse objects and diverse determinations. For the conceptions of color, taste, odor and texture are not united; it is not the case that the color I saw is this very texture I feel, and the texture I felt is this very color I see. Nor when Devadatta has seen something is what is seen unified with Yajnadatta. For it is not the case that what Devadatta saw, I Yajnadatta see. Why so? Because [these are] determinations of objects in distinct minds. According to those who hold the non-self theory there are no [selves] having distinctly determined objects with mutually exclusive forms, and thus unification is not appropriate. Therefore what unites is the self.

What if it is objected that unification is owing to there being the cause-effect relation? So you [the opponent] think that unification is not because of oneness of the agent. What then?

[The Buddhist opponent:] It is because there is a cause-effect relation. From distinct earlier mental events, other successively later mental events come into existence instilled with the whole mass of powers in conformity with the powers of the earlier mental events. Hence even though there is diversity, there is unity due to the existence of the cause-effect relation, as with the seed. Thus the sprout becomes manifest immediately after the grain of rice. Its conformity with the power of rice is established by what comes before it [the grain of rice]. Afterwards, in conjunction with the material elements, a new grain of rice is produced, not a grain of barley, for that is not what came before. Likewise here the unification of mental events in a single series is due to the establishment of the cause-effect relation, and this excludes mental events in another series because they are not what come before [in this causal series]. The unification is not, however, due to there being a single agent, since that is not perceived. This unification being otherwise [than you claim], it cannot establish the existence of a self.

[Uddyotakara's reply:] This is not right, since diversity has not been excluded. That is, stating that the unification is due to the cause-effect relation does not exclude diversity. How so? The existence of the cause-effect relation indeed supports diversity [since cause and effect are distinct], and where both sides in this dispute accept diversity, no unification is to be found. Why is that? Because what one has experienced is not remembered by another, and it is not possible to unify what is not remembered, for it is not established where there is no cause-effect relation.

[Opponent:] But we do not say that where there is the cause-effect relation there unification is seen. What we say is rather that it [unification] is not seen in the absence of the cause-effect relation, because there is nothing prior to that [to explain unification]. Thus this objection is not in accord with our meaning.

[Reply:] This is wrong, for the reason that is in dispute is not made clear. What you say does not make the reason distinct. What I have said is that [unification] is not seen where there is diversity. You have said no, it is not seen where there is diversity because of the absence of the cause-effect relation. Because there is uncertainty about the reason, the disputed reason has not been made clear.

[Opponent:] The same applies to you as well: by saying 'because it is not seen where there is diversity', neither have you made the reason clear.

[Reply:] Because of your acceptance [of diversity], you are without a response; it was by your saying 'the same [applies to you as well]' that you accepted this.

[Objection:] Not so, it was due to lack of proof [on your part]. That is, I have not proven that unification is because of the cause-effect relation. Rather it is that because it [unification] might occur otherwise [than due to a single agent] that your reason is said to have the defect of not proving what it is meant to prove.

Both sides agree that in the remembering of past experience there is a sense of unification: it feels as though what does the remembering must be what had the experience. The Naiyāyika claims this shows there must be a self. The Buddhist objects that the phenomenon might instead be explained through there being a cause-effect relation between the elements that occurred at the time of the experience, and the elements occurring at the time of remembering. Uddyotakara responds that since cause (for example, a rice seed) and effect (for example, a rice sprout) are distinct things, this cannot explain unification. You can't use diversity to explain unification. The Buddhist then says they are not required to explain the feeling of unification, all they need to do is cast doubt on the Nyāya inference. And their point about causation does this. When a grain of rice is planted, eventually a new grain of rice is produced, and it is easy to mistake that for the original grain of rice. So maybe the feeling of unification is like that. Since this possibility is not ruled out, the Nyāya argument does not prove its conclusion. Uddyotakara now responds by clarifying what is meant by unification:

[Reply:] Not so, for you have not understood the meaning of that reason. You have not grasped the specific nature of that reason, but have said the reason is defective, saying 'it may be otherwise', only due to the reason taken in general. But this unification has been specifically qualified: there is unification by means of memory through there being one object of both earlier and later cognitions; and such memory cannot occur on your thesis.

Why is that? Because one does not remember what another has experienced. That is, there is no remembering by one of what another has experienced; it is not the case that someone remembers what a distinct person experienced. And there is memory. Hence it is reasonable for unification to be affirmed on the side of the thesis according to which memory is possible.

[Objection:] You attribute to us the view that memory does not occur; but on our thesis it is not the case that memory is not possible. How so? It is due to there being the cause-effect relation that the series of psychophysical elements in which memory and experience occur is, as series of psychophysical elements, both rememberer and experiencer.

[Reply:] Not so, because of the impermanence of mental events: that which is preserved by something putting it away [that is, storing it] is seen to be permanent, and there is no permanence among mental events. And because of the absence of contact: that which is preserved is in contact with what puts it away somewhere, but in the case of mental events there can be no contact with what [supposedly] places it somewhere.

The nuts that a squirrel stores are things that endure from the time that the squirrel puts them away until they are retrieved. And nuts are physical, the sorts of things that can be picked up and put somewhere. The mental events that are involved in experience and memory are neither physical nor enduring. So the Buddhist is not entitled to say memory involves storing something away:

> Perhaps it is held that the impression is something having production of consciousness through a distinctive power. That is, it is thought that because of a distinctive mental force accompanied by a prior consciousness, a consciousness arises characterized by the distinctive prior power, that is called the impression of that [prior mental force] that has production of consciousness through a distinctive power. But it is in reference to this that [I] said, 'because of the impermanence of mental events', and 'because of the absence of contact'. That mental force that coexisted with the earlier consciousness performs no useful function in connection with consciousness in the present or future. Why so? Precisely because, as it comes into existence in the present, without alteration, just so it is annihilated, and so is not connected with the future; and what is unconnected does not put things away. Thus to say there is memory because of the cause-effect relation is an impression resulting from a non-education!

On the Buddhist view that Uddyotakara is contesting, cause and effect are two distinct things that occur at distinct times: first the cause exists, then it goes out of existence and the effect comes into existence. So not only is there no physical contact. There is also no temporal contact. The two events don't overlap in time. How then, Uddyotakara asks, can the cause produce the effect? How can it influence the way that the effect is?

> And for this additional reason there is no memory on your thesis: because a property is dependent on a property-possessor. Every property depends on a property-possessor, as does production from action-ness. Now the property-possessor with respect to remembering could be either the object of an action or else an agent: in the case of the object of an action, for instance, the cooking of the rice; in the case of an agent, for example, the going of Devadatta. But [in the case of remembering, the property-possessor] is not the object of the action, for

there may be [remembering] even when that [object] does not exist. That is, when one remembers something that is not presently existing, then memory obtains without [its object as] substratum. So then the agent is its substratum, in which case it accords with our thesis not yours. Why so? Because you do not accept an agent. You do not posit an agent in order to account for memory. This being your thesis, that memory is indeed without locus, there is no inference [from the cause-effect relation], for there is not seen an effect without substratum. All effects are seen to have substrata, e.g., color etc. Remembering is such, and so has a substratum.

[Objection:] But the conventions 'property' and 'property-possessor' apply to effect and cause. The moment of the effect is a 'property', and the causal moment is a 'property-possessor'. And so what property-possessor need be additionally posited?

[Reply:] But that is not the case, due to temporal distinction. For cause and effect, occurring at distinct times, cannot be related as locus and locatee, like a bowl and jujube fruits and the like.

[Objection:] But then it may be like this: origination is what is called the property, and that which originates is what is called the property-possessor. Memory also originates, so its origination will be a property, while as what originates it will also be called a property-possessor.

[Reply:] This is also wrong, both because of contradiction and because of lack of agreement. If origination is distinct from memory there is a contradiction [with your position], and then the intrinsic nature [of origination] must be stated; for you hold that origination is not distinct from what is originated. So if your thought is that origination is after all distinct, then its intrinsic nature must be stated. And to state its intrinsic nature would contradict your treatise. Why is this? Either origination is related to existence by its own cause, or existence has a distinct relation with its cause, and both these contradict what is accepted in your treatise.

Then is it preceded by an origination that is no different from the memory?

In that case, what functions where? The designation is empty.

The origination is the property, and what originates is the memory?

To say so would make sense only if one were to say that the origination of a memory comes about by means of a property. But if memory is the property, then it [the origination] must be the property-possessor. Why? Because, as was said earlier, a property depends on a property-possessor. Therefore on your thesis memory is not at all possible, and without memory there is no unification. But there is unification, the agent of which is therefore another object, the one self.

Notice how Uddyotakara's argument uses the Nyāya categorial scheme. Memory is a property in the same way in which qualities, actions and universals are properties. As such it requires a property-possessor, something to serve as its substrate. The Buddhist says that 'property' and 'property-possessor' are mere convenient designators, but Uddyotakara requires that the Buddhist identify something ultimately real that these terms designate. The Buddhist then suggests that the origination of the memory (that is, its arising) is the property, and the memory itself (that which arises) is the property-possessor. That is, origination is something that happens to memory. But Uddyotakara points out that the Buddhist holds origination and the thing that originates are not ultimately distinct (for reasons that we will explore in the next chapter). So this will not work.

> The verse may also be interpreted as a positive inference: Devadatta's cognitions of color, taste and touch bear the mark of one and many, because they are unified by [the notion of] 'mine' together with memory, just like the many simultaneous cognitions, on the part of the elders who have made a convention, when the eyebrow of the dancing girl is drawn together. As the variously based cognitions of various agents who have made a convention are unified because of the oneness of the target brow of the dancing girl, so here as well the various objects are brought together due to the oneness of a ground, and that ground is the self.
>
> Or 'Desire and aversion, effort, pleasure, pain and cognition are the marks of the self' may be explained differently: desire etc. are qualities. That qualities are dependent is reasonable. Their being qualities is known by differentiation [by process of elimination]: they are not universals, or individuators, or inherence, because they are impermanent. And they are not substance or motion, because they inhere in a concomitant substance, as does sound. The inference is established as one of general concomitance. Due to impermanence, the dependency of desire, etc., and also because of being an effect, as in the case of color etc. Because they belong to a substance that lacks quantity [i.e., extension], their being qualities of the body is excluded. That being denied, they can only be qualities of the self. Thus by differentiation is it proven that there is a self. [NV on NB on NS I.1.10]

The analogy of the dancing girl is colorful but not especially helpful. The idea seems to be that people watching the dance have entered into an agreement to all act together in some way when the dancer's eyebrows converge. The point would then be that there cannot be coordinated action without some one central focus to serve as unifier. The argument of the final paragraph is more interesting. Mental events like volitions and feelings are shown to belong to the category of qualities by elimination. Since they are impermanent, they cannot belong to the categories of universal, individuator or inherence, for these are all permanent. And a mental event inheres in just a single substance, whereas when a substance or a motion inheres, it inheres in many substances. So mental events must be qualities. And qualities require a substance as substratum in which to inhere. This substance must, moreover, be indivisible, so it cannot be the body. Hence by elimination mental events must inhere in a simple non-physical substance, that is, the eternal self.

What should we make of this exchange? Clearly the Buddhist needs an adequate response to the problem of unification. It is only my own experiences that I remember, not those of others.[8] And when I remember an experience, it seems that

---

[8]There is, of course, a sense in which we do remember the experiences of other persons. I might remember seeing you eat your first mango. But what I remember is not what it was like for you 'from the inside'. I can only remember my own experiences of seeing you eat it and hearing you describe it. I can only remember how it was for me 'from the inside' when this took place. It is this sense of 'experience' to which the restriction applies.

what is now remembering is the same thing as what earlier had the experience. There seems to be a single subject for the two mental events. Uddyotakara knows that the Buddhist will try to explain this away using the notion of a causal series and the idea that some things may be mere conceptual fictions. But the uses to which Uddyotakara has the Buddhist put them in this passage are inadequate. Can the Buddhist do better? In the next chapter we will look at what Abhidharma philosophers have to say on the subject. But for the moment you might want to consider whether the distinction between the two truths has been used effectively on the Buddhist side. Could it be used to bolster their position on the problem of unification?

Further Reading

For an excellent introduction to the overall Nyāya system see Part One of: *Indian Metaphysics and Epistemology: The tradition of Nyāya-Vaiśeṣika up to Gaṇgeśa. Encyclopedia of Indian Philosophies*, Vol. 2. Edited by Karl H. Potter (Princeton, NJ: Princeton University Press, 1977).

For the debate within Indian epistemology between Nyāya and its critics, see Bimal Krishna Matilal, *Perception* (Oxford: Clarendon Press, 1986).

For the Nyāya categorial scheme see Chapter 3 of William Halbfass, *On Being and What There Is: Classical Vaiśeṣika and the History of Indian Ontology* (Albany, NY: SUNY Press, 1990).

For an introduction to the problem of universals in Western philosophy see: D.M. Armstrong, *Nominalism and Realism: Universals and Scientific Realism*, Vol. 1. (Cambridge: Cambridge University Press, 1978). As Armstrong is himself aware, his own view resembles that of Nyāya in important respects.

For a recent formulation of the Nyāya argument for the existence of the self from synthetic unity, see Arindam Chakrabarti, 'I Touch What I Saw', *Philosophy and Phenomenological Research* **52** (1992): 103–16.

CHAPTER SIX

Abhidharma: The Metaphysics of Empty Persons

The subject of this chapter is a movement in Buddhist philosophy that grew out of efforts to systematically interpret the discourses of the Buddha. We call this movement 'Abhidharma' because that is the name of the collection of texts laying out the results of those efforts. *Abhidharma* is the third of three groups of texts in the Buddhist canon. The first is *Sūtra*, which collects together all the discourses of the Buddha. The second is *Vinaya*, which lays out the rules of monastic discipline. The texts in the first and second sets were composed, at least in part, around the time of the Buddha. *Abhidharma* texts came later. They reflect difficulties that Buddhist practitioners faced in sorting out all the entities that the Buddha discussed in his teachings. Over time subtle differences emerged in the solutions proposed. These differences of interpretation led to the formation of several different schools. But all shared a common approach to interpreting the Buddha's teachings, and a common philosophical outlook. In this chapter we will examine that common outlook. We will also look at a few of the more philosophically important disagreements among the schools of Abhidharma.

As the subtitle of this chapter indicates, our chief interest will be in the metaphysics of Abhidharma. In the last chapter we saw Nyāya challenge the metaphysical basis of the Buddhist doctrine of non-self. The Abhidharma responds by coming up with an innovative view about what is ultimately real. We will look at the theory of *dharmas*, its foundations and some of the disputes over which *dharmas* there are. We will also look at an important epistemological dispute over the nature of perception. But we begin with an important piece of unfinished business from Chapter 3: proving that wholes are unreal and only impartite entities are real. The Buddhist view of persons is based on this mereological reductionism, the view that wholes are reducible to their parts. This is what is behind the idea that the person, as a whole made of parts, is a mere conceptual fiction. But this claim about wholes was not argued for in early Buddhism. Abhidharma metaphysics begins with such an argument.

6.1

Abhidharma metaphysics is based on the claim that only impartite entities – things with no parts – are ultimately real. So it is crucial to Abhidharma that there be an argument for this claim. To see how this goes, we will be pulling together ideas from several different sources. For Abhidharma authors the most important part of the argument is the part that shows that a real whole could be neither identical with nor distinct from real parts. And we will look at a text that lays out an important component of this part of the argument. But first we need to stand back and look at the overall framework that the argument uses.

The basic question we are confronting is one of ontology: what is it that is fundamentally real? In this case the question is narrowed down to one concerning the reality of wholes and parts. This means there are just four possible answers:

1   Wholes and parts are both real.
2   Wholes are real, parts are unreal.
3   Neither wholes nor parts are real.
4   Wholes are unreal, only parts are real.

The strategy will be to show that (4) is true by showing that none of (1)–(3) can be true. The argument is one of proof by elimination. For this strategy to work, it must be the case that these are the only possible alternatives. But this is easy to show. We have two categories: wholes and parts. And each one could be either real or unreal. So there are just four possible combinations: that both are real (1), that both are unreal (3), and two mixed views ((2) and (4)). Since these are the only possible views, one of them has to be true. Hypothesis (1) turns out to be the most important of the rivals to (4). But let us set that aside for the moment and start with (2).

Hypothesis (2) says that the only real things are the wholes that are made up of parts. The parts that make them up are not themselves really real. The chariot is real, but its parts are not, the tree is real, but the roots, branches and leaves are not. If we were to ask someone who believed this why it still seems to us that leaves and branches are real, they might say that we've been misled by a process of mental abstraction. We've divided the tree up into useful-sized chunks, and then forgotten that something can be a branch only by being part of a tree. But there is one major difficulty this hypothesis faces. By its logic, there is really just one thing: the One Big Thing. This is so because most of the things that we think of as wholes are actually parts of larger wholes. The room you are in is a whole made of parts: floor, walls, ceiling, furniture, etc. But the room is a part of a building. The building is part of a city or town. The city or town is part of something bigger, etc. The resulting view is what is called absolute monism. It holds that the ultimately real is one and indivisible. There have been philosophers who were absolute monists: in India, Śaṅkara, founder of the Advaita Vedānta school; in the West, the pre-Socratic philosopher Parmenides. But they faced an apparently intractable difficulty. Why should it even seem to us that there is a plurality of things in the world? Why should acting on that assumption turn out to be useful? If everything is really just one, then for instance it should make no difference whether I drink beer or bleach. The distinction between the two is just a mental superimposition on the One Big Thing that is, in itself, undifferentiated. Perhaps we might agree that there is one big thing – the cosmos, the universe as a whole. But to explain the facts about our experience with things like beer and bleach, we need to suppose that the universe can really be divided up into parts – some of which are more toxic than others. So (2) seems to be false.

Hypothesis (3) says in effect that nothing whatever exists. Every existing thing must be either made of parts (a whole) or not made of parts (an ultimate part). (3) says neither sort exists, so it says that nothing exists. This is the view called metaphysical nihilism. And it is pretty obvious that it has to be false. If it were true, then the thought that it might be true could not occur. For a thought can occur only if it is itself an existing thing (of some sort or other) or takes place in an existing thing. We are right now considering metaphysical nihilism, so the thought that it might be true is occurring. Hence metaphysical nihilism must be false. (3) can safely be set aside.

Hypothesis (1) says that wholes are real and the parts they are made up of are also real. The bicycle is real and so are the seat, handlebars, pedals, chain, etc. that it is built of. You might point out that a bicycle seat is itself a whole made of parts: springs, frame, padding, cover, etc. This is true. But let's ignore it for the moment, and pretend that things like seats and spokes are the ultimate parts of bicycles. We're exploring the hypothesis that they and the bicycle they compose are equally real. But here is a further question. If the bicycle and the parts are equally real, then they must be either identical or distinct. So is the bicycle identical with its parts or distinct from them? Of course there wouldn't be a bicycle if the parts were not related to one another in a certain way: seat attached to frame, spokes attached to rim, etc. So what we're really asking is whether the bicycle is identical with or distinct from the parts when they are attached to one another in the 'assembled-bicycle' way. We'll call the assembled parts 'the parts in relation'. Hypothesis (1) can then be split into two alternatives:

1a   Whole and parts are both real and the whole is identical with the parts in relation.
1b   Whole and parts are both real and the whole is distinct from the parts in relation.

We need to examine each in turn.

Hypothesis (1a) will seem appealing only if we mistake it for a very different hypothesis. We might think it means that, for instance, there actually is a bicycle, but it is really just the parts in relation. When we say one sort of thing 'really just is' some other sort of thing, though, what we are saying is that the one thing can be reduced to the other – that strictly speaking there is nothing more to reality than the latter. To say this about the bicycle would then be to affirm (4), not (1a). It would be saying that the bicycle is a conceptual fiction, that it is really just the parts that are real. What (1a) says is that the bicycle is just as real as the parts, but that it is identical with the parts.

And this could not be true. To see why not, consider the principle of the indiscernibility of identicals:

PInId: If x and y are numerically identical, then x and y share all the same properties.[1]

To say that x and y are numerically identical is to say that 'x' and 'y' are really just two names for one and the same thing. And if this is so, then everything that is true of x must also be true of y. For how can a single thing both be and not be a certain way?[2] When we apply this to (1a), we get the result that everything that is true of the bicycle must also be true of the parts in relation. The bicycle, though, has the property of being one thing, while the parts in relation do not. They have the very different property of being many things. How could one thing be identical with many things?

This makes (1b) seem more reasonable. It says the bicycle is a separately existing thing. When the parts are assembled together, a new thing comes into existence, a bicycle. The parts still exist, but the bicycle exists over and above them. As we saw in the last chapter, this is the view that Nyāya holds. And the positions of Nyāya are generally quite reasonable and common-sensical. So (1b) seems quite tempting. There are, though, some challenges that must be overcome. The first concerns the question of evidence for the existence of this new thing, the bicycle. Is there any evidence that is not equally evidence for the existence of the parts in relation? All of our experiences with respect to the bicycle can be explained in terms of facts about the parts in relation. When we see a bicycle, for instance, what we see is certain of the parts in relation. When we ride a bicycle, what transports us are the parts in relation. We agree that the parts exist. Unless we have evidence for the existence of the whole that cannot be explained in terms of facts about the parts in relation, the principle of lightness dictates that we reject (1b) in favor of (4).

The second challenge concerns the question of where the bicycle exists. Its location clearly overlaps that of the parts in relation. The question is whether it is the bicycle as a whole that exists in each of the parts, such as the seat, or it is only part of the bicycle that exists in the seat. Now the first possibility might seem odd. How can something as big as a bicycle exist in something the size of a seat? But the second possibility has its own problems. If it were just a part of the bicycle that existed in the seat, then we would have to say that the bicycle itself – this separately existing whole

---

[1]This principle is to be distinguished from the principle of the identity of indiscernibles, which states that any two things that have all the same properties are numerically identical, so that if there is no way of telling two things apart, then they must really be just one thing. This principle is controversial. That of the indiscernibility of identicals is not. The principle of the indiscernibility of identicals is also known as Leibniz's Law, after the eighteenth-century philosopher Gottfried Leibniz.

[2]If you believe there are enduring substances that undergo qualitative change, you might think these are a source of counter-examples to PInId. Suppose x is a leaf in June, and y is the same leaf in October. Isn't it then true that x has a property that y lacks, the property of being green? No, not if we understand properties as temporally indexed, as things that are had by a substance at a time. Then both x and y have the property of being green in June. They likewise both have the property of being red in October.

– contains parts. This bicycle-whole would be something that could be divided up into the part of the bicycle-whole that is just where the seat is, another part of the bicycle-whole that is just where the left pedal is, etc. And these parts of the bicycle-whole must be separate from the seat, the pedals, etc. For we are asking about how the bicycle itself is related to the seat, the pedals, etc. If we have to say that it itself has these parts occurring where the seat, etc., are, then we are using these parts to explain the relation between the bicycle and the seat, pedals, etc. If we call the seat, pedals, etc., 'parts$_1$', then we should call these 'parts$_2$'. Since it is the parts$_2$ that are supposed to explain the relation between the parts$_1$ and the bicycle-whole, they must be separate from the parts$_1$. But then we will need to ask about the relation between the bicycle-whole and the parts$_2$. Does only part of the bicycle-whole exist in each of the parts$_2$? And the same reasoning will lead us to posit yet more parts, parts$_3$, and so on.

So it looks like we must say that the whole exists in each of its parts. Nyāya holds this view; it would say the whole is related to each of its parts in the same way that a universal is related to each of its instances. Take all the patches of yellow color there are. If there is such a thing as *yellowness* that explains their all being yellow, then this *yellowness* must be a single thing that is equally present in each of them. Someone who holds (1b) would say that the bicycle is likewise equally present in the seat, the left pedal, the right pedal, etc.

We can now give the argument against (1b). This is found in a passage of the text *Abhidharmakośabhāṣya* by Vasubandhu. We will have more to say about this text and its author later, but for now let us examine Vasubandhu's criticism of the Nyāya view that the whole inheres in its parts. The context is a discussion of the Nyāya view of causation. According to their view, cause and effect are distinct things. Now anyone who holds this must then explain why a given effect can only be produced from a certain cause. If a sprout is the effect of a seed, why does the seed produce just this kind of effect and not some other? But Nyāya denies that the seed is the cause of the sprout. The sprout's cause, they claim, is the atoms that make it up. We can only get a sprout from a seed, they hold, because the atoms that make up a sprout are capable of being rearranged in such a way as to yield a sprout. Now this view depends on the Nyāya theory that a complex substance such as a sprout is a distinct thing that inheres in the substances that are its parts, the atoms of which it is composed. This is just what Vasubandhu will attack.

> But they [the Naiyāyikas] do not accept that the origination of sprouts etc. is from seeds etc. From what then? Just from its parts, which arise from their parts, and so on down to the atoms. What then of the capacity of the seed etc. to produce the sprout etc? It [the sprout] does not occur anywhere else [than where the seed is] because of the gradual movement of the atoms of that [seed]. What do they accept as cause? They say there is no possibility [of origination] from something different in nature. Why not? Because it would be irregular, in this way there would be no regularity of capacity. As for instance the origination of black salt from sound [which is impossible]. The characterizing quality [produced] may be different [from the originating cause], but substance is not so. One sees only

origination of similar substances from the similar, as for instance a mat from grass or cloth from threads.

   This is incorrect. That is considered unfit for proving which is itself unestablished. What is here unestablished? That the mat is distinct from the grass, the cloth is distinct from the threads. It is just these [grass or threads] that, assembled, receive this or that conception [as 'mat' or 'cloth']. Like a row of ants.

The Nyāya explanation depends on the assumption that the cloth is distinct from the threads. Vasubandhu says they can't use this assumption in their explanation, since it has not been established. That is, there is another possible view of the relation between cloth and threads: there are just the threads, and 'cloth' is merely a convenient designator for woven threads. Just as a row of ants is really just the ants together in a line, so the cloth is not a distinct substance, but only a conceptual fiction. Why should we accept this view rather than the Nyāya assumption? Vasubandhu continues:

   How is this known? One does not cognize the cloth where there is [sensory] contact with a single thread. What then prevents one from seeing the cloth? If it is that it is in an incomplete state, then it is just a part of the cloth, not the cloth. And then the cloth would be merely the collection. And what part of the cloth is different from the threads? There being [sensory] contact with just the fringe, and in dependence on contact [of the fringe] with the locus of the many [parts], there would be perception of the cloth, but this never happens, due to lack of sensory connection with the middle and the extreme parts. Nor would there be cognition of the whole due to visual contact with the parts in successive connection. [For if we suppose this is how the whole is cognized,] then the awareness of that [cloth], based on perception of the whole through successive connection, is only found in the parts, as with the whirling firebrand.

Suppose there is a piece of cloth on the floor, but I can only see a single thread of its fringe. We would not say that I then see the cloth. Why not? If it is because I am seeing just one part of the cloth, then the cloth as a whole is not in that thread. To see the cloth I must see more than just one thread. And if it is a large piece of cloth, I may never see all the threads at one time. It is only by seeing first the threads at this end, then the threads in the middle, then the threads at the other end, that I see the cloth. But if I never see the cloth as a whole, then it is something that is put together by the mind, not something existing in reality. Vasubandhu gives the example of the whirling firebrand. When someone twirls a torch rapidly, it appears as if there is a circle of fire. In fact there is just the fire at the tip of the torch. It is only because that fire is moving so rapidly that it seems to us there is a ring of fire. The ring of fire is the mind's interpretation of what we actually see, fire at many distinct locations in rapid succession. By the same token, the cloth might be the mind's interpretation of what we actually see, distinct but connected threads seen in rapid succession:

[The cloth cannot be distinct from the threads] for it is impossible for the color etc. of the cloth to arise where the threads are of distinct color, kind and function. There being variegated color and the like, the origination would also be of different kinds, and either there is no seeing of the pot when the outside and the interior are indistinguishable, or there is variegated seeing. The function as well is variegated, there is excessive difference. Heat and illumination being different, there is no perceiving of both the color and the touch of that throughout by means of the light of fire. [AKBh III.100ab, Pradhan, pp. 189–90]

Suppose our cloth is woven from blue and red yarns. If the cloth is a substance distinct from the threads, it must have its own color. What color is the cloth? To this question Nyāya responds that the cloth has its own distinctive color, called 'variegated color'. This is the color that is supposedly produced when something is made of parts of differing colors. But if the cloth is equally present in all its parts, how can this variegated color be present in blue yarn? There are similar difficulties for a whole the parts of which have different functions. The inside of a pot holds liquids in, while the outside keeps other things out. But the pot, as a whole made of these parts, does both. So if the pot is in all its parts equally, the function of keeping things in must be found at the outside of the pot. Similarly, fire both illuminates and heats. But it is different parts of the fire that do these two things. For a hot fire may fail to illuminate. (We would say it is different parts of the radiation spectrum that produce heat and light.) If we think of fire as a single substance with both functions, we must suppose that both are equally present in all its parts, even though some perform only one function, and some perform only the other. All these difficulties are avoided, on the other hand, if we suppose that the whole is a mere conceptual fiction, the product of the mind's aggregating activity.

Consequently, (1b) turns out to be just as problematic as the other alternatives to (4). We are thus invited to conclude that the whole is a mere mental construction, that only impartite entities are ultimately real. You might still be wondering just what these impartite entities are like. Indeed you might suspect that there are equally grave difficulties with the view that there are such things. It is time to look at the Abhidharma account of a *dharma* or ultimately real entity.

6.2

What are the ultimately real impartite entities? The Abhidharma answer is that they are *dharmas*. A *dharma* is defined as what has intrinsic nature (*svabhāva*). In the following passage Vasubandhu makes this point by contrasting what is ultimately real with what is merely conventionally real.

> 4. Anything the idea of which does not occur upon division or upon mental analysis, such as an object like a pot, that is a conceptual fiction. The ultimately real is otherwise.

That is a conceptual fiction the idea of which does not occur when it is divided into parts. Like a pot: there is no idea of a pot when it is broken into shards. And that is also to be known as a conceptual fiction the idea of which does not occur when properties are stripped away by the mind. Like water: there is no idea of water where properties such as shape and the like have been excluded by the mind. And with respect to these, the convenient designators being formed through the power of convention, saying that pot and water exist is true, one does not speak a falsehood, this is conventional truth. What is other than this is ultimate truth. Where there is the idea even upon division, as well as upon exclusion of other properties by the mind, that is ultimately real. Like *rūpa* (physical things): even when it is divided up into atoms, and even when the mind takes away properties such as taste and the like, there is still the intrinsic nature (*svabhāva*) of *rūpa*. Feeling, etc., should be seen in the same way. Because this exists in the highest sense, it is called ultimately real. As one grasps that by a transcendent cognition, or by a subsequent convention, it is ultimate truth. [AKBh VI.4, Pradhan, p. 334]

The key to finding the *dharmas* lies in seeing why it is that a conventionally real thing is not ultimately real. According to Vasubandhu, this is because it 'disappears under analysis'. That is, when we physically remove its parts, or when we distinguish among its distinctive properties, what remains is not something to which the concept of the thing applies. For instance, there is no longer a pot when we separate the neck from the bowl. This is not true of water. When we take away drops from a glass of water, what remains is still water. But suppose there were water when what was left was too small to be further divided. (This is what it means to think of water as an element.) Ordinarily, by 'water' we mean something that is colorless, has the shape of its container, is wet, may be hot, lukewarm or cold, etc. So that tiny drop of water that is not further divisible physically can still be analyzed into a set of distinct properties: shape, color, wetness, etc. Just as something's being a chariot depends on there being wheels, axle, body, etc., put together in the right way, so something's being water depends on the properties of shape, color, wetness, etc. all occurring together. We think of water as the 'thing' that has these properties. But take away the properties and the water disappears.

Abhidharma philosophers express all this by saying that a conceptual fiction borrows its nature from something else. This is their way of making the point that concepts like that of the chariot and water are aggregative: they involve the mind putting together separate things and then constructing some one thing to hold them all together. This is what is shown by the fact that the 'thing' disappears under analysis. We think of a chariot as the thing that has the wheels, axle, etc., as its parts. But when these are taken away the chariot disappears. We think of water as the 'thing' that has color, shape, wetness, etc. as its properties. But when these are excluded the water disappears. This shows that the chariot and the water were just mental constructions. But something that did not disappear under analysis would not borrow its nature from other things. It would not be a mental construction, and so it would be ultimately real.

It would be something that exists independently of our interests and cognitive limitations. It would have an intrinsic nature.

The Sanskrit term we translate as 'intrinsic nature', *svabhāva*, literally means 'own nature'. To say that *dharmas* have intrinsic natures is to say that their natures are entirely their own, not borrowed. What this means is that something's being the *dharma* it is does not disappear under analysis. If it is something physical, it continues to be the kind of thing it is when we take away bits of it. It is also not capable of being conceptually analyzed into a plurality of distinct properties. We know we have reached *dharmas* when we have arrived at existents that cannot be reduced to other sorts of things. One way we might put this is to say that *dharmas* can only be known by acquaintance, not by description. That is, we could come to know what is meant by the name for a certain kind of *dharma* only through having direct experience of it. We could not learn this just by having someone describe it to us. Someone who has never seen a chariot can come to understand what one is by hearing a description: two wheels connected by an axle, etc. But this is possible precisely because the chariot borrows its nature from its parts. The description works by explaining how those parts are arranged. With *dharmas* this avenue is not open to us. You must experience it for yourself to know what kind of thing it is.

6.3

To get a better idea of what this means, we should look at some examples of *dharmas* recognized by the Abhidharma schools. It is natural to assume that among these will be atoms. But these are not exactly the atoms you might have expected. Of course they are truly impartite, unlike the things called 'atoms' by today's science.[3] But they are also unlike the atoms of Nyāya, which are substances. Like Nyāya, Abhidharma recognizes four kinds of atoms, those of earth, fire, water and air. But for Nyāya an earth atom is a substance having the quality of solidity inhering in it. In the Abhidharma ontology there is no category of substance. So an earth atom *dharma* is not a tiny solid particle. It is just a particular occurrence of solidity. Likewise a fire atom is not a hot thing, it is just a particular occurrence of heat. This point comes out in the following passage, which continues the extract from *Abhidharmakośabhāṣya* that we looked at earlier. Vasubandhu is discussing the empirical evidence for the existence of atoms, which he knows are required if we are to agree that wholes like the pot are unreal:

> And while the atom is imperceptible, there is the perception of the aggregate, as there is their initiation of an effect with respect to vision and the like, and there is the perceiving of a mass of hairs on the part of those with cataracts. And because

---

[3]See Chapter 5, §I.

there is the occurrence of the perception of atoms only where there is color, etc., it is proven that the destruction of that is the destruction of the atoms.

[Objection:] The atom is a substance, and the substance is distinct from color, etc., there being the destruction of those [qualities], the destruction of that [substance] is not proven.

[Reply:] This is wrong, the distinctness of that is not at all ascertained by anyone in the form 'These are [the substances] earth, water, fire, those are the color, etc. of these'. It is what is grasped by seeing and touch that is cognized. The ideas of wool, cotton, safflower and saffron only arise where there are different colors, etc., for there are no such ideas when these are burnt. The recognition of a fired pot [as the same pot that was unfired] is due to similarity of shape. For there is lack of recognition in the absence of seeing a characteristic. [AKBh III.100ab, Pradhan, p. 190]

The objection comes from a Naiyāyika, who wants to preserve the categorial distinction between substances and qualities. Vasubandhu has said that when we feel the solidity of a pot, it is actually the solidities of all the atoms making it up (the 'aggregate') that are causing our perception. So, he concludes, when all the sensible properties are destroyed, so are the atoms. The opponent wants to maintain that a substance can survive change of its qualities, e.g., that a clay pot still exists when its white color is destroyed and it takes on the new color of red after being fired in a kiln. They can then use this in their effort to establish that the whole exists distinct from its parts. This is why the Naiyāyika claims the atom is a substance that can survive destruction of its qualities. Vasubandhu responds that there is no empirical evidence for the existence of substances, only of qualities. In the case of a thread of saffron, what we are aware of through vision is the red color, not the thing having that color. What we cognize through smell is the pungent odor, not the thing that is pungent. What we call the saffron is really just a bundle of these sensible qualities all occurring together. There is no underlying substrate that unifies them all by being their bearer. We ordinarily speak of a pot undergoing a qualitative change when it is fired: its white color is destroyed and it acquires red color. But this is just a way of speaking. What we actually have is one bundle of properties followed by another. The first bundle includes white color and pot shape, while the second bundle includes red color and pot shape. It is the similarity of shape (along with factors having to do with our interests) that makes us assign a single convenient designator, 'pot', to both bundles. This is why we think there is one substance that first was white and now is red. A substance like a pot is a mere conceptual fiction. What is ultimately real is the solidity we experience when we come in contact with the earth atoms.

The idea that there are no substances, only qualities, takes some getting used to. Our common-sense conceptual scheme is organized around the idea of substances as the bearers of qualities. This is why the Nyāya system of categories seemed so sensible. Abhidharma claims, though, that we can make do perfectly well with just the qualities and without the substances. The substances are useless cogs in the machine, they explain nothing. What are real are the solidity we feel, the red color and round shape we see. These, it must be emphasized, are just like Nyāya's qualities: they are particulars that only exist at a certain place and time. According to Nyāya, the red color I see when I look at the pot is one quality, and the red color just like it that I see when I look at the book is another quality. When the pot is smashed and ground up, that red color ceases to exist, while the red color belonging to the book still exists. Abhidharma agrees about the quality-particulars, but adds that these are all we perceive.[4] So why suppose that there is also this extra unperceived thing, a substance such as a pot or a book, that they inhere in?

Abhidharma will grant that it is certainly useful to have a word like 'pot' to express what we perceive when we see red color and round shape, feel solidity, etc., all together in the same place. But this is just because when these *dharmas* occur together, we can reliably predict certain other experiences. Take the experiences we ordinarily call pouring milk into a pot. The 'milk' is itself a bundle of *dharmas*, including the wetness *dharmas* called water atoms. When we have the experience of this bundle going into the 'pot' bundle, we can count on not feeling the wetness *dharmas* on the table around the 'pot' bundle. (The milk, we would say, stays in the pot and doesn't go all over the table.) Since we want to have experiences that go this way, it is useful for us to collect the red color, round shape, etc., under the 'pot' convenient designator. This explains why we think there is a pot. But it also shows why the pot is just a useful fiction, something that is only conventionally real.

An atom, then, is not a substance. Nothing is a substance, for the category is just a conceptual construction. An earth atom is not a very small solid thing. What is it? An occurrence of solidity in a very small region of space. A fire atom is likewise a very small occurrence of heat. You might wonder what color a fire atom is, but this would be a mistake. Heat is something only perceptible by touch. Color is perceptible only by vision. A fire atom is only perceived by the sense of touch, so it is not the sort of thing that could be some color. The same holds for the other three types of atom, all of which are just occurrences of tangible qualities. They are also only perceived by touch. There are no color atoms. But a patch of color is a *dharma* nonetheless. That patch of red is among the *dharmas* in the bundle we call 'pot'. Particular instances of qualities like color, shape, odor, taste and the like are all *dharmas*. They may occur whenever there are sufficiently many of the four kinds of atomic *dharmas* occurring. Where there are enough atoms to make what we call a pot, there will occur that red color or some other color. It is important not to think of the atoms as supporting the red color *dharma* though. That would be thinking of the atoms as substances. Instead we should think it's just a law of nature that the color *dharma* doesn't occur unless there are a certain number of atom *dharmas* occurring in the same place. The 'pot' is a bundle consisting of all four kinds of atom *dharma*, plus the red color *dharma*, the round shape *dharma*, etc.

This, at any rate, is the official position of the more conservative sectors of

---

[4]Recently, philosophers have coined the term 'trope' for quality-particulars. For more on trope theory, see the suggested readings at the end of the chapter.

Abhidharma. But it is not the view of all. It is said that at the height of this movement in Buddhist philosophy there were 18 different schools. Since each such school was built around some distinctive interpretation of the original texts, there are many disputed matters in Abhidharma. Most of those disputes lack any major philosophical significance.[5] So for our purposes we may safely ignore most of the 18 schools. There are three that deserve mention, though: Theravāda, Vaibhāṣika and Sautrāntika. Theravāda is the form of Buddhism that is practiced today in Śri Lanka and much of South East Asia. It is probably the most conservative of the three. That is, it is the least likely to embrace philosophical innovations that are not directly supported by the Buddha's own teachings. Vaibhāṣika is somewhat less conservative, as can be seen from the other name by which it is known, 'Sarvāstivāda' or 'the doctrine that everything exists'. It gets this name from its innovative theory of time, according to which past and future exist just as much as does the present.[6] Still more innovative is Sautrāntika, which can occasionally be quite ruthless in using the principle of lightness to whittle down the number of kinds of *dharmas*.[7] Vasubandhu is widely thought to have been a Vaibhāṣika. But his comments on Vaibhāṣika positions often reveal strong Sautrāntika tendencies.

The view of atoms just presented is the official view of Theravāda, and it was also held by most Vaibhāṣikas and some Sautrāntikas. But there were dissenters. Some Vaibhāṣikas held that strictly speaking, among physical things only the four kinds of atoms are ultimately real. And there were also those, probably Sautrāntikas, who denied the existence of atoms and claimed that only property-particulars such as visible color, tangible heat and solidity and the like are *rūpa dharmas*.[8] Both views

---

[5]For instance, one early dispute concerned the question whether an *arhat* can have a 'nocturnal emission' (that is, a wet dream). What was at issue here was whether one is responsible for the content of one's dreams. If so, then the occurrence of an erotic dream would be evidence that the dreamer is still subject to attachment and clinging, and hence is not genuinely enlightened.

[6]It thus teaches what is sometimes called a 'block universe' account of time. It adopted this view in order to account for the fact that the Buddha is said to have been able to directly cognize certain past and future facts. If only existing things can be directly cognized, this means that past and future things must exist. While things exist whether they are past, present or future, only the present ones are functioning. The past ones have functioned, while the future ones will function. The difficulty with this view is that it then needs to be explained what is meant by 'are functioning', 'have functioned' and 'will function'. These expressions seem to presuppose real differences among the three times. Vaibhāṣikas worked very hard to try to resolve this problem.

[7]By the name it called itself, it sought to cloak its innovative tendencies in a mantle of orthodoxy. 'Sautrāntika' literally means 'derived from the sūtras'. The name was meant to suggest that the school gave greater weight to the sūtras, or discourses of the Buddha, than to Abhidharma texts. But this was to no avail. Its rivals referred to it as 'Dārṣṭāntika', or 'school of the example'. This came from the Sautrāntikas' tendency to insist that a controversial claim be supported by an example (*dṛṣṭānta*), and not just by a quotation from the sūtras.

[8]Sautrāntikas deny that shape is a *dharma*. The reason seems to have been that this leads to problems having to do with infinite divisibilty. We will have more to say about this in Chapter 8.

were probably motivated by the fact that it is difficult to explain the relation between atoms of the four elements on the one hand, and sensible properties like color and odor on the other, if both are ultimately real. For there is the fact that the sensible qualities like color are said to depend on the atoms, which makes the former seem less real than the latter. And there is also the fact that atoms are never themselves perceived but only inferred, whereas sensible qualities like color are directly perceived. Someone of an empiricist bent might conclude from this that atoms are conceptually constructed, and only sensible property-particulars are ultimately real.

The Abhidharma schools also had difficulty completely abandoning the substance view of common sense, the view that takes a property-possessing substance as the basic model of an existing thing. For instance, there is an extensive debate over whether the atom has size or is a mere geometrical point. There are difficulties with both views. But the deeper problem is that when we ask whether an earth atom has a certain size, we are thinking of it as a thing that has such properties as solidity and size. To think of an atom this way is to think of it as a substance, something in which properties inhere. Abhidharma clearly intends to reject the view that there are substances of any sort; *dharmas* are to be understood more along the lines of the Nyāya category of quality. But it is not always clear that it has succeeded in making this work.

The same difficulty emerges with respect to the impermanence of *dharmas*. The Buddha taught that everything dependently originated is subject to origination, duration and cessation. (Some interpretations include a fourth state, ageing.) Since this must apply to conditioned *dharmas* (those originating in dependence on conditions), it follows that these pass through three (or four) phases. This was the view of Theravāda. To think of a *dharma* in this way, though, is to think of it as a substance that has three (or four) distinct properties at different times: the property of originating at one time, that of enduring at another, etc. The Vaibhāṣikas thus concluded that origination, etc., should be thought of as separate *dharmas*. Take, for instance, the red *dharma* that is part of the 'pot' bundle. Suppose it originates when the 'pot' is fired. According to Vaibhāṣika, just as we should not think of red as a property of a substance, the pot, so we should not think of the origination as a property of the red. Just as we think of the red as one member of the bundle that we call 'pot', so we are to think of origination as another *dharma* alongside the red *dharma*. Origination interacts with the red *dharma* to make it available for interaction with other *dharmas*. Similar things are said about duration and cessation (and ageing) as *dharmas*. This view is clearly meant to keep us from thinking of *dharmas* as substances. There is a difficulty, though. If origination is a conditioned *dharma*, then it must itself be subject to origination, since all conditioned *dharmas* are subject to origination. So to account for the origination of the red when the 'pot' is fired, we will need a second origination. Won't that require a third? This will lead to an infinite regress, and the red color *dharma* will never get off the ground. Vaibhāṣikas tried to stop the regress at the second origination, but there are problems with the strategy they used. Sautrāntikas concluded that distinguishing among three (or four) phases of the *dharmas* is just a useful way of talking. In reality a *dharma* just exists for an instant.

In addition to rejecting substances, Abhidharma also rejects the Nyāya categories of universal, individuator, inherence and absence. Universals are rejected because they would have to be permanent. In fact, Sautrāntikas eventually develop an argument meant to show that nothing permanent could exist. The argument is that for something to exist it must be the cause of some effect; and anything that was permanent could not have effects. For if it had any effect, it would produce that effect over and over again for all eternity, which is absurd. So permanent things like universals can't exist. Hence only particular things can. This in turn means that there is no need for individuators. And inherence is also unnecessary, since there are no universals to inhere in *dharmas*. Finally, absences are rejected on the grounds that they clearly depend on our expectations. I am aware of the absence of the pot on the table only if I expect there to be one. To see the table as bare is just to see the table when I expect to see a pot. A defender of real absences may object that I must at least notice that my expectation has not been met. To do this I must notice an absence, namely the absence of the satisfaction of my expectation. So it may look like absences will still be needed. But to this the Buddhist responds that what I am aware of is just the frustration of my expectation. And the feeling of frustration is something positive, not an absence.

Finally, a word should be said about the non-physical *dharmas*. These include such occurrences as feelings of pleasure and pain, volitions like hunger and attentiveness, and cognitions such as the awareness of a patch of red That they are *dharmas* is easy to show, for each has its own distinctive nature. A pain sensation *dharma*, for instance, just is the occurrence of a mental state with the distinctive feeling of painfulness. The most important point to make about the non-physical *dharmas* is that they are not states of something, such as a mind. There is no such thing as the mind. There is just the causal series of mental state *dharmas* to which we attach the convenient designator 'mind'. There is relatively little controversy among the Abhidharma schools about any of this. The one interesting Sautrāntika innovation has to do with the problem of explaining continuities among our dispositions in the absence of an enduring mind. For instance, I may retain the ability to speak a language I have not used for years. Put in the right environment, I suddenly find myself understanding and speaking it again. How is this to be explained if there is no enduring substance, the mind, in which that ability is lodged? The Sautrāntika answer is that our actions create mental *dharmas* called 'seeds'. These replicate themselves in the mental stream until such time as conditions cause them to ripen. The ripening of a seed then brings about the appropriate mental event, such as understanding the word I just heard. We will later (in Chapter 8) see this theory get put to a very different use.

6.4

We have been discussing the development of an Abhidharma ontology that is meant to replace both our common-sense conceptual scheme and the Nyāya system of categories. A key move in this development is the rejection of the idea of substance in favor of the idea of *dharmas* as property-particulars. But there is more to the rejection of substance than we have discussed so far. For the concept of substance has two distinct strands. One is the idea of substance as property-possessor. This is what is expressed in our use of the subject-predicate form. When we describe the pot, for instance, we say, 'The pot is round', first introducing the subject, the pot, and then predicating a property of it, being round. This idea is also expressed in the Nyāya claim that qualities, universals and individuators all inhere in substances. A second strand, though, is the idea of substance as something that endures. This is expressed in the ordinary use of the word 'substantial' to mean something that will last. We can also see it at work in the Nyāya claim that simple substances must be eternal. Now these two strands come together in the claim that substances persist through qualitative change. When we think of some one thing, the pot, as first being white and then later being red, we are thinking of the pot both as a property-possessor and as something that endures. It is by combining the two strands that we get a solution to the problem of change. We have to think of the pot as something that has a variety of properties, and we must also think of it as something that persists from one time to another, if we are to think of it as having the property of being white at one time, and then losing that property and acquiring the different one of being red at another time. Our discussion so far has focused on the rejection of substance as property-possessor. But when we employ the concept of substance, we are also committed to the view that at least some existing things endure. Abhidharma claims the only ultimately existing things are *dharmas*. We have seen that *dharmas* are not property-possessors. But might they endure?

To ask if *dharmas* could endure is not to ask if any *dharmas* could be eternal. Sautrāntikas deny this. (Theravādins and Vaibhāṣikas allow a few minor exceptions.) They believe the Buddha was right to claim that everything is impermanent. But as we saw earlier (in Chapter 3), something might be impermanent and still last for some time. The question is whether *dharmas* could exist for more than a moment, whether they could persist from one moment to the next. We think of a pot as something that, while clearly impermanent, can last for a while. Abhidharma tells us there really is no pot, just the bundle of *dharmas* to which we have attached the convenient designator 'pot'. Among these is the red color that comes into existence when the so-called pot is fired. We ordinarily think this red color will persist as long as the pot does. Are we right? The surprising answer is that we are not. According to Sautrāntikas, this red color *dharma* goes out of existence immediately upon its coming into existence. Like all *dharmas*, it is momentary: it lasts only an instant. Why do we think it lasts? Because at the next moment we see what is actually a new red color *dharma*, and mistake it for the one that existed a moment ago. One *dharma* has gone out of existence, but another one just like it has come into existence in its place. The process is too rapid for us to discern, just like the succession of frames in a motion picture. When we see a movie, we think we are seeing a continuous image, but we are not. It is actually a succession of distinct images, each flashed for just an instant, then immediately succeeded by another image resembling it. According to Abhidharma, *dharmas* work the same way. They create the illusion of continuously existing things.

This is the theory of momentariness. According to this theory, all existents last only a moment. Existing things (that is, *dharmas*) come into existence and then go out of existence immediately afterwards. Why should we accept this theory? The argument begins with the claim that all existing things are conditioned, that is, come into existence in dependence on causes. Now the dependence of conditioned things on other things makes them impermanent: not only have they not always existed, but they also go out of existence sooner or later. What the argument seeks to do is show that it is sooner rather than later. Let us look at how Vasubandhu puts the argument. The context is a discussion of the claim that nothing ever really moves. This is a corollary of the claim that everything is momentary. (For if everything is momentary, then nothing would last long enough to move from one place to another; apparent motion would really be the coming into existence of a new thing at a different place, just like the apparent motion in a motion picture.) So to show there is no motion, Vasubandhu will try to show that nothing lasts longer than an instant:

> 2c.   There is no going, since the conditioned is momentary,
> What is this 'moment'? Immediate cessation upon having obtained existence. What exists in this fashion is momentary. Indeed nothing conditioned exists later than its acquisition of existence. It perishes just where it was born. Its movement to another place would be impossible. Thus there is no bodily action of going.
>
> [Objection:] This would be so if universal momentariness were proven.
>
> [Reply:] It is proven that conditioned things are momentary. How? With respect to the conditioned, necessarily,
> 2d.   Because it perishes.
> For the cessation of conditioned things is spontaneous. Why is this? A cause is of an effect. And cessation is an absence. What is there to be done with respect to an absence? Therefore destruction does not depend on a cause.

The core argument is deceptively simple. If we agree that every existing thing is impermanent, then we must also agree that every existing thing perishes. What explains the perishing or cessation of an existing thing? There are two possibilities:

1   An existing thing goes out of existence due to a cause, e.g., the hammer blow that destroys the pot.
2   The cessation or going out of existence of an existing thing is spontaneous; it is part of the nature of an existing thing to self-destruct.

But if (1) were true, then the cause would have as its effect the absence of the existing thing. And absences are not real. Nothing can be a cause that does not have a real effect. So nothing could be the cause of the going out of existence of an existing thing. The hammer blow might be the cause of the coming into existence of shards, for they are real things. But the hammer blow cannot be the cause of the cessation of the pot. Hence (2) must be the correct explanation of cessation. Existing things inherently self-destruct:

> If it were not so with respect to what has just arisen, there would likewise be no destruction later, for it would still be the same.
> [Objection:] But an existing thing changes [so it can go out of existence later, in dependence on its changed state].
> [Reply:] It is wrong to say of something that that very thing can be otherwise. For how is it possible that it itself is different from that?

If cessation is spontaneous, it must happen immediately upon the coming into existence of an existent. Otherwise there would have to be some reason to explain why the cessation happened later rather than sooner. The reason cannot be that the thing itself changes over time. To say it could change is to say that while it continues to exist, it loses one property and gains another. This could only happen if it were a substance. And substances have been shown to be mere conceptual fictions. So if cessation is part of the nature of existing things, that cessation must come immediately. (Perhaps one might say that it takes time for cessation to come about. But that would be saying that the time it takes is the cause of the cessation. And it has already been shown that nothing could be the cause of cessation.)

> [Objection:] But surely it is seen that there is destruction of wood and the like due to contact with fire, etc. And there is no means of knowledge more important than perception. Not all cessation is spontaneous – how can you think, 'I see the cessation of wood and the like due to contact with fire and the like'?
> [Reply:] Because one doesn't see them [being destroyed by contact with fire and the like]. This is to be reflected upon: Is it that wood etc. are not seen because they were destroyed due to contact with. fire etc.; or that they are not seen because, they having themselves ceased, others have not arisen in their place? As with a lamp [that has been blown out] through contact with the wind, or the sound of a bell [that has stopped] through contact with the hand.

While we say we see the fire burning up the wood, what we actually see is first the fire touching the wood, and then later a smaller amount of wood. We infer from this that the cause of the destruction of the wood is the fire. Call this explanation (1) of what we see when we see less wood. But there is an alternative explanation: (2) existing things are momentary. But under ordinary conditions, when a piece of wood goes out of existence, another one just like it comes into existence in the next moment. When there is contact with fire, different conditions obtain. What then comes into existence in the next moment is heat, smoke and ashes. The wood goes out of existence in either case. All that changes is what replaces it. So which explanation is correct, (1) or (2)? This can only be settled by inference.

> Therefore this matter is to be decided through inference.
> [Objection:] But what is the inference here?
> [Reply:] As was already said, because an absence is not an effect. Moreover,
> 3a.   Not without a cause would anything [cease]
> If cessation were universally due to a cause, then nothing whatever would stop without a cause, such as origination. The cessation of momentary things such as thoughts, sounds and flames is seen to be spontaneous, it does not depend on a cause. As for the notion that the cessation of a thought is due to another thought, that of a sound is due to another sound, that is wrong. For the two thoughts do not occur together. For there is no mutual contact of the states of doubt and certainty, of pleasure and pain, of desire and hate. And when a strong thought or sound is followed by a weak thought or sound, why would the weak *dharma* destroy a stronger one of the same kind? If it is thought with respect to the last two cases that cessation is due to the absence of a cause of persistence of flames, or due to virtue and vice [that is, karmic merit and demerit], that is incorrect. For absence is not capable of being a cause. And it is not possible that the arising or cessation of virtue could at one moment prevent the occurrence of something [when it is unfavorable] and at another moment bring about its occurrence [when it is favorable]; and likewise for vice. It is possible to apply this reasoning to all constructed things, so enough of this discussion.
> If, moreover, the cessation of wood and the like were because of contact with fire and the like, then with respect to the arising, in what is more and more heated, of [successively more intense] qualities produced by heating,
> 3b.   The cause would also be the destroyer.
> Why is that? Either those [distinct] heating-produced qualities that arise successively in grass and the like through contact with fire are all just due to what is the same [heat], or else their destruction is in the arising of the more and more heated, precisely the cause would be their destroyer, there would be no difference in causes. And it is not right that what their existence is from should also be just what their non-existence is from. That would be to imagine that within flames there are distinct causes.
> [Objection:] What is it that is thus effected in the case of the arising of heat-produced differences through contact with lye, snow, acid, sun, and the watery? In the case of boiling water that grows less, what is it that contact with heat does there?
> [Reply:] By virtue of its contact with fire, through the force of the fire, the heat element – which is present in water – increases; and increasing, causes the mass of water to be reborn in quantities more and more reduced, until being totally reduced, the series does not renew itself. This is what contact with fire does to water. Therefore there is no cause for the destruction of things. It [destruction] is just intrinsic. Ceasing because of their transitoriness, being just arisen they go out of existence. Destruction in an instant is thus proven, and from destruction in a moment, the absence of motion is proven. There is the conception of movement,

however, when there is an uninterrupted arising in different locations, as with a grass fire. [AKBh IV.2c–3b]

Vasubandhu gives a second reason why cessation could not be caused. Not only is this impossible because the cause would have an absence as its effect. It is also a matter of observation that some things do cease spontaneously, without an external cause. His examples are thoughts, sounds and flames. He explores various alternative ways of trying to show that their cessation is due to causes, and claims these all come up short. But there is another argument, namely that then origination would also continue ceaselessly. After a seed produces a sprout, its productive activity ceases. Why? If cessation required a cause, there would have to be a cause to explain the cessation of the seed's production. But that cause would function by originating this cessation of the seed's production. Why does this originative activity cease? It looks like yet another cause will be required, and we are headed toward an infinite regress. This is a bad sign.

Vasubandhu also objects to the claim that one and the same thing could be both the cause of origination and the cause of destruction. When the pot is fired, its white color goes out of existence and red color comes into existence. A given cause can only have one effect. So either we say that the fire causes the destruction of white color, and red color just spontaneously appears, or else we say that the white color self-destructs, and the fire causes the coming into existence of a red color rather than the usual white color replacement. The evaporation of water that is heated can be similarly explained.

Finally, notice the example of a grass fire that is meant to illustrate the illusory nature of motion. We ordinarily say that the fire moves across the burning field. But strictly speaking this is incorrect. For the fire is a mass of individual flames, and each flame is on just one stalk of grass. The apparent motion is the result of a flame on one stalk causing another flame on an adjacent stalk. What we take to be a moving fire is really a causal series of stationary things. If everything is momentary, then what we take to be a falling stone is likewise just a causal series. It is one set of *dharmas* in one location causing the occurrence of another similar set of *dharmas* in an adjacent location when the first set has gone out of existence.

6.5

We have now covered enough of Abhidharma metaphysics to be able to follow their response to the Nyāya critique of non-self. In what follows, Vasubandhu's opponent is a Naiyāyika with the same sorts of concerns that Uddyotakara expressed in his comments on *Nyāya Sūtra* I.1.10:[9]

---

[9]This passage is taken from Chapter 9 of *Abhidharmakośabhāṣya*, which may have been written as an independent work and then attached to Vasubandhu's commentary on *Abhidharmakośa* as a kind of appendix. My translation of this passage substantially follows that of Kapstein; cf. Chapter 5, n. 7.

> [Objection:] If, then, there is no self whatsoever, then how is it that among momentary cognitions there occurs memory or recognition of objects experienced long ago?
> [Reply:] Due to a distinct cognition [that is, a seed] that is connected to a conception of the object of memory.
> [Objection:] From what sort of distinct cognition is it that memory immediately arises?
> [Reply:] From one having a conception that is connected with the enjoyment of that and resembles that, and whose power is not destroyed by distinctive features of its support, grief, distraction, etc. For though it resembles that, a distinctive cognition not connected to it is not able to produce that memory, and even one that is connected to it but which resembles something else is unable to produce that memory. When both conditions are met there is the capacity, and thus there is memory, for the capacity is not seen elsewhere.

This is an example of the Sautrāntikas theory of seeds being put to use to explain memory. If an experience is striking and one is not distracted immediately afterwards, then a seed is formed that has the power under the right circumstances to create a memory image or bring about the experience of recognition. Like all *dharmas*, this one goes out of existence in an instant. But it causes a successor seed, which causes another, etc., in a causal series, until such time as the memory is triggered. Note that the occurrence of a memory image or the feeling of recognition is not by itself enough to make something a memory. The cause of that memory must be part of a causal series that stretches back to the original experience. Otherwise it's just a pseudo-memory.

Suppose I am now remembering my first experience of eating a mango. On this account, none of the *dharmas* that now make up me existed at the time of that experience. These present *dharmas* were caused by the ones that existed then. But they are numerically distinct *dharmas* all the same. This leads to an objection. We all know that one person does not remember the experiences of another person. But the Abhidharma account of memory says that it is one thing that has the experience of eating the mango, and another thing that remembers it. So isn't there a problem here? Notice how Vasubandhu's reply will make implicit use of the idea that the person is a conceptual fiction constructed out of a causal series of *dharmas*.

> [Objection:] Now, how is it that what has been seen by one mental event is remembered by another? For then what was seen by a mental event of Devadatta, a mental event of Yajñadatta might remember.
> [Reply:] No, for there is no connection. For with respect to these two [mental events] there is no connection, for they lack the cause-effect relation that would hold between events in a single mental stream. Nor do we say, 'What was seen by one mental event is remembered by another'. Rather, from the cognition that sees, a distinct memory cognition arises. There is the transformation of the causal series, as has been said; what fault is there in that case? And recognition occurs only owing to memory.

[Objection:] If there is no self, who remembers?

[Reply:] What is the meaning of 'remembers'?

[Objection:] One grasps the object by means of memory.

[Reply:] Is that grasping distinct from memory?

[Objection:] What then does the remembering?

[Reply:] It was said that what does that is the distinct cognition that is the cause of the memory. What is then expressed as 'Caitra remembers' is so called having perceived that [this distinct cognition] occurs due to the causal series called 'Caitra', it is thus said, 'Caitra remembers'.

[Objection:] If there is no self, whose is the remembering?

[Reply:] What is the meaning of the genitive case [of 'whose']?

[Objection:] It means the owner, that is, someone is the owner of something, e.g., Caitra with respect to a cow [in the expression 'Caitra's cow'].

[Reply:] How is he her owner?

[Objection:] Because he controls her use, as a draught-animal or for milking and the like.

[Reply:] But then what is memory to be used for, if we are then looking for its owner [who must use it for something to be an owner]?

[Objection:] For the object to be remembered.

[Reply:] For what purpose is it to be used?

[Objection:] For the purpose of remembering.

[Reply:] Oh, what gems from the mouths of those who have been well-raised! So it is to be used for that purpose. Well, how is it to be used? For production [as the cow is used for milk], or for moving something [as when the cow is used as a draught-animal]?

[Objection:] Because memory is without movement, for production.

[Reply:] But then it must be the cause, as owner, that obtains the effect, as owned, since there is power of the cause over the effect, and by means of the effect the cause is its possessor. Thus, what is the cause of the memory is its [possessor]. So having taken as one that causal series consisting of collections of elements that is called 'Caitra', it is called the owner of the so-called 'cow'. Though one thinks of him as being thus a cause of the production of [the cow's] movement and change, there is nonetheless no one called 'Caitra' nor is there a cow. Hence, even in that case, there is no possessor relation apart from the causal relation.

[Objection:] In that case, who cognizes? Whose is the consciousness? This and more must be stated!

[Reply:] The cause of that, the respective sense faculty, object and attention, this is what is distinctive.

[Objection:] But it may be said: 'Because a property depends on an existing thing, all properties are dependent on existing things. Just as with "Devadatta goes", the property of going depends on the goer, Devadatta. And consciousness is a property. Therefore it must exist by means of that which cognizes.' It should be said what this [cognizer] is.

[Reply:] What is this 'Devadatta'? If the self, then indeed that remains to be proven. Or the conventionally designated person? That too is not at all one, for it is those elements [in the series] that are so called. In that case, Devadatta cognizes just as he goes.

[Objection:] And how does Devadatta go?

[Reply:] The momentary elements in an unbroken series that are regarded by simple persons as 'Devadatta' through their grasping it as a single being as a whole, these, as the cause of the series' own existing in another place, are what are expressed as 'Devadatta goes'. And that arising in another place is what is called 'going'. Just as 'it goes' designates the movement of a series of flames or sounds. Just so as well, the existing things that cause the cognition are expressed as 'Devadatta cognizes'. And so as well are they referred to by the Noble Ones for the purpose of conventional communication.

Recall that in his commentary on *Nyāya Sūtra* I.1.10, Uddyotakara demanded that the Buddhist supply a subject for the experience of remembering. (See Chapter 5, §3.) Has Vasubandhu satisfactorily responded to that demand? Uddyotakara also argued that cognitions like that of the taste of the mango are qualities, and as such require a substance in the form of the self. In this he was employing the Nyāya system of categories. Vasubandhu's response clearly rejects that set of categories. But what is his alternative? And does it work as well as the Nyāya conception to account for the nature of our experience?

[Objection:] As for what it says in the sūtra, 'Consciousness cognizes', what in that case does consciousness do?

[Reply:] It does nothing whatever. Just as the effect is said to conform to the cause by virtue of being similar in nature but without having done anything, so 'Consciousness cognizes' is said due to being similar in nature without having done anything.

[Objection:] But what is its similarity?

[Reply:] Its having the form of that [its object]. It is for just this reason that we say it [the object] is cognized, and not the sense faculty, since the object of awareness [*viṣaya*] arises from its sense faculty. Is it not true that here as well there is no fault in saying that consciousness cognizes? For there is a causal relation when there is a cognition in a causal series of cognitions, and there is no fault in applying an agent-term to the cause. Just as in 'the bell sounds'. Moreover, as a light moves, so it is said that consciousness cognizes.

[Objection:] And how does a light move?

[Reply:] 'Light' designates a continuum of flames. Its arising in different places is what is expressed as 'It moves to that place'. 'Consciousness' likewise designates a continuum of cognitions. Its arising in different intentional objects is what is expressed as 'Consciousness cognizes that object'. Again, just as when it is said that *rūpa* arises and persists, there is no object apart from the state of becoming [to serve as agent of arising and persisting], so it could be as well in the case of consciousness.

The difficulty with saying 'Consciousness cognizes' is that it makes it sound like consciousness is an agent, a substance that performs acts of cognizing. That turns consciousness into something dangerously like a self. So Vasubandhu must show that this is just a way of talking that does not reflect the ultimate reality involved. Notice how he uses the theory of two truths in his attempt:

[Objection:] If consciousness arises from consciousness and not from the self, then why does it neither always arise only similarly, nor always arise according to a fixed order, e.g., sprout, shoot, leaf, etc.?

[Reply:] Because the mark of the conditioned is that what persists becomes otherwise. For this is the nature of the conditioned, namely that necessarily there comes about difference in a continuous series. For otherwise, for those who are absorbed in deep meditation would not reemerge [from meditation] by themselves, for in the arising of similar bodily states and cognitions [in meditation] there is no difference between the first moment and later ones. Also because the series of cognitions is indeed determined. The arising of something is only from that from which it is supposed to arise. Similarity of form is a capacity for some sort of arising due to a distinct class. So if, following the thought of a woman, the thought that that body is corrupting, or the thought of her husband, son, etc., should arise, then when later on, owing to the transformation of the continuum, the thought of a woman arises again, then it is capable of giving rise to the thought that that body is corrupting, or the thought of her husband, son, etc., because it is of that class. Otherwise it would not be capable. Moreover, when from the thought of a woman a great many kinds of thoughts have arisen in succession, then that which is most frequent arises, or else that which is closest. For it has been most forcefully cultivated. It is otherwise when there are simultaneous special conditions external to the body.

[Objection:] Why does that which has been most forcefully cultivated not perpetually bear fruit?

[Reply:] Because the mark of the conditioned is that what persists becomes otherwise. And the being otherwise of that conforms to the fruition of other cultivations. But this is merely an indication concerning the forms of all cognitions. For the buddhas [fully enlightened beings], though, there is abundance in the cognition of immediate causes, as is said:

The cause, in all its aspects, of a single eye of a peacock's feather
Is not knowable by one who is not omniscient, for the cognition of that is the power of omniscience. [AKBh IX, Pradhan, pp. 402–404]

The example of what follows after the thought of a woman is related to a common concern among male meditators: occurrences of sexual desire can disrupt one's efforts to remain in focused concentration. This helps explain the two thoughts that Vasubandhu says might subsequently arise. Both are strategies for dismissing the thought. The thought that the woman's body is corrupting is not necessarily an expression of misogyny. It may just reflect the idea that sexual desire is unhelpful for those on the path to nirvāna. (So a female meditator might equally dismiss intrusive sexual desires by reflecting that the male body is corrupting.) The thought of her husband or son is part of an alternative strategy of banishing the thought by thinking of the man whose role it is (under classical Indian patriarchy) to protect the woman's chastity. But the point of the example is just to illustrate the fact that the causal connections operating in a mental causal series (that is, a 'mind') are extremely complex. A mind and a stone are both conceptual fictions, each constructed on the basis of a causal series. But the 'stone' series is much simpler. The *dharmas* occurring at one moment in the causal series that we call a stone are usually just like those that occurred the moment before. This is not true of a mental causal series. Still there are patterns, and these patterns give us some insight into what the causal laws governing a mental stream are.

6.6

In the passage we have been looking at, Vasubandhu has tried to answer the opponent's question who it is that remembers. The answer is basically that it is those parts of the causal series that cause the memory that get treated as the subject of experience. In doing so, Vasubandhu seems to treat as legitimate the opponent's demand for something that could be an experiencer. And we can raise the question whether he is right to do so. Of course Vasubandhu does not actually think there is some ultimately real thing that has experiences and later remembers them. What are ultimately real are just the *dharmas* in the causal series. It is to these that words like 'I' and names like 'Devadatta' get attached, thereby fostering the illusion that there is something that first experiences and then remembers. Still he never comes right out and says that the opponent's question is really ill formed. Would this be a useful strategy for an Ābhidharmika to pursue?

We can see how this strategy might work by looking at what another Abhidharma philosopher says about the idea of an experiencer. The philosopher is Buddhaghosa, whose *Visuddhimagga* is one of the most important Abhidharma manuals in the Theravāda tradition. The passage we are about to look at is discussing the Theravādan account of rebirth. Buddhaghosa makes the usual point that there is nothing that travels from one life to the next. Instead rebirth is just the continuation of the causal series through the mechanism of karmic causal connections. The opponent raises two objections. The first is that then the person who reaps the karmic fruit does not deserve it. We looked at this objection, as well as Nāgasena's response, earlier (Chapter 3, §8). But the second objection is new. It is that karma makes no sense without an experiencer, something the Buddhist does not countenance. The idea is that in order to say a certain feeling of pleasure or pain is a karmic fruit, we must be able to say that the pleasure or pain is experienced by someone. The question here is not whether this is the same person as the one who did the deed in an earlier life (and so deserves the fruit). That question was the focus of the first objection. The question here is rather whether it could make sense to say that there is pleasure or pain without someone to experience them. The opponent thinks not. Here is Buddhaghosa's reply:

> Now as to what was said, 'If there is no experiencer, whose is the fruit?' consider the following:

'As there is the convention, "It bears fruit"
When fruit arises on a tree;
Just so there is the convention of calling *skandhas* an experiencer,
When karma's fruit arises.'

Just as it is simply because of the arising of tree fruit, which is one portion of the *dharmas* that are designated 'tree', that it is said 'The tree bears fruit', or 'The tree has fruited', so it is simply because of the arising of the fruit consisting of pleasure and pain, designated 'experience', which is one portion of the *skandhas* designated 'god' or 'human being', that it is said, 'A god or a human being experiences or feels pleasure or pain'. There is therefore no need here for any superfluous experiencer. [VM XVII.171–72]

It may look like there is nothing new here. Buddhaghosa seems to be saying just what we saw Vasubandhu say: that 'experiencer' is just a convenient designator for a causal series of *dharmas*. But think about the example of the tree that bears fruit. There are many parts that make up a tree over the course of a year: roots, trunk, bark, branches, leaves, fruit.[10] Suppose we were to collect all these parts together into one set. Would that set be what 'tree' is a convenient designator for? No. That set includes the fruit. And when we say, 'The tree bears fruit', 'tree' cannot designate the fruit. The fruit cannot be among the things that we say bear that very fruit, since that would violate the anti-reflexivity principle. The relation of bearing is non-reflexive: the bearer and the thing that is borne must be distinct things. So in the sentence, 'The tree bears fruit', 'tree' could only designate those of the parts that remain after excluding the fruit.

Now consider the sentence, 'The tree has shed its leaves'. What does 'tree' designate in this case? Not the same set of parts as the one that 'tree' designates in 'The tree bears fruit'. That set contains leaves. And it would not make sense to say that that set has shed its leaves. How could leaves be among the things that shed those very leaves? So here 'tree' must designate the set of parts that remain after excluding the leaves. Suppose the tree in question retains its fruit after shedding its leaves. Then in this sentence, 'tree' will designate a different set of parts than it does in 'The tree bears fruit'. Where the leaves occur in the one set, the fruit occurs in the other. Here is the situation for the tree:

1 'The tree bears fruit': 'tree' designates {roots, trunk, bark, branches, leaves}.
2 'The tree has shed its leaves': 'tree' designates {roots, trunk, bark, branches, fruit}.

And we need not stop here. There are other things we say about the tree that require

---

[10]We are now thinking about the tree and its parts in common-sense terms. Of course a leaf is itself a whole made up of further parts. Ultimately these can all be reduced to *dharmas*. The point we will make could be made by talking about those *dharmas*. But it is simpler to make the point in common-sense terms.

'tree' to designate still other sets, as when we say that the tree has grown some new branches. What this makes clear is that there is no one set of things that the convenient designator 'tree' always designates. But to say this is not to say that the word 'tree' is hopelessly unclear. The word works perfectly adequately for ordinary purposes. It does so because there is always substantial overlap among the parts it designates on one way of using it, and those it designates on another way. In (1) and (2), for instance, both sets include roots, trunk, bark and branches. We can also understand why it would be useful to have a word that can shift its meaning like this. The point is just that we should not expect there to be one set of things that the word always designates.

Now apply this lesson to the relation between conceptual fictions in general and the ultimately real things that constitute them. Whenever the conceptual fiction in question is a substance that can endure over time, we can expect that our convenient designator for that substance will pick out a different set of *dharmas* on different occasions. There is no collection of *dharmas* that our name for the conceptual fiction will always pick out. So we cannot say precisely which ultimately real things the concept corresponds to. Yet we can still explain why we have the concept, and how it can be useful for us. There are no *dharmas* that the concept of a subject of experience can always be mapped onto. If we take the set of all the *dharmas* that ever occur in a 'person' series, then 'experiencer' will sometimes refer to one subset of this set, sometimes to another subset. We can now see that there is nothing strange in this. But it also means that it is illegitimate for the opponent to demand that we supply something ultimately real to take the place of our common-sense concept of the subject of experience. We can understand why common sense would include this concept. It can be useful to be able to partition the 'person' *dharmas* in this way. But there are no ultimately real things that 'experiencer' designates every time we apply it to a particular causal series. Instead there are many sets with overlapping members.[11]

6.7

It seems to have been the Sautrāntikas who first articulated and defended the doctrine of momentariness. We have seen how the doctrine helped Abhidharma put the theory of non-self on a firm philosophical footing. But the Sautrāntikas also used it to establish a view about the nature of sense perception, namely the theory known as representationalism. This is a theory about what it is that we are aware of when we cognize something using our external senses. But before stating the theory we need to introduce a technical term for this expression 'what it is we are aware of'. When we have sensory experience through a sense faculty like vision or touch, we ordinarily use the word 'object' for what it is we are aware of. We would say that we see and touch an object. The difficulty with this word is that we also use it to mean something

---

[11]Consider how this would apply to the 'shifting coalitions' strategy discussed in Chapter 3, §4.

physical. And what the representationalist claims is that in sense perception we are not aware of physical objects – at least not directly. So let's use the expression 'intentional object' to mean whatever it is that one is directly aware of when one has sensory experience. And let's also agree to use 'external object' to mean a physical object, something that exists outside the mind.[12] Then we can state representationalism as follows:

> **Representationalism**: the theory that in sense perception, the intentional object is not an external object but a representation.

We now need to know what a representation is. Here's a definition:

> **Representation**: a mental image that is caused by contact between a sense faculty and an external object, and that resembles the external object.

Representationalism is not the view of common sense. According to common sense, when I have experiences through my external senses, what I am directly aware of is the external object my sense faculty has come in contact with.[13] The common-sense view is that the intentional object just is the external object. We will call this view 'direct realism'. According to direct realism, in external sensory experience our senses inform the mind about things in the external physical world. When I pass the bakery, what I smell is the odor of the freshly baked *baguettes*. When I buy one, tear off a warm bit of crust, and eat it, it is the warmth of the bread that I am aware of through touch, and the flavor of the bread that I am aware of through taste. The odor, the warmth and the flavor are all there in the bread. Things are a bit more complicated in the Abhidharma form of direct realism. According to Abhidharma, the bread is a conceptual fiction, so it can't be either sort of object. What really exist are very many atoms, plus such other *dharmas* as the odor, the flavor, etc. But Abhidharma thinks of all these *dharmas* as things existing outside the mind. So an Ābhidharmika who is a direct realist would say that the intentional object of my touch experience is the warmth, which is among the many external object *dharmas* making up the *baguette* conceptual fiction.

Now a representationalist does not deny that through our sensory experiences we become aware of things existing outside the mind. What they deny is that these are what we are directly aware of. Representationalists draw a distinction between being directly aware of something and being aware of it only indirectly. This is a distinction

---

[12]The intentional object is called in Sanskrit the *viṣaya* or *ālambana*; the external object is called the *artha*.

[13]Remember that in Indian psychology there are six senses, not five. But everyone agrees that the intentional object of the inner sense is not an external object. Inner states like pleasure and pain, for instance, are not external objects. What the representationalist and the direct realist disagree about is the intentional object of sensory experiences involving the five external senses.

that a direct realist can also draw. When we are trying to be careful in describing our experience, we distinguish between what it is that we actually perceive, and what it is that we infer from our sense perceptions. We say that we heard the footsteps on the stairs, and only inferred that someone was coming up. That we saw the footprints in the sand, and only inferred that a dog walked on it. Since the intentional object is what we are directly aware of, then in these cases the direct realist would say that the intentional object is the sound of the footsteps and the shape of the footprints. But the direct realist still thinks of these as external objects. The sound is something that exists out there in the external world. It is something that occurs regardless of whether or not someone is there to hear it.

The representationalist agrees that the sound made by a foot on the stairs is an external object, something that would exist even if no one were aware of it. But the representationalist claims that for that very reason, it cannot be the intentional object of auditory experience. It is something that we can become aware of only indirectly. First we must be aware of a representation, something that can only exist in the mind. And then, based on our awareness of that, we can infer the existence of that sound. What exactly is a representation? Our definition called it a mental image, but what does that mean? Well, consider the case where you look up and see two moons in the sky, perhaps because your eyes are out of focus. We know there is only one moon, so what is it you see when you see a second? It can't be another moon; there isn't one. It can't be the white color of the moon; there's only one of those too. It can't be anything external, yet you are aware of something. So that 'something' must be something in the mind – a mental image. Likewise when you hear a high-pitched whine after you've operated a power saw. The sound you hear isn't coming from the saw, which is off. You hear it, but others don't. What is it that you are aware of? A mental image; in this case an auditory mental image.

These are cases of illusion or non-veridical perception. But we can be taken in by them. The branch sticking in the water really does look bent. The representationalist takes this to show that the intentional object in veridical perception cannot be different in kind from the intentional object in non-veridical perception. If we can't tell *just by how the branch looks* that it is not bent, then what we're aware of when we see the branch correctly must be the same sort of thing. But we agree that what we're aware of when the branch looks bent is a mental image. So that must be what we're aware of in the normal case of perception as well. According to representationalism, the difference between illusion and veridical perception is not that the illusion is in the mind while non-illusory perception grasps what's out there. The intentional object in both cases is something in the mind. The difference is rather that in veridical perception the mental image resembles what's out there, while in illusory perception it doesn't.

According to the representationalist, in perception we are only indirectly aware of the external object. We are directly aware of a mental image, and from our awareness of the image we infer the existence of something out there that is like it. Usually we are right about this. It's because our senses are working properly, and our senses cause us to have mental images like the external objects they come in contact with, that we have the sensory experiences we do. Here is an analogy that may help explain what the representationalist is saying. Nowadays large department stores use surveillance cameras to spot shoplifters. There are cameras mounted in strategic locations throughout the store, and each camera is hooked up to a monitor in some central location out of sight of the sales floor. We might say that the person watching the monitors sees someone shoplifting, but that isn't completely accurate. It would be more accurate to say that they see an image on the monitor, and from this image they infer that someone is shoplifting on the sales floor. Of course the inference would probably be correct, but that isn't the point here. The point is to give an accurate account of what actually goes on in the perceptual process. According to the representationalist, in perception the intentional object – what we're directly aware of – is like the image on the monitor, only it's inside the mind. Our senses are like the surveillance camera. They have the capacity to produce images in the mind that are copies of what the external object is like. Like any piece of hardware, they can sometimes go astray and produce mental images that misrepresent how things are in the external world. Then we have illusions like seeing a double moon or hearing the high-pitched whine. Usually, though, they get it right. When they do, we can tell what the external object is like from the nature of the intentional object. Then we can say that we hear the sound of the feet on the stairs. What we're really aware of, though, is not the sound but the representation that the sound causes in our mind.

By now we should be used to philosophers contradicting our common-sense views. So it should not come as a shock to discover that some Abhidharma philosophers embraced representationalism. But why should we believe them? For that matter, why should any Buddhist believe this theory about sense perception? Early Buddhism didn't embrace it, nor did many of the Abhidharma schools. What convinced the Sautrāntikas that the direct realist picture of perception is wrong and should be replaced by representationalism? One argument, the time-lag argument, uses the doctrine of momentariness. The basic idea behind the argument is that since there is always a tiny gap between when the sense comes in contact with the external object and when there is sensory awareness, what we are aware of can't be the external object that the senses were in contact with, since it no longer exists. In outline the argument looks like this:

1   The intentional object of perceptual cognition must be (a) capable of being directly present to the cognition that cognizes it, and (b) what is responsible for the cognition's having the content it has.

2   In the perceptual process there is a time lag between the moment of contact between sense faculty and external object and the moment at which there is cognition of what is perceived.

3   Hence at the time of perceptual cognition the external object that the sense faculty came in contact with no longer exists (since all things are momentary).

4   The external object with which the sense faculty came in contact is not the intentional object, since it does not now exist, like the horns of a hare.
5   An external object that presently exists is not the intentional object, since it is not responsible for the cognition's having the content it has, like events occurring on the other side of the world.
6   Hence the external object with which the sense faculty comes in contact is not the intentional object.
7   But since in perceptual cognition we are directly aware of something, there must be an intentional object of perceptual cognition.
C   Therefore the intentional object of perceptual cognition must be a representation.

The first premise imposes two requirements on the intentional object of perception (that is, what it is we are aware of when we perceive). Requirement (a) says that it must be the sort of thing that we can grasp directly and not just through an intermediary. The idea here is that perception is the most important means of knowledge precisely because it is the one that directly cognizes the object. Other means of knowledge like inference and testimony give us the object indirectly, at some remove. They come into play only when we can't get at the object itself, and have to go by way of our cognition of something else. But if perception is a way of directly cognizing its object, then the object must be something that can be present to the cognition that cognizes it; it must be the sort of thing that can stand right before the cognition to be scrutinized. Requirement (b) then adds that the object must also be what accounts for the content of the cognition. Suppose there is a red round spot on the wall in front of me, that my eyes are functioning properly, and the light is good. Suppose that because of this, I have the perceptual cognition that is reported as 'There is a red round spot.' Requirement (b) says that the intentional object of this cognition must be something that explains why I say what I see is red and round.

The second premise says there is a time lag between sense-object contact and perceptual cognition. The reason is that the perceptual process always takes some time. For even in something that seems perfectly simple, like seeing a spot, there is a certain amount of cognitive processing that has to be done. According to the Theravāda tradition, this process requires at least 17 moments.[14] But we need not accept Abhidharma psychological theories in order to accept this premise. For we know that sense perception involves transmission of the sensory stimulus from the sense organ to the brain, followed by some brain processing. This means that sensory cognition will always occur slightly later than stimulation of the sense organ. The time lag will be very short, but it will always be there. The third premise then brings the doctrine of momentariness to bear on this situation. It means that when I have the cognition that I report as seeing a red round spot, the red round *dharma* on the wall

---

[14]That is, 17 atomic moments. An atomic moment is the shortest duration possible, given that everything is momentary. It is the length of time it takes for something to come into existence and immediately go out of existence.

that my eyes came in contact with will have gone out of existence. There is still a red round *dharma* on the wall, but it's not the one that stimulated my vision. The one that exists now is a successor *dharma* to the one that my eyes came in contact with. If my eyes are directed toward it, this will result in another perceptual cognition of a red round spot a very short time from now. But it can play no role in the perceptual cognition of a red round spot that is occurring right now.

The fourth and fifth premises then show that neither of these external objects could be the intentional object of my perceptual cognition. Premise (4) points out that the red round *dharma* that stimulated my vision does not meet requirement (a), since it no longer exists. It's impossible for something that doesn't exist, such as the horns of a hare, to be present to cognition. Premise (5) points out that on the other hand the red round *dharma* that does now exist (and so could meet requirement (a)) does not meet requirement (b). It cannot contribute anything to the content of my cognition. The earlier red round one might have been replaced by a purple triangular *dharma* and my present perceptual cognition would still be exactly the same. Of course if it were a purple triangular *dharma* that is there now, then the perceptual cognition I would have a very short time from now would be of a purple triangle. But what I now cognize is a round red spot. Because of the time lag, no presently existing external object can explain why that is what I cognize. It can have no more to do with what I now see than do events taking place on the other side of the world.

The remainder of the argument draws the consequences of this. The only external object that could be the intentional object of my perceptual cognition is a red round *dharma* on the wall. The one that my sense of vision came in contact with a little while ago can't be the intentional object. Neither can the presently existing one. So no external object can be the intentional object. Yet there must be something I am directly aware of in perceptual cognition. For otherwise I could never be indirectly aware of anything. Indirect awareness requires that one use what one is directly aware of in order to grasp something else. So if the intentional object of perceptual cognition is not an external object, it must be something internal or mental. It must, in short, be a representation. Since this is something mental, it is something that can be directly present to cognition. And it is because it is the image of a red round patch that my perceptual cognition has the content it does. A representation can meet both requirement (a) and requirement (b).

How strong is this argument? There is one loophole. Think about premise (3). If there were some way to show that the external object that the sense faculty comes in contact with still exists at the time the perceptual cognition occurs, then this external object could meet both requirements for the intentional object. Theravāda claims that *rūpa dharmas* are an exception to the doctrine of momentariness. They teach that a *rūpa dharmas* lasts not just one moment but 17 moments. If this were true, then the red round *dharma* that my sense of vision came in contact with could be the intentional object. Unfortunately, Theravāda gives no reason for its claim that *rūpa dharmas* last longer than other *dharmas*. No reason, that is, other than that this would make their direct realism consistent, which hardly counts as a good reason.

Vaibhāṣika does better in this department. This school does not deny that all conditioned things are momentary. But it holds a direct realist view of perception: external objects like the red round *dharma* are the intentional objects of our perceptual cognitions. This is possible because it denies (3). Given the Vaibhāṣika view of time, the red round *dharma* still exists when the perceptual cognition occurs. They can say this because they hold that all past objects (as well as future objects) exist. (See §4, especially note 6.) Past objects no longer function; that is what makes them past and not present. But existence is something that an entity has timelessly. On this view, the red round *dharma* is still available to be directly present to a perceptual cognition. It can no longer bring about any effects, but it still is. And since it can also explain why the cognition has the content it does, it may be the intentional object. So if you are willing to embrace the Vaibhāṣika view of time, then you could consistently hold a direct realist view of perception despite the existence of a time lag.

Representationalism is well known in the Western tradition. Indeed the question of what we are aware of in perception is among the core issues that define modern philosophy. It is interesting to note, though, that the considerations that led the Sautrāntikas to embrace representationalism are quite different than those that led British empiricists like Locke to the same conclusion. With the latter, two arguments seem particularly prominent: the argument from illusion (which of the two moons is the 'real' one?), and an argument based on the distinction between primary and secondary properties. The latter is based on the idea that there is nothing in the physical object resembling the color we see or the flavor we taste. From this it is concluded that the experience of properties like color and flavor is just the cognition of a mental image or representation, and this conclusion is then generalized to cover all properties.

The Sautrāntikas have other arguments for representationalism, but we will not look at them. Our final question is how representationalism fits into the larger scheme of things. In the case of modern Western philosophy, the answer is fairly clear. The representationalist account of sense perception grew out of attempts at reconciling the difference between the common-sense picture of the world and the view that was emerging from new scientific discoveries. It gives us a way of explaining why, for instance, physical objects look colored to us when color is not a scientifically respectable property. In the case of the Sautrāntikas, though, things are not so clear. By now we have grown used to Buddhist philosophical theories serving some soteriological purpose. We saw this, for instance, with the doctrine that the whole is ultimately unreal, and likewise with the claim that everything is momentary. Both views help support the doctrine of non-self, which is central to the Buddhist enlightenment project. It is not clear, though, that representationalism is linked to attaining nirvāna and overcoming suffering. Perhaps the Sautrāntikas embraced it simply because they thought it was true. Philosophers have been known to do such things, after all. And this should not be surprising. To philosophize well, one must be committed to following the argument wherever it leads. Perhaps the Sautrāntikas simply found that their thinking about the nature of perceptual cognition led them to this surprising conclusion.

Further Reading

For the history of the 18 schools making up the Abhidharma movement see Chapter Nine of: A.K. Warder, *Indian Buddhism* (Delhi: Motilal Banarsidass, 1970).

For more on the theory of tropes (quality-particulars), see the critical survey by Chris Daly, 'Tropes', in D.H. Mellor and Alex Oliver, eds, *Properties* (Oxford: Oxford University Press, 1997). A more sympathetic treatment is in Jonathan Schaffer, 'The Individuation of Tropes', *Australasian Journal of Philosophy* **79**: pp. 247–57. Two discussions of the interpretation of *dharmas* as tropes are in Jonardon Ganeri, *Philosophy in Classical India* (New York: Routledge, 2001), pp. 101–02; and also Charles Goodman, 'The *Treasury of Metaphysics* and the Physical World', *Philosophical Quarterly* **54** (2004): 389–401.

CHAPTER SEVEN

The Rise of Mahāyāna

We turn now to Mahāyāna Buddhism, the third of the three major phases in the history of Buddhist philosophy. In this chapter we will examine the key philosophical concepts by which Mahāyāna sought to set itself apart from the Abhidharma movement. In subsequent chapters we will look at how these concepts are expressed in the three major schools of Mahāyāna philosophy. The Mahāyāna movement encompasses much more than philosophy, though. It also represents a transformation in the understanding of Buddhist practice. And this transformation led to changes in Buddhist institutional arrangements. So far in this book we have had little to say about Buddhist institutions and their history. But in this case it would be useful to begin with a brief discussion of the genesis of Mahāyāna as a distinctive expression of Buddhist insight. This will help us avoid some common confusions concerning the relationship between Mahāyāna and other forms of Buddhist practice.

7.1

The first thing to be said about the rise of Mahāyāna is that there is little that can be said on the subject with much certainty. In European history we can place the beginning of the Protestant Reformation to within a span of a few decades in the sixteenth century. In Indian history, by contrast, scholars have a hard time even pinning down the century in which Mahāyāna arose. This is largely because we lack good historical records for classical India. But it also reflects the fact that at the outset, Mahāyāna did not portray itself as innovative.[1] So even if we had better historical sources, there may well not have been anything like the definitive break with tradition that we find in the actions of a Luther or Calvin. The earliest Mahāyānists did not wish to be seen as decisively breaking with existing Buddhist institutions.

We can see signs of this in the texts that represent our first clear-cut indication of Mahāyāna tendencies. Starting sometime in the first century BCE, there began to appear a new kind of Buddhist sūtra. In the Buddhist context a sūtra is a prose text containing a discourse of the Buddha or one of his immediate disciples.[2] According

---

[1]Something similar might be said about the origins of Christianity. The earliest followers of Jesus thought of themselves as belonging to a variant form of Judaism. It is only in retrospect that we call them Christians.

[2]In the orthodox Indian tradition, the sūtras are the foundational texts for the schools. *Nyūya Sūtra*, for instance, lays out the basic tenets of the Nyāya system. These sūtras (unlike those in the Buddhist tradition) are in verse form, and are extremely concise. This makes it quite difficult to understand a philosophical

to the traditions of the Abhidharma schools, the sūtras were collected and recited in a large assembly of monks that took place shortly after the death of the Buddha.[3] So presumably the collection of the sūtras should have been complete by the late fifth or early fourth century BCE. Yet some four centuries later we find previously unknown sūtras beginning to appear. These often take the form of discourses by the Buddha. But sometimes it is some Buddha other than 'our' Buddha, Gautama, who is represented as speaking. Likewise the setting is sometimes not the India where Gautama lived and taught, but another world entirely. And the nature of the teaching is often quite different from what we find in the collections of sūtras recognized by the Abhidharma schools. Much stress is placed, for instance, on the claim that everything is 'empty' or lacking in essence. In the earlier sūtras the doctrine of non-self was sometimes put as the claim that the person is empty of essence. But in these new sūtras we are told that not just the person but all things are empty of essence. We likewise find frequent use of paradoxical statements, such as the claim that nirvāna and *saṃsāra* are really one and the same. There are also new ethical ideals put forth. For instance, in place of prescriptions to follow the eightfold path, we find admonitions to develop the six (or ten) perfections of the *bodhisattva*. For, we are told, one should strive not to be an *arhat* but a *bodhisattva*, someone destined to become a Buddha. In short, these new sūtras are radically different, in form and in content, from those previously considered authoritative expressions of the Buddha's teachings. These look to be new creations, not real records of the Buddha's teachings at all. Yet they are presented by their authors as authentic sūtras nonetheless. What is going on here?

One answer that one sometimes encounters in these sūtras is that they are examples of the Buddha's expedient pedagogical methods (*upāya*). We saw (in Chapter 3) that the Buddha was said to be an especially gifted teacher, in that he always adapted his teaching to the needs and capacities of his audience. While his exercise of this *upāya* never led to his saying things that are false, he did sometimes stop short of the full truth when he knew his audience was not yet ready for it. So, for instance, for those at the earliest stage of progress toward nirvāna he might teach the doctrine of karma and rebirth, without adding that rebirth takes place without a transmigrating self. By the

---

system from its foundational sūtra alone; one must read a commentary as well. In the case of *Nyūya Sūtra*, for instance, there is an extensive commentary by Uddyotakara, which is what we used in Chapter 5. It is likely that the sūtras were originally preserved in oral form, and only later written down. This would explain their form, which is easier to memorize than a lengthy piece of prose. But a student who was memorizing a sūtra would also receive an oral explanation from their teacher. When the literature of a school was finally committed to writing, the genre of the oral explanation became the basis of the written commentary.

[3]In the Theravāda tradition the sūtras are referred to collectively as the *Nikāyas*. There is another collection of sūtras, existing only in Chinese translation, referred to collectively as the *Āgamas*. This collection was probably drawn from those sūtras considered authoritative by a number of different Abhidharma schools. There is extensive but not complete overlap between the two collections.

same token, it is sometimes claimed that the new teachings found in Mahāyāna sūtras are another instance of the Buddha's expedient methods: these are the deeper truths that underlie and complete the teachings taken by Abhidharma as definitive. So for example, on many occasions the Buddha exhorted his hearers to follow the career of the *arhat*, someone who practices the eightfold path, realizes enlightenment, and eventually attains cessation without remainder. Yet if the teachings of the Mahāyāna sūtras are to be believed, it is the very different career of the *bodhisattva* that one should aspire to. This discrepancy, we are told, came about because the Buddha recognized that few would be initially attracted to the arduous career of the *bodhisattva*; only after making progress toward *arhat* status is one likely to grasp the necessity of *bodhisattva* practice. So the Buddha taught the *bodhisattva* path to only a select few, those at a sufficiently advanced stage to be able to benefit from the teaching. The 'new' Mahāyāna sūtras thus aren't really new at all. They are records of those 'private' teachings. Presumably we are to suppose that they were initially available to a select few, but were later made public when it was felt that enough people might benefit from them.

We may be suspicious of these claims. Other strategies were also used to try to explain away the gap of four or more centuries between the collection of the sūtras and the appearance of these Mahāyāna texts. Sometimes the author of a new sūtra claims that the Buddha dictated it to the author in a dream or a trance state. But this strategy requires us to accept that the Buddha still existed centuries after the Parinirvāna. This looks like a significant departure from Buddhist orthodoxy. To make sense of it we need to say more about the ideal of the *bodhisattva*.

The key difference between an *arhat* and a *bodhisattva* is this. While both have attained the sort of enlightenment described by the Buddha in the original sūtras, the former attains cessation without remainder at the end of the life in which they became enlightened, while the latter does not. The *bodhisattva* chooses to be reborn instead. Why would someone able to avoid rebirth choose to remain in *saṃsāra*? Because while suffering has been overcome in this particular causal series, there are many other sentient beings who still suffer. And someone with the sort of insight required to reach the *arhat* stage is capable of perfecting the further set of skills necessary to help others overcome suffering. These include insight into the emptiness of all things, great compassion, and mastery of expedient pedagogical methods. Development of the requisite perfections may take several lifetimes. Once they have been mastered, there will be countless opportunities to help the unenlightened overcome suffering by attaining nirvāna. So the career of the *bodhisattva* may be very lengthy. Now the Mahāyāna sūtras claim that the *bodhisattva*'s career is superior to that of the *arhat*. But it would be inconsistent to say this and also say that at the Parinirvāna the Buddha attained cessation without remainder. If *bodhisattvas* are supposed to undergo further rebirth out of compassion, shouldn't the same hold for the Buddha? This seems to be the reasoning that led early Mahāyāna to the view that the Buddha is still in some sense available, and so might have dictated new sūtras.

Modern scholars have several different theories about the origin of the new *bodhisattva* ideal. One is that this reflects the growing power of lay followers in Buddhism. Within Abhidharma the lay follower's role is confined to following a set of basic precepts, and giving alms to support monks and nuns in their quest for nirvāna. (The payoff is that these actions supposedly earn the lay follower a rebirth in which it will be easier to seek nirvāna themselves.) Now the *bodhisattva* is presented in the Mahāyāna sūtras as spiritually superior to those monks and nuns who seek the status of *arhat*. But a *bodhisattva* might spend an entire lifetime as a householder, never renouncing worldly existence and becoming a monk or nun. While it might be necessary for the *bodhisattva* to have spent at least part of one lifetime in monastic retreat, the insight and powers they acquire in developing the perfections of *bodhisattva* practice will be retained in future lives. This means that a lay follower might actually be a *bodhisattva*, the spiritual superior of the monks or nuns to which lay followers are subordinate in the Abhidharma scheme. This has led some scholars to speculate that the Mahāyāna *bodhisattva* ideal grew out of the increased influence of lay followers in some Buddhist institutions.

This theory no longer has wide acceptance. For there is evidence that in its early stages Mahāyāna was primarily a movement of monks and nuns, not of lay followers. Interestingly, these early Mahāyāna monastics seem to have lived side-by-side with their Ābhidharmika co-religionists. And despite the name of the movement – *Mahāyāna* means 'great vehicle' – they made up only a minority of the Buddhist practitioners of their day.[4] Some scholars now believe that Mahāyāna grew out of a kind of competition among monastic Buddhists for material support. It stands to reason that as Buddhism became more popular, it would need to find new ways to support monks and nuns. Remember that a monk or nun has renounced the productive life of a householder, and devotes all their time and energy to the task of attaining nirvāna. The original pattern, wherein each practitioner made a daily round in search of a donor to give them their meal, could only be sustained when the ratio of monastics to lay followers was quite small. As monastic institutions grew in size, and the lives of renunciants became more settled, there would have been a need to develop more reliable sources of donations. There thus developed the idea that certain forms of worship might earn lay followers the sort of good rebirth that made nirvāna more likely. Out of this idea grew first the worship of stūpas (burial mounds supposedly containing relics of the Buddha), and somewhat later the worship of images of the Buddha. There then ensued a kind of arms race among Buddhist institutions – competing claims as to whose practices might earn devotees the most

---

[4]Mahāyāna texts have several different names for non-Mahāyāna Buddhism (what we are here calling Abhidharma). Two of the most common are *Hīnayāna*, 'inferior vehicle', and *Śrāvakayāna*, 'vehicle of the hearers'. Since the former term is a pejorative, it should not be used. (Calling a Theravādan a 'Hīnayānin' would be rather like calling a Roman Catholic a 'Papist'.) The latter term is historically accurate enough, and more nearly neutral in emotive force. It classifies Abhidharma as that type of Buddhism descended from the practices of those who heard Gautama teach the Dharma. But we will continue to use the name 'Abhidharma' for this phase of Buddhist philosophy.

karmic merit. It seems plausible that in this atmosphere there might develop the seeds of what would later become Mahāyāna devotionalism. For instance, the *bodhisattva* is sometimes described as having accumulated huge amounts of merit, as well as the power to transfer some of that merit to others out of compassion. Worship of the *bodhisattva* (through pilgrimages to places associated with his cult, and the appropriate material support of institutions located there) might thus be presented as a way for lay followers to make progress toward release from suffering.

The growth of these practices does not explain the appearance of new Mahāyāna sūtras, however. For one thing, the rise of the worship of stūpas and Buddha-images seems not to have been associated with any particular school or sect. Some scholars thus suggest that Mahāyāna arose out of a variant on the worship of stūpas and images, that is, the cult of books. One finds in many Mahāyāna sūtras the claim that copying, memorizing or reciting this text will earn one great merit. The theory is that this formula reflects a new form of worship aimed at attracting lay followers and their material support. Unfortunately there does not seem to be any independent evidence for this. The presence of such a formula in a text would help explain how it came to be perpetuated even if it attracted relatively little by way of a following. A more plausible theory is that the early Mahāyāna sūtras reflect the thinking of forest-dwelling meditation masters. As such they would constitute a reaction to the growth of monastic institutions near urban centers, and their associated practices. This would help explain, for instance, why these texts reject some key tenets of Abhidharma philosophy. For it may have seemed to those who had taken up the relatively ascetic life of a meditator in a forest retreat that the scholastic theories of Abhidharma reflected the more lax conditions prevailing in the better-supported monasteries in urban centers.

7.2

Mahāyāna defines itself in terms of two key ideas: the *bodhisattva* ideal, and the doctrine of emptiness. Partisans of the Mahāyāna sometimes claim that the *bodhisattva* ideal shows Mahāyāna to be morally superior to Abhidharma. But it is not clear that this claim is justified. What is claimed is that the *bodhisattva*'s compassion reflects true selflessness, in contrast to the apparent selfishness of *arhats*, who seek nirvāna only for themselves. The first thing to be said about this is that if there is a difference between the two ideals, it is one that can only show up over the course of many lives. The aspiring *bodhisattva* will have to devote the greater part of at least one lifetime to their own enlightenment before they can even begin developing the perfections needed for *bodhisattva* practice. Indeed the aspiring *bodhisattva* must first cultivate precisely the kind of insight into non-self that Abhidharma considers definitive of the *arhat*'s enlightenment. We can see why this would be so by thinking about the argument for compassion that we discussed earlier (in Chapter 4, §4). That argument was taken from a Mahāyāna text, the title of which might be translated as 'Introduction to the Practice of *Bodhi*'. Yet the argument makes use of stock Abhidharma ideas. Apparently it is only after one has attained the understanding that Abhidharma considers constitutive of *arhat*-hood that one can embark on the *bodhisattva* path. And that path, Mahāyāna claims, requires many lives. So if one does not believe in karma and rebirth, the difference between the two ideals cannot seem all that great.

Then there is the fact that the Abhidharma schools also stress the importance of cultivating compassion and equanimity. For them these virtues are important tools in the struggle to bring about full realization of non-self.[5] Now this is different in one key respect from the view of compassion found in the argument of Chapter 4. That argument treated non-self as a tool that helps bring about full realization of compassion, and not the reverse. And the realization of non-self is what is supposed to bring about cessation of suffering for the *arhat*. So the partisan of Mahāyāna might claim that the Abhidharma still values ending one's own suffering over ending that of others. But it could be replied that this misses an important point about the relation between wisdom and compassion in the path toward enlightenment: that the relation is reciprocal. That is, perhaps it cannot be said that one of the two must be deemed of greater importance, with the other valued only because of its instrumental role. It might be that each serves to sustain and further develop the other, and that both are equally valuable. So from the fact that Abhidharma extols compassion as a virtue needed for full realization of non-self, it would not follow that they place greater emphasis on ending one's own suffering than on ending that of others. It might be that the *arhat* will naturally work to help others overcome suffering, and will do so all the more effectively precisely because they have understood that they themselves are empty persons.

So it is not clear that the alleged difference in the ethical ideals of the two movements actually amounts to all that much in practice. Things are different on the metaphysical side. There the Mahāyāna doctrine of emptiness does mark a substantive break with Abhidharma. It is central to Abhidharma that the person is seen as lacking an essence, that is, a self. But in explaining how this could be, Abhidharma makes crucial use of the concept of a *dharma*. And *dharmas* are things that bear their own intrinsic nature. This is what is supposed to make them ultimately real and not mere conceptual fictions. Mahāyāna claims to go beyond Abhidharma in claiming that not just persons, but *dharmas* as well, lack essences. If they are right about this, then the teachings of Abhidharma cannot represent the ultimate truth. Remember that a statement cannot be ultimately true (or ultimately false) if it asserts or presupposes the existence of any mere conceptual fictions. And if *dharmas* lack essences, they can only be conceptual fictions. So all those Abhidharma discussions of the *dharmas* and the causal connections among them could at best be

---

[5]This may be seen, for instance, in the ninth chapter of the important Theravāda text *Visuddhimagga*, which is devoted to the cultivation of loving kindness, compassion, sympathetic joy and equanimity. See *The Path of Purification*, trans. Bhikku Ñyāṇamoli (Berkeley, CA: Shambala, 1976), pp. 321–53.

conventionally true. What, then, is the ultimate truth? According to the early Mahāyāna sūtras, the fact that all things are empty. The contrast with Abhidharma could not be clearer.

But this raises a major difficulty. On this way of understanding things, to say of something that it is empty is to say it is merely conceptually constructed: it is something we take to be real only because we have learned to clump several distinct things together under a single, useful concept. It cannot be ultimately real, because our minds have played a central role in its creation. This was the Abhidharma view about persons and other wholes. Could this be true of everything though, as the Mahāyāna sūtras seem to assert? Could everything be conceptually constructed? If so, then what are things constructed out of? In order for some of the things that we take as real to be conceptual constructions, wouldn't there have to be other things that are not mere conceptual fictions but are ultimately real? Won't ultimate reality have to contain some basic building blocks? The doctrine of emptiness seems to lead straight to metaphysical nihilism, the view that nothing whatever really exists. And we have already agreed (in Chapter 6) that metaphysical nihilism is absurd. Could this really be what the Mahāyāna sūtras mean to assert?

It is over this question that the Mahāyāna philosophical schools diverge. The Madhyamaka school takes the doctrine of emptiness at face value. It then seeks to show why the absurd consequence of metaphysical nihilism does not follow. (We will examine this understanding of emptiness in Chapter 9.) The Yogācāra school holds that metaphysical nihilism does follow if the doctrine of emptiness is taken literally. It then tries to reinterpret the doctrine so it will not have this absurd consequence. On their reinterpretation, to say all things are empty is to say that all things lack the natures that are attributed to them through our use of concepts. They hold, that is, that whenever we cognize something by identifying it as falling under some concept, we are in some sense falsifying it. Yogācāra identifies two reasons why all conceptualization should involve falsification of what is ultimately real. The first is that when we conceptualize, we impose a subject-object dichotomy on reality: we think in terms of an object 'out there' and a cognizing subject 'in here'. This dichotomizing structure falsifies reality because, Yogācāra claims, there is no external world. The second reason is that, according to Yogācāra, ultimately real things are by nature unique and so ineffable. To apply a concept to something is to say it belongs together with other things that also fall under that concept. To say something is red is to say it resembles certain other things in respect of its being red. But if everything is unique, this can never be true. Yogācāra philosophers developed arguments for both claims about conceptualization. (We will examine them in the next chapter.) But the second reason, the one based on the idea that ultimately real things are unique and so ineffable, was only fully developed by the Yogācāra-Sautrāntika school. (We will look at its metaphysics and epistemology in Chapter 10.)

Further Reading

For more concerning current research on the early history of Mahāyāna see Paul Williams, *Mahāyāna Buddhism: The Doctrinal Foundations* (London: Routledge, 1989), pp. 1–33.

For more on the ideal of the *bodhisattva*, see R. Ray, *Buddhist Saints in India* (Oxford: Oxford University Press, 1994).

For the translation of a major early Mahāyāna sūtra see Edward Conze, *The Perfection of Wisdom in Eight Thousand Lines and its Verse Summary* (Bolinas, CA: Four Seasons Foundation, 1973).

For a skeptical response to the question whether compassion is compatible with emptiness, see Paul Williams, 'How Śāntideva Destroyed the *Bodhisattva* Path', Chapter 5 of his *Altruism and Reality: Studies in the Philosophy of the Bodhicāryāvatāra* (Richmond, Surrey: Curzon Press, 1998).

CHAPTER EIGHT

Yogācāra: Impressions-Only and the Denial of Physical Objects

We saw in the last chapter that the most philosophically important of the new Mahāyāna ideas is the doctrine of emptiness. The Yogācāra school represents one way of trying to make sense of that doctrine. It does this by developing a theory that denies the existence of external objects. In this chapter we will examine that theory, and the arguments that Yogācārin philosophers gave to support it. Then we will look at how the resulting view might be connected to the claim that all things are empty, and what all this might have to do with attaining nirvāṇa.

8.1

Yogācāra is one of the two chief schools of Mahāyāna Buddhism. It is not, however, the earlier of the two. The ideas that became the basis of Madhyamaka, the other major school, began appearing in sūtras perhaps as early as late in the first century BCE. And these ideas received their first philosophical formulation, in the work of Madhyamaka's founder Nāgārjuna, in about the mid-second century CE. By contrast, the sūtras that first express distinctively Yogācāra ideas seem to have appeared no earlier than the second century CE. And the founders of the school, Asaṅga and Vasubandhu, are generally dated around the middle of the fourth century CE. Why, then, are we discussing Yogācāra before Madhyamaka? (Madhyamaka will be the subject of Chapter 9.) In large part this is because Yogācāra philosophy represents an extension of the Abhidharma project that we investigated in Chapter 6. It is true that some elements of Yogācāra developed in reaction to ideas of the earlier Madhyamaka school. So we will have to say something about Madhyamaka in order to understand certain facets of the Yogācāra project. But for the most part, once we have understood what Abhidharma is all about, we will have little problem seeing what Yogācārin philosophers are up to.

This is not surprising if, as the tradition maintains, the Vasubandhu who co-founded the school is the same person we encountered in Chapter 6 as the author of *Abhidharmakośa* and its commentary. The tradition holds that Vasubandhu was converted from his Abhidharma views to the Yogācāra by his brother Asaṅga. Some modern scholars believe that there were actually two distinct Vasubandhus, one the author of the *Abhidharmakośa* and the other the Yogācārin.[1] What is clear is that the

---

[1]Many scholars also dispute the historical existence of the third traditional founder of Yogācāra, Maitreya.

146

Vasubandhu whose works we will be examining is very much at home in the Abhidharma problematic. What Vasubandhu will do is use a set of questions that had already arisen within Abhidharma to argue for one simple (though seemingly radical) change in the overall Abhidharma picture: that instead of the five *skandhas* there are actually just four, there being no *rūpa* or corporeality.

The name of this school, 'Yogācāra', literally means 'the practice of yoga'. But the school goes by several other names as well: 'Vijñānavāda', 'Cittamātra' and 'Vijñaptimātra'. The first of these means 'the doctrine of consciousness' (the fifth of the five *skandhas*), the second means 'consciousness only' (*citta* and *vijñāna* are synonyms), and the third means 'impressions-only'. (We will come shortly to what a *vijñapti* or 'impression' might be.) Now the '-only' in the last two names suggests that this school holds that nothing exists other than mental things. It suggests, in other words, that Yogācāra is a form of idealism.[2] And that is indeed the central claim of Yogācāra. But what does this have to do with 'the practice of yoga'? What seems likely is that Yogācāra metaphysics grew out of speculation concerning the content of yoga or meditation. Here it is important that the higher stages of meditation involve focused awareness of purely mental objects. Since meditation is recognized as playing a key role in attaining enlightenment, perhaps it seemed to some meditation-masters that the ignorance that must be overcome to attain nirvāna has to do with our belief in things existing independent of consciousness, physical things. Perhaps they thought that if we could come to see the world as only impressions, then the temporary surcease from suffering that is attained in meditational trance states could be extended to our daily lives.

Our job, though, is not to speculate about the historical origins of the impressions-only doctrine. What we want to know is what reason there might be to believe it. How could anyone possibly accept such a bizarre view? Isn't it simply obvious that there are rocks and trees, houses and cars, the earth, the sun? And what about us, how could we exist without bodies and brains? Perhaps by now we have come to accept that ultimately there are no such things as trees and cars, bodies and brains. These are, after all, wholes made up of parts. But what about the ultimate parts that a conceptual fiction like a tree is made of, the *rūpa dharmas*? Surely they must exist if the mind is going to perform its constructive activity of collecting them together to form aggregates? (See Chapter 4.) Surely it's obvious that there is *something* out there that we are aware of when we have sensory experience?

The first thing to be said in response to these (perfectly legitimate) questions is that

---

[2]In philosophy 'idealism' names the metaphysical claim that nothing exists that is independent of the mind. The best-known Western proponent of this view is the eighteenth-century British philosopher George Berkeley. But sometimes the rather different position of the nineteenth-century German philosopher Hegel is also called 'idealist'. To differentiate these, views like Berkeley's are called subjective idealism, while the Hegelian variety is referred to as 'absolute idealism'. But since we won't be concerned with Hegelian idealism at all here, I shall use 'idealism' to mean just the Berkeleyan variety of subjective idealism.

Yogācārins like Vasubandhu will pick up where the Sautrāntikas left off. Recall (from Chapter 6) that Sautrāntikas developed the view of sense perception called 'representationalism'. This is the view that what we are directly aware of in waking sensory experience is not the external object, but rather a mental image that resembles the object and is caused by sense-object contact. Since our waking awareness of a mental image is typically the result of such contact, we are usually justified in inferring the existence of an external object that is like the image. We may then say that we are indirectly aware of an external object, something physical that exists independently of the mind. So in veridical sensory experience – experience that is not the result of distorting factors like defective senses or hallucination – we do perceive physical things. But notice that this is only indirect. We are never directly aware of the external object that we think we perceive. It is always something whose existence we only infer. What an impressions-only theorist like Vasubandhu wants to know is what reason we have to trust this inference. They will claim that when we examine it in detail, it will turn out to deserve no credence.

The 'impression' in 'impressions-only' is like what the representationalist calls a representation: a mental image that is the intentional object in our sensory cognitions. The impressions-only theorist is an idealist, while the representationalist is a realist (someone who affirms the existence of external objects). They disagree in their ontological views. But they agree about what it is we are directly aware of in our sensory experience. It is important to be clear about this at the very outset. Common sense – not just ours but probably that of every culture – is realist in its metaphysics. Here common sense sides with the representationalist. But common sense strongly disagrees with representationalism about how it is that we cognize the external objects that both parties believe exist. The common-sense view is direct realism – the view that in waking sensory experience we are directly aware of the external object. It is because most people hold this view that they think it is easy to show that there are physical objects: all we need to do is look. When Samuel Johnson, the eighteenth-century British lexicographer, heard of Berkeley's idealism, he reportedly kicked a stone and said 'I refute it *thus*'. But if you have understood the arguments that support representationalism, you will understand why it is not so easy. No doubt Dr Johnson had sensory experiences that he interpreted as the kicking of a stone – an external object. But were those sensory experiences a matter of direct awareness of a stone? If representationalism is correct then they were not. All Dr Johnson was directly aware of were mental images. The representationalist holds that these images were caused by the sense-object contact between Dr Johnson's foot and the stone. But to know that the stone exists we would have to show that the experience was caused in this way. Just having the experience is never enough.

This is where Vasubandhu begins his argument for impressions-only. The text we are about to examine is called *Viṃśatikā* ('20-versed'), which is the first part of a two-part work the overall title of which is *Vijñaptimātratāsiddhi*, or 'The Proof that There Are Only Impressions'. *Viṃśatikā* begins as follows:

1. This [world] is nothing but impressions, since it manifests itself as an unreal object,
   Just like the case of those with cataracts seeing unreal hairs in the moon and the like.   ·

When someone with cataracts looks at the moon, they have the experience of seeing the moon as covered with hairs. Their sensory experience is just like what someone with normal vision sees when they look at a head of hair that's been blown about by the wind. So from the content of their sensory experience, the person with cataracts would say they see hairs on the moon. But there are no hairs on the moon, so it can't be true that that is what they are seeing. They are seeing something, though; there really is something that they are aware of. No one ever has the experience of seeing a round square or the son of a barren woman. If what they are aware of is not an external object (hairs on the moon), what is it? What it seems we have to say at this point is that they are aware of a mental image. Vasubandhu agrees, but he calls it an impression, and adds that it manifests itself as an external object when there is actually no such thing outside the mind. This is what he means when he says that the person with cataracts is aware of an impression that 'manifests itself as an unreal object'. What they are aware of is just an impression: it's not a physical object, nor is it a representation of a physical object. But the impression presents itself to the person with cataracts as if it were an external object. So unless they knew better they'd be just like Dr Johnson: they'd say, 'Of course there are hairs on the moon, I can see them!'

So much for Vasubandhu's example of hairs on the moon. He says there are many others like this one, and we can imagine the sort of thing he has in mind: the yellow color that someone with jaundice sees when looking at a white shell, the snake we see in the yard at dusk when looking at the garden hose, etc. But notice what else he is saying: that the whole world of our sensory experience is like this. That is, he is arguing:

> The content of a sensory experience presents itself as an external object when no such object exists.
> Anything presenting itself as an external object when no such object exists is only an impression, like the hairs on the moon seen by one with cataracts.
> ∴ the contents of sensory experience are only impressions.

So what he is saying is that when we have sensory experiences, what we are aware of are just mental images (with this the representationalist would agree), and these mental images are not representations of external objects. Why not? The hairs seen by the cataract sufferer are not representations, since there aren't any such hairs in the external world. And all our sensory experiences are just like that: they seem to be presenting something that's really in the external world when there isn't any such thing.

8.2

But how does Vasubandhu know that there aren't any external physical objects? Isn't that what he was supposed to be trying to prove? At this point we may suspect that Vasubandhu has begged the question. What he's actually done, though, is laid down a challenge for the representationalist realist opponent: what evidence is there that the images we are aware of in sensory experience are caused by contact with external objects? Vasubandhu recognizes that the argument he gave in v.1 won't convince a realist. He gave the argument in order to stimulate the opponent to raise objections against the impressions-only theory. Here he is simply following the standard format for Indian philosophical works: state your own position and briefly indicate the evidence in its favor, then allow the opponent to raise objections and see if you can successfully defend your theory in response to them.

The objections that the opponent is about to give are all meant to be reasons why we should believe our sensory experience – the mental images we are aware of in perception – are caused by physical objects. Before looking at the ones the opponent gives, it might be useful for you to stop and see what reasons you can think of to support the claim that there are physical objects. (Remember that 'Because I can see them!' doesn't count.)

> Here it is said [by the opponent]:
>   2. If an impression is devoid of external object, then it should be without
>   spatial and temporal determination,
>   It should be without determination in the mental stream [of the perceiver]
>   and it should not have efficacy.
> What does this mean? If an impression of color-and-shape etc., occurs in the absence of any external object such as color-and shape etc., it is not arisen from the external object color-and shape etc.; then why does it occur at a certain place, not everywhere? And why, it occurring at that place, does it occur at a certain time, not always? And why does it occur in the mental streams of all who are there at that time and place, not just in that of one alone, just as the appearance of hairs and the like in the mental streams of those with cataracts does not occur [in the streams] of others? The hairs, insects, and the like seen by those with cataracts do not produce effects; it is not the case that things other than these are not productive. The food, drink, garments, poison, etc., seen in sleep do not produce the effects of food, etc; and it is not the case that these do not ordinarily produce effects. It is because of its unreality that the city of the Gandhārvas gives rise to no effects; it is not the case that other cities are unproductive [of effects]. Thus in the absence of an external object, spatial and temporal determination, determination of mental stream, and efficacy are unexplained.

Though there are four reasons here, we could combine the first (spatial determination) and the second (temporal determination) into one, spatio-temporal determinacy. The idea is that our waking sensory experience conforms to certain rule-like patterns. Only at certain determinate places and times do we have certain kinds of experiences. We are not aware of the smell of bread baking unless we are in the kitchen; and even there, it's only when the bread is in the oven (or just come out) that we have the experience. Why is this thought of as evidence for the existence of physical objects? The thought here is that a realist can explain these facts about our experience but an idealist cannot. The realist will say that our sensory experience exhibits spatio-temporal determinacy because it depends on contact with external objects that are located in different parts of space. And since it takes time for our bodies to move from one region of space where one object is located to another, we can also explain why there's usually a time gap between my deciding to go to the pool and the experience of smelling the chlorinated water. The realist doesn't see how the impressions-only theorist can explain these features of our experience though.

A word should be said here about how to formulate objections. The opponent has put the objection from spatial determinacy as the claim that sensory experiences only occur 'at a certain place'. This is a question-begging way of stating the objection. As an impressions-only theorist, Vasubandhu denies the existence of spatial locations. Only physical objects can have spatial location. When the opponent says that our experiences have spatial determinacy, they are in effect assuming what they set out to prove, that there are external objects. There is something to this objection though; it just needs to be reformulated in a way that doesn't beg the question.

To do this we need to remind ourselves of what the realist and the idealist agree on. Both sides accept the view that sensory experience consists in immediate awareness of mental images. So it must be that we construct our conception of space from features of those images. Consider, for instance, the visual experiences we have when we say we are in the kitchen. While we are accustomed to describing these experiences in terms of physical objects (seeing the sink beside the stove, etc.), we can instead describe them as the awareness of images of certain colors and shapes (yellow and oval, white and rectangular, etc.). We can then describe these color-and-shape images as bearing different relations to one another in the visual field (above, to the left of, etc.) Of course the visual field itself changes over time, so we will need some way to keep track of these changes. But we can do this once we notice that certain features regularly recur. For instance, after the yellow oval patch disappears from the left edge of the visual field, a similar patch may emerge on the right. (This is the sort of experience we actually have when we say we have turned a complete clockwise revolution.) What we can do, in short, is construct a purely phenomenal language, one that captures all the features we ordinarily describe in spatial terms, but does so just in terms of the features of pure phenomena – what we are immediately aware of in sensory experience. The objection from spatio-temporal determinacy could then be put in that language. Such a language might be cumbersome and awkward to use. But if we want to object to Vasubandhu's argument, we need to be sure we're not just assuming that an external world exists. We need to put our objection in neutral terms, terms that both we and our opponent can accept as an unbiased description of the evidence. Stating the objection from spatio-temporal determinacy in a purely phenomenal language would be a way to do that.

The next realist objection brings up what we might call intersubjective agreement: the fact that under similar circumstances different perceivers (different mental streams) have similar sensory experiences. This is not true of those experiences that we all agree are only impressions – such as seeing hairs on the moon or seeing the shell as yellow. So, the realist will say, there must be some difference between those cases and normal sensory experience that explains why there is only intersubjective agreement with the latter. And the only explanation the realist can see is that normal sensory experiences are caused by things that are publicly observable and hence exist independently of mental streams. So explaining this feature of our experience requires us to suppose that there are physical objects.

The final objection concerns something called efficacy. It also involves comparing experiences that are acknowledged to be only impressions with normal sensory experience. Here the difference is that the latter have effects that the former do not. When I 'see' the snake in the garden at twilight, I do not subsequently have the experience of feeling a snakebite, whereas if I had a similar visual experience under better lighting conditions I might. The waking experience of eating a large meal is followed by the feeling of fullness, whereas a similar dream experience is not. (This objection also needs to be carefully formulated in a purely phenomenal language in order to avoid question-begging. The realist can't simply say that we only feel full after we eat 'real food'.)

Are there other objections that could be raised against Vasubandhu's argument? One common response to any form of idealism is that if it were true then sensory experience would be just like imagination. This comes up because the idealist denies that sensory experiences are caused by things existing independently of our minds or mental streams. So the images we are aware of in sensory experience must be somehow created by the mind. And this makes sensory experience seem just like imagination. When we daydream about winning the lottery or being with someone we find attractive, it is desires in our mental stream that determine which images appear. Sensory experience is not like that. While we may have some control over our perceptions – we can always close our eyes or hold our nose or walk away – it is obviously nowhere near as complete as the control we have over the contents of our imaginings. Now the objection from efficacy could be construed as making a similar point. But we might want to count the objection from imagination as a separate challenge for the impressions-only theorist: 'Isn't this equivalent to saying (absurdly) that we make it all up?'

8.3

Now that we have clarified the sorts of objections that a sophisticated realist might raise, it is time to let the impressions-only theorist respond. There are two things you need to know in order to understand Vasubandhu's replies in the following section. The first has to do with the *preta*s, those miserable creatures whose diet consists of feces, urine, pus and blood. One might wonder why it is that a *preta* is unable to drink anything but urine, pus and blood. The Buddhist realist answers that where we see a river full of water, *preta*s see a flow of vile liquids. And this is not because the *preta* lives on some other world where all rivers are polluted. This is because a *preta*'s karma causes it to see and taste urine, pus and blood when we would see and taste water. The second point concerns those who are consigned to hell. As retribution for their evil deeds, these beings are subjected to constant torture by various demons. But how did the demons get there? Remember that all sentient beings are subject to karma and rebirth, so if the demons who torture the inhabitants of hell are sentient beings, their status must also be the result of karma. But this struck Buddhists as decidedly odd. Presumably someone confined to hell for a lifetime must have done serious evil in their past life, yet the demons do not suffer. So it became the orthodoxy that the demons are not sentient beings after all. Instead they are constructed by the karma of the *preta*s – a sort of mass hallucination if you like. The same device helps explain other odd things about hell, such as the fact that it sometimes rains fire. It is not as if the laws of physics are different in hell; instead it is karma that makes things appear to work so differently. In answering the realist's objections, Vasubandhu will use these two points in the Buddhist realist conception of how karma works.

[We reply:] These are not at all unexplained.
3. Spatial determination, etc., are established as in dreams; again as with *preta*s
    Is determination of mental stream [explained], for they all see rivers of pus, etc.
How is it established by analogy with sleep? In sleep, in the absence of an external object, there are seen an insect, a grove, a woman, a man, etc., but only at a determinate place, not everywhere. And being just at that place, they are seen just at a particular time, not always. Thus are spatial and temporal determination established without an external object. And how is determination of mental stream established by analogy with *preta*s? Rivers of pus are rivers full of pus, the word being a compound like 'ghee-pot'. *Preta*s, who are descended as the result of similar karma, all see a river full of pus; it is not just one *preta* alone [who sees the river of pus]. As it is filled with pus, so it is filled with urine, excrement, etc., and they are guarded by persons bearing sticks and swords – this is what is indicated by the word 'etc.'. Thus is determination of mental stream explained though the object of impressions be unreal.
4. There is production of an effect as with wet dreams; or as in hell
    All see the guardians of hell, etc., and there is affliction from them.
It should be understood that the production of effects is proven by analogy with wet dreams. Just as in sleep, without sexual intercourse there are wet dreams marked by emission of semen. In this way, by means of such examples, are the four [objections] of spatial and temporal determination, etc., to be answered. Again, it should be understood as proven 'as in hell, all ...' How is it established? 'Seeing the guardians of hell, and suffering afflictions from them.' Just as it is granted that the inhabitants of the hells see the guardians of hell at determinate

times and places. By 'etc.' is meant that they also see dogs, crows, mountains of iron and the like coming and going about. And this is seen by all of them, not just by one. And it is established that these things cause that affliction, though the guardians of hell etc. be unreal, because of the efficacy of the result of equivalent deeds [in a prior life]. Thus should it be understand that the four [objections] may be answered in other ways as well.

[Objection:] But why is it not allowed that the guardians of hell, dogs, and crows are real?

[Reply:] Because they cannot have earned it; since they do not experience suffering as [the *preta*s do], they cannot have earned habitation in hell. [If the guardians were real and hence suffered,] there would be no telling one from another among those suffering – 'these are the inhabitants of hell, those are their guardians'. And if among those suffering there were similarity [of guardians and inhabitants] in shape, strength, and weight, then there would be no fear [of the guardians, etc.]. And how would those [guardians], themselves unable to endure the suffering of burning while on the same ground made of burning iron, cause others to suffer there? And how is it possible that those who are not [determined by karma to be] inhabitants of hell are in hell?

[Objection:] But for that matter how is it possible for animals to attain heaven? By the same token, [if there can be animals in heaven] it should be possible for there to be different species of animals and *preta*s as guardians, etc., in the hells.
[Reply:]
5. While animals can attain heaven, not so hell,
    Since they do not experience suffering, it not being produced as it is with
        the *preta*s.

Those animals who attain rebirth in heaven are beings who there experience the pleasures produced therein because [in their past life they performed] deeds capable of producing the pleasures belonging to that realm. But the guardians of hell, etc., do not in the same way experience the suffering of hell. Thus is it that such birth [in hell] is not attained by animals, though it is by *preta*s.

[Objection:] The inhabitants of hell have perceptions of guardians, etc.; it is by means of their karma that there arise in hell different elements with distinct color-and-shape, weight, and strength. Then when these various elements are transformed and are seen performing such actions as scattering the hands, etc., fear arises [in the *preta*s]. Similarly they [are transformed into] mountains in the form of the Meṣa demon which fly back and forth, and thickets of iron-thorn trees whose thorns point upward and downward. But this does not mean that these things are not real.
[Reply:]
6. If you allow the possibility of elements being produced by the karma of the
        inhabitants of hell,
    Why do you not instead allow the transformation of consciousness?

Why not thus allow that it is just their consciousness that has been transformed by their karma? Why, instead, invent [material] elements [produced by karma]? Moreover,
7. You suppose that the effect is someplace other than where the karmic trace
        is.

What reason is there for not saying that it is precisely where the trace is? It is supposed that there is the production there [in hell] of elements in such a manner by means of the karma of the inhabitants of hell; and these are transformed. Their karmic traces are contained in the mental streams [of the inhabitants], they are nowhere else. And its effect is just where the trace is – why not allow that it is thus a transformation of consciousness? What reason is there for supposing that its effect is where the trace is not?

As Vasubandhu says in introducing v.3, his strategy will be to show that the phenomena of spatio-temporal determinacy, etc., can be explained without supposing that there are physical objects. One way he seeks to do this is to show that there are cases of mere impressions which exhibit the features that the opponent thinks prove the existence of external things. Dreams, for instance, can exhibit spatio-temporal determinacy as well as efficacy. When we see something in a dream, it is at a particular place and time in that dream, not always and everywhere.[3] Some dreams also have the same sorts of effects as do waking sensory experience of the same kind. Both a vivid erotic dream and an equally intense erotic experience had while awake, for instance, might be followed by the experience of feeling wet bedding. But we all agree that what we are aware of in dreams are only impressions: while they present themselves as external, they are entirely mental in both nature and cause. So the fact that waking sensory experiences have the properties of spatio-temporal determinacy and efficacy does not show that these must be caused by physical objects.

Does this really answer the objections from determinacy and efficacy? There is a sense in which this is a successful response. The realist opponent claimed that spatio-temporal determinacy and efficacy were features that proved our waking sensory experiences were external in origin. So all Vasubandhu needs to do is find cases that have those features but that the opponent would acknowledge are only impressions. But we may not be satisfied by this response. Why not? Well, most dreams lack efficacy. And the spatio-temporal determinacy of our dreams seems different from that of waking sensory experience. It would be nice to have some explanation of these differences. The dream examples don't satisfy our need for an explanation of the features of waking sensory experience.

Vasubandhu tries to address that need with his examples of *preta*s and inhabitants of hell. Intersubjective agreement and efficacy are to be accounted for not by supposing we are all seeing and feeling the same publicly observable object, but rather by the similarity in our karma. How does that work? Well, suppose we had been born as dogs rather than humans. In that case we would now be having very different sensory experiences. Our hearing and sense of smell would be much more

---

[3]You might think that nothing in a dream could have spatial determinacy, since the dream is 'all in the mind', that is, the things we 'see' in a dream have no spatial location. But consider the fact that a dream can be described in a purely phenomenal language. And recall what was said above about putting the objection from spatial determinacy in such a language. The fact that the contents of a dream can be described in the same language shows that dreams can also exhibit spatial determinacy.

acute, for instance, and our color vision less refined. If we believed it is karma that determines the situation into which we are born, then we would say it is due to our (good) karma that we have the kind of color experiences we do. And notice the word 'we'. You and I and most other humans share common features of our visual experience because (presumably) we have similar good karma. So here is a start toward addressing our need for a real explanation.

But does this work? Suppose we are together in one room. Since we are humans, we will have similar visual experiences. Had we been born as dogs we would be having certain smell experiences instead. But that, we might think, is just because as humans we were born with certain kinds of sense organs; had we been born as dogs we'd have different sensory apparatuses. And this explanation of the difference still requires us to suppose that there is a single physical environment that those sense organs are operating on. It's because the carpet is blue that we all see blue (but dogs don't, since they are color-blind). What Vasubandhu needs is a non-realist way of explaining what generates the experiences. And this is what the example of the inhabitants of hell is meant to give. All these creatures share similar (singularly bad) karma. Because of that karma, they all have similar experiences of seeing demons and the like. But these demons are themselves just the product of the karma of the inhabitants. Now the realist Buddhists who first came up with this theory about the demons no doubt thought of the demons as physical objects (assemblies of 'elements') that were somehow produced by the karma of the sufferers. But, Vasubandhu asks, why suppose that the demons exist outside the mental streams of the inhabitants? Karma is, after all, something mental. It is the desire or volition behind an action that causes the karmic fruit to eventually be produced. If the karmic seed is in the mental stream, wouldn't it be 'lighter' to suppose its fruit is there too? When the inhabitants of hell all see a demon, they are experiencing a kind of collective hallucination.

What Vasubandhu is saying, then, is this. The desires that motivated our past actions produced karmic seeds. These seeds, like all existents, are momentary. But typically when a seed goes out of existence it causes a similar seed to come into existence in that mental stream. Karmic causal laws specify the conditions under which a seed will ripen and bear fruit. The fruit of a karmic seed is an impression – a mental image that presents itself as an external object. Since the same karmic causal laws govern all mental streams, similar karma will lead to similar sensory experiences. The uniformity of the karmic causal laws will likewise account for spatio-temporal determinacy: the seed that causes the seeing of a rose image will only ripen after certain other experiences, such as the ones we interpret as 'walking into the garden' experiences. We can also use karmic causal laws to explain efficacy. The desire that produces a dream of eating is simply not strong enough to produce the karmic fruit of a feeling of fullness; the desire that leads to a waking experience of eating is. We can even explain the fact that waking sensory experience is not under our control in the same way that imagination is. If it is our past desires that cause our present experience, then since we can't change the past, it's no wonder that we have little direct control over the nature of our present perceptions. Thus all the features of our sensory experience can be accounted for by the hypothesis that they are impressions caused by karmic seeds in accordance with causal laws.

So what? Perhaps you are thinking that Vasubandhu is perfectly welcome to his explanation of sensory experience, but you prefer your own. Even if we accepted karma (and we will come to that question shortly), still we would just have two competing explanations of experience: the impressions-only explanation in terms of karmic seeds and karmic causal laws, and our familiar explanation in terms of sensory interaction with physical objects in an external world. Why reject the familiar model that everyone else accepts in favor of some weird alternative? But Vasubandhu has one more card to play. Remember the question he asks in v.6: Why invent material elements? This might have struck you as a strange question, but it is legitimate. In the debate between the representationalist realist and the impressions-only theorist, physical objects are indeed unobservable entities that are posited by the realist in order to make their theory work. They are unobservable because all we are ever directly aware of are mental images (what the realist calls representations). Physical objects are never directly observed, they can only be inferred from the nature of what we do directly observe, *viz.* the mental images that make up our sensory experience. And the inference that leads to our belief in physical objects is just the one that the realist explanation is based on: because our experiences have such-and-such features, they must be caused by external objects. If the representationalist is right about how our belief in an external world is formed, then physical objects are indeed unobservable entities that are posited on the basis of a certain theory. And now Vasubandhu can employ our old friend, the Principle of Lightness:

> **Principle of Lightness**: Given two competing theories each of which is equally good at explaining and predicting the relevant phenomena, choose the lighter theory, that is, the theory that posits the least number of unobservable entities.

This is what is behind Vasubandhu's question, Why invent (that is, posit) material elements? The impressions-only theory and the representationalist realist theory both offer explanations of the same set of phenomena, our sensory experience. They agree on what the observables are: mental entities, including mental images but also such things as desires and feelings. They also agree that karma plays a role in explaining our experience. The realist theory, though, has an additional posit: physical objects, things that are in principle unobservable. If the two theories are equally good at helping us predict the future course of our sensory experience, then by lightness the impressions-only theory is preferable.

Notice, by the way, that this is not an argument from skepticism about the external world. Those who have studied modern Western philosophy might expect that Vasubandhu would argue like this: 'We can't prove that physical objects do exist. (How could we conclusively prove this if we can never be directly aware of them?

For all we know we might be in a completely closed system of virtual reality.) So we have no reason to say they do exist. Therefore we ought to conclude that they don't exist.' But his 'argument from lightness' is actually quite different from this skeptical argument. It isn't skepticism about the external world that he thinks gives support to impressions-only. It's the principle of lightness. The idea behind that principle is that when we posit superfluous entities, this is most likely to be the mind superimposing its interests on the world. Vasubandhu's argument is not based on epistemological considerations (skepticism is an epistemological position), but on considerations that are strictly metaphysical.

Does the argument work? Here is one of those places where it does seem to make a difference whether or not one accepts the theory of karma and rebirth. Vasubandhu's explanation of sensory experience requires that there be karmic seeds and karmic causal laws. So if we have little or no reason to accept that idea, then it might seem that his argument from lightness won't work. Are there any alternatives that a modern impressions-only theorist might use instead? Berkeley used God to account for the regularities in our sensory experience. According to Berkeley, sensory images (Berkeley called them 'ideas') are caused to occur in our minds by another more powerful mind, that of God. And the orderly patterns in which these ideas occur in us are testimony to God's concern for our welfare. But such an explanation would not appeal to a Buddhist. For Berkeley's minds (ours and God's) are thinking substances – just the sort of thing the Buddhist theory of *anātman* denies.

Might a modern Buddhist adapt Vasubandhu's basic idea to a culture skeptical about karma? Perhaps. We might be able to make sense of the idea that mere impressions are caused by past desires. Consider the famous hand-washing scene in Act 1 of Shakespeare's *Macbeth*. Why does Lady Macbeth see blood on her hands when neither her husband nor we in the audience see any such thing? Clearly because of the guilt she feels due to the part she played in getting her husband to commit murder. So at least in this case we can understand how a desire might serve as cause of a later impression. So there must be at least some causal laws connecting past desires with present impressions by way of triggering conditions. And perhaps such causal laws might play a larger role than we suspect in our experience – leading not just to what we call hallucinations but to more ordinary kinds of experiences as well. Then similarities among the past desires of distinct mental streams could also explain intersubjective agreement. These are the sorts of things a modern impressions-only theorist might say to try to make Vasubandhu's argument from lightness work. Would it then succeed? This is a question we will come back to later. For there is at least one more twist to the argument, having to do with the question how we tell whether two competing explanations are 'equally good'. That twist won't come out till we reach v.18 and the notion of 'mutual determination of mental streams'.

8.4

We will now skip over verses 8–10 (to which we will return later), and examine a second major argument for impressions-only, presented in verses 11–15. Here Vasubandhu goes on the attack, seeking to show that the hypothesis that there are physical objects is incoherent. He begins with a new objection: even the Buddha holds that there are physical objects. The Buddha spoke often of such things as the *āyatanas* of color-and-shape, etc. That suggests he believed there are physical objects that cause our experiences of seeing colors and shapes, smelling odors, etc. Of course Vasubandhu has his own theory about why the Buddha said such things. (We'll come to it later.) But the opponent wants to know why we shouldn't just accept the most obvious explanation: the Buddha said these things because he was a realist. Now this isn't a serious objection to impressions-only, unless you already believe that the Buddha's testimony is authoritative on questions concerning the ultimate nature of reality. So this is not a philosophically interesting objection. But what Vasubandhu has to say in response is philosophically interesting. What Vasubandhu will do is look at two different theories concerning the nature of *rūpa dharmas*: atomism and the property-particulars theory. (See Chapter 6 for these two theories.) In verses 11–14 he will try to show that atomism could not explain our sensory experience, and in verse 15 he will argue that the property-particulars theory couldn't either. So if we're right to think that only *dharmas* can be ultimately real, it will turn out that neither of the available realist theories can be correct.

> [Reply: We should not take the Buddha to have been referring to physical objects] because,
> 11.   That [*āyatana*] is not one, nor is the intentional object a plurality made up of atoms,
>   Neither do they aggregate, since the atom is unproven.
> What is meant by this? If the *āyatana* of color-and-shape etc. were respectively the intentional objects of impressions of color-and-shape, etc., then they would be individuals, like the 'whole' posited by the Vaiśeṣikas, or they would be pluralities made up of atoms, or they would themselves be the aggregates of atoms. But the intentional object is not an individual, since one never apprehends a whole which is distinct from its parts. Neither is it a plurality, since one does not apprehend atoms individually. Nor, finally, do the aggregates [of atoms] become the intentional object of perception, since there is no establishing that the atom is an individual real.
> Why is it not established? Because,
> 12ab. The atom must have six parts, for it joins simultaneously with six others.
> The atom will have six parts if it joins simultaneously with six atoms from six sides, since it is impossible that where one is another should be.
> 12cd. [Otherwise] it would be a mass having the size of one atom, because all six would be in the same place.
> Or else the space [occupied by] one atom is that of all six. Then because all are in the same place, they would all together be a mass the size of one atom; then

because of lack of mutual separation, no mass whatever would be visible.

[The opponent:] The atoms do not at all unite, since they are partless. Hence the fault does not arise as a consequence [of our position]. Aggregates, however, do join. So say the Vaibhāṣikas of Kashmir.

They should be replied to as follows: The aggregate of atoms is not an object distinct from those [atoms].

13.   If the atoms do not join, then with respect to their aggregates, of what is there this [joining]?

It cannot be shown that their joining does not take place because of their partlessness.

Suppose that the aggregated things do not join with one another. Then it should be pointed out that it is not right to deny joining on the grounds of the partlessness of the atoms, since one could not then acknowledge the joining of the aggregate, even though it has parts. Thus it does not follow that the atom is a distinct substance. Moreover, regardless of whether one allows that atoms join or not,

14.   There is no individuality of that which can be divided into distinct spatial parts.

On the opposite assumption, why is there shade and obstruction? If the mass is not distinct, these two do not characterize it.

In other words, if there are distinct spatial parts of the atom such as the east part, the upper part, etc., then how should there be any individuality of an atom with such a nature?

If each atom has no distinct spatial parts, then how is it that upon the appearance of the sun, in one place there is shade, in another there is sunlight? There would be no place at which it is different from where the sunlight is. And how can there be obstructing of one atom by another if distinct spatial parts are not posited? The atom has no other parts whatever where, by having come there, it could be resisted by another. Then as has been said [above], in the absence of resistance, the entire aggregate would be the size of an atom, since all would occupy the same place.

[Objection:] Why not say this, that shade and obstruction pertain to the mass, not to the atom?

[Reply:] What mass could possibly be posited as distinct from the atoms yet characterized by these two [shade and obstruction]? None, and thus it is said, 'If the mass is not something distinct, these two do not characterize it.' That is, if the mass is not posited as something distinct from the atoms, then these two will not characterize it.

[Objection:] The atom, the aggregate, and the like, are fabricated constructions, what is the point of considering them when the characteristics of color-and-shape cannot be denied?

[Reply:] What, then, are their characteristics?

[The opponent:] The property of being the intentional object of vision, etc., and blueness, etc.

[Reply:] That is precisely what is being deliberated upon, whether what is taken to be the intentional object of vision, etc., is a single substance or a plurality.

[The opponent:] What do you say?

[Reply:] The fault involved in plurality has already been indicated.

15. If it [the intentional object] were an individual, there would not occur (1) going progressively, (2) simultaneously grasping and not grasping, (3) the appearing together of distinct things, and (4) the not seeing of minute things.

(1) If we were accordingly to suppose that the intentional object of vision is not a plurality, but one undivided substance, then there would not be such a thing as going progressively across the ground, that is, walking. For with a single step one should have traversed all at once. (2) Again it would be impossible for one simultaneously to grasp the near part of something and not grasp the far part. Grasping and not grasping of one and the same thing at one time cannot be. (3) Nor can there be the occurrence of a plurality of distinct things, e.g., elephants or horses, in distinct places. Since the one is just where the other is, how can it be thought that the two are distinct? Alternatively, since an empty space is apprehended between two things, how can that which is both occupied and not occupied by them be considered to be one? (4) Nor should there be invisibility of tiny aquatic animals which are the same color as gross ones, if it is supposed that distinctness of substance is determined only by difference in characteristics, not in other ways [such as quantity, position, time, etc.].

Thus necessarily, distinction [among substances] requires the positing of atoms. And that [atom] cannot be proven to be an individual existent. That being unproven, the objectness of the [supposed] intentional objects of sight, etc., namely color-and-shape, etc., is unproven; thus it is shown that impressions alone exist.

In v.11 Vasubandhu mentions three things an atomist might say about how atoms contribute to our sensory experience. The first is that the intentional object of perception is a whole existing over and above its atomic parts, and the second is that the intentional object of perception is the individual atoms themselves. Vasubandhu dismisses them for the obvious reasons that the whole is unreal, and individual atoms are too small to detect with the senses. But the third is something new: atoms combine to form aggregates, and in an aggregate the individual atoms are able to do something collectively that they are unable to do on their own. The idea is roughly like this: if a single snowflake fell on you it probably wouldn't register, but if enough snowflakes are stuck together to make a snowball, you'd probably feel them when they struck. The key thing here is that the aggregate is not supposed to be a whole existing over and above the parts. That's why the atomist realist calls it an 'aggregate': as a way of making clear that we're really just talking about all those individual atoms (which are the only ultimately real physical things the atomist recognizes). The 'aggregates of atoms' option is supposed to combine the benefits of the 'one whole' option (something big enough to see and feel) and the 'pluralities of atoms' option (real atoms to act as causes), while inheriting the defects of neither.

Now we might wonder whether this view is really distinct from the one that says the object of perception is the whole. But Vasubandhu is willing to set that question aside, since he sees a more pressing difficulty. How exactly do the atoms come together to make an aggregate that is larger than any of its constituent atoms? As you may recall, Ābhidharmikas discussed a number of possible approaches to this problem. Vasubandhu argues that none of them will work. The argument begins with v.12, where he considers what appear to be the basic options the atomist has. To understand what he is saying, you need to understand that the standard model of an aggregate of atoms has it consisting of seven atoms: one in the middle, one in each of the four cardinal directions (north, south, etc.), and one each above and below. We might imagine other configurations of atoms making up an aggregate, but the number doesn't matter. What does matter is the question how we get something bigger when atoms come together. And what Vasubandhu is saying in v.12 is that this can only occur if the individual atom has some finite size. If the atom has no size – if it is a mere geometrical point, something with no length, breadth or height – then putting other atoms together with a central atom to form an aggregate will not result in anything bigger than our original atom. This is his point in v.12cd: if the central atom has no size, then where the one to the east touches it must be the same place as where the one to the west touches it. So those three atoms will be no bigger than the one we started with. The atoms must have some size if aggregates are to be big enough to detect with our senses. But, he says in v.12ab and again in v.14ab, if an atom has size then it must be a whole made of parts. So then the atom would not be a real entity.

Why must the atom have parts? Imagine three atoms, the first one M in the middle, a second one L touching it on its left side M_L, and a third one R touching M on its right side M_R. Now if the three atoms together are going to be bigger than M, M_L and M_R must be on two different sides of M. So there must be some distance inside M to separate these two sides. The interior of M must, that is, contain distinct spatial regions, the region adjoining M_L, and the region adjoining M_R. And Vasubandhu is saying these distinct spatial regions inside the atom count as parts.

We might find this last claim dubious. We could agree with Vasubandhu that it is hard to imagine that atoms have no size whatever, that they are mere geometrical points. But isn't an atom something with a size so small that it can't be divided up into anything smaller? (Remember that by 'atom' we here mean something genuinely indivisible, and not what we (mistakenly) call by that name today.) We can grant that the atom must contain distinct spatial regions within itself: one bordering the left side, another bordering the right side, etc. But since these spatial regions cannot be physically separated from one another, why should they be called parts? Wasn't it Vasubandhu himself (speaking as a Sautrāntikas) who said that the test of something's being ultimately real is that it cannot be broken up like a pot can be broken? (See Chapter 6.) Why should our ability to mentally distinguish among the different regions of the atom show that the atom has parts and so isn't ultimately real if the atom is something truly indivisible?

Vasubandhu will answer that the true test of something's being ultimately real is that it not borrow its nature from other things. This is what he meant when he said in *Abhidharmakośabhāṣya* that we reach the *dharmas* when we reach something that not only cannot be broken up like a pot can be broken, but also cannot be conceptually analyzed. Something showing qualitative complexity, such as a complicated mental state, might be physically indivisible simply because it isn't a physical object and so doesn't have any spatial size. It can nonetheless be analyzed into distinct components. And this shows that it borrows its properties from those components; it is a whole made of parts and so not ultimately real. Vasubandhu is now saying this applies to the atom as well. Even if it cannot be split up into parts, insofar as it contains distinct spatial regions it borrows its nature from its components. When we rule out the atom as a mere point, we commit ourselves to saying that having a certain (very small) size is the intrinsic nature of an atom. But that nature turns out to be borrowed from the (smaller) sizes of the spatial regions making it up. So an atom could not be a *dharma*.

It won't help to propose that the real *rūpa dharmas* are these smaller spatial regions that make up the atom. For exactly the same reasoning will apply to them as Vasubandhu used against the reality of the atom. Each must have a finite size, and so must be made up of yet smaller spatial regions. This process will never come to an end. This is a consequence of the infinite divisibility of space: between any two points, no matter how close, there are infinitely many distinct points.

So maybe it's time to revisit the option of saying the atom has no size at all. We saw that if the point-atoms touched they would all wind up in the same place, so no matter how many atoms made up the aggregate it would never get any bigger. But what if the atoms didn't touch? What if an aggregate were seven point-atoms each at some distance from the rest? Then the aggregate would have some finite size, and it could serve as the building-block of still larger physical objects.

In v.13 Vasubandhu points out a problem for this proposal. If we allow that the atoms in an aggregate don't touch, we must still say that one aggregate touches another. For how else are we to explain the fact that two distinct aggregates occupy different spatial locations – which we must do if adjoining aggregates are to make up larger things? When two aggregates come into contact, what is to stop the one from occupying the same space as the other? An aggregate must be able to obstruct other aggregates. You might think this is no problem, since the aggregate has size. We can distinguish between the one side of the first aggregate where a second one touches it, and the other side where the second is obstructed from going. We can do this because we agree that the aggregate is made up of distinct spatial regions between the one side and the other. It is the atom that we are supposing has no size, not the aggregate. The problem is that the aggregate is itself a mere conceptual fiction. The only really real things in this picture would have to be atoms, and only really real things can do any real work. So if one aggregate is to obstruct another, individual atoms must be obstructing other individual atoms. And Vasubandhu wants to know how this is possible if atoms are mere points.

This is the question Vasubandhu is raising in v.14cd. He cites two problems for the atomist, those of shade and obstruction, but they are really a single difficulty. In order for one thing A to obstruct another thing B, A must prevent B from moving beyond A's near side and reaching A's far side. In order for the dam to hold the water back, it must stop the water at the upstream side; if the water reaches the downstream side of the dam then the dam has not succeeded in obstructing the water, and the water will flow past the dam. But now imagine a dam that is just one atom thick, and suppose that the atoms are mere points. Then when a water atom touches the upstream side of one of the earth atoms making up the dam, it will already have reached the downstream side of that atom. So that earth atom hasn't succeeded in obstructing the water. Adding a second layer of earth atoms to our dam won't help either, since they will be equally unable to prevent the water from reaching their downstream sides. On the hypothesis that atoms are points, no amount of atoms can ever obstruct anything. Likewise, no matter how many such atoms make up a tree, when the sun shines on the south side there should not be shade but sunlight on the north side of the tree.

At this point we might ask whether Vasubandhu has considered all the possible atomist scenarios. Perhaps he has a point about the hypothesis that the atom has size, but has he really refuted the view that atoms are mere points? Might the atomist not say that atoms need not touch in order to obstruct one another? Perhaps the atom exerts a repulsive force on other atoms, and this is what keeps them separate. This would explain how the earth atoms in the dam prevent the water atoms from flowing downstream: because of mutually repulsive forces, the water atoms never touch those earth atoms on the upstream side of the dam at all. It would also explain how the atoms making up the tree prevent the sunlight from reaching the ground to the tree's north. Vasubandhu says nothing about this hypothesis. And the idea of forces acting on particles seems like a plausible view; it is, after all, something like what modern physics tells us. So it seems Vasubandhu hasn't yet succeeded in refuting atomism.

There is, though, a reason why Vasubandhu didn't give this sort of view serious consideration. It involves what is called 'action at a distance': one object acting on another when the two are not themselves in contact and there isn't some third thing transmitting the action from the one to the other. Modern physics does posit various kinds of action at a distance, such as gravity. But this is an idea that most people have great difficulty making sense of. That's why we tend to think of gravity as a sort of invisible hand that reaches out and pulls objects down. We think of gravity this way because we find it hard to see how the earth could act on something it isn't in contact with, such as the skydiver who has just left the airplane. We thus think of gravity as a force, and we think of forces as invisible things that reach out and push or pull. Classical Indian philosophers did discuss the case of magnetism, which is a phenomenon that suggests action at a distance. There is even a dispute in Abhidharma over whether vision must touch its object for perception to take place. But when it came to phenomena such as obstruction the assumption seems to have been that contact is required.

Although this may explain why Vasubandhu did not consider the view that atoms obstruct through repulsive forces acting at a distance, we still want to know whether the view might be true. Were Vasubandhu presented with this hypothesis, what could he say to refute it? There is at least one difficulty he could point out: applying the inverse square law to the hypothesis leads to absurd results. The inverse square law says that the force exerted by A on B is inversely proportional to the square of the distance between A and B. So if we double the distance between them, the force A exerts on B is one fourth what it was. Conversely, if we halve the distance the force is quadrupled. Now remember that space is infinitely divisible. This means that if atoms are mere points, the space between two atoms A and B may be halved infinitely many times. So as B approaches A, the force that A exerts on B will rapidly approach infinity. And this seems absurd. How could something with no size at all contain within itself more force than there should be in the universe?[4]

In v.14 a new opponent agrees with Vasubandhu that atomism will not work. Atoms and aggregates of atoms are, this opponent says, 'mere fabricated constructions', entities we invent as part of our efforts to make sense of the experience of putting things together and taking them apart. Atoms are, after all, in principle unobservable. So if we are to be good empiricists we should be wary of positing them, only doing so if there are no other, lighter ways of explaining the phenomena. This opponent thinks the property-particulars theory is such a way. On this theory, ordinary physical objects are bundles not of aggregates of atoms but of property-particular *rūpa dharmas*. The impartite things out of which a table is composed are not tiny indivisible 'things' like earth atoms (hunks of hard stuff), but rather occurrences of properties such as hardness, whiteness, smoothness, etc. Remember that these property-particulars are thought to exist whether we perceive them or not. When my vision does come in contact with the whiteness property-particular, that causes a mental image that resembles the whiteness that exists 'out there'. And it's because this whiteness tends to occur together with certain other sorts of property-particulars such as a certain shape, a certain smoothness, etc., that we construct the conceptual fiction of the table as a 'thing' that we think of as supporting all these properties. The truth is just the opposite of what we think, though: it is the really existing property-particulars that 'support' the fiction of the table. Now this theory of the *rūpa dharmas* has the advantage that it only mentions things we can observe: colors, shapes, textures, smells and the like. And it looks like these things might not be subject to the same divisibility problems that atoms fell victim to. Things like whiteness and smoothness are qualitatively simple – they're the sorts of things that could only be known by acquaintance. And it just doesn't make sense to say that a certain smoothness is made up of smaller things. What could they be, smoother smoothnesses? So perhaps this view – which sounds initially quite odd – is worth considering.

Vasubandhu presents four difficulties for the view in v.15. The commentary discusses these in terms of our ordinary 'thing' language, but they are better

---

[4]Notice that this does not refute the view that there is action at a distance. What it refutes is the combination of that view and the claim that the atom that acts is a mere point with no size. Action at a distance will work in combination with the view that the material particles have finite size. For there will then be only finitely many times one can halve the distance between the centers of the particles before they come in contact. The difficulty Vasubandhu will see here is just that an atom with size must have parts.

represented if couched in terms of a phenomenal language. (The property-particulars theorist would say the nouns of a phenomenal language are all names of *rūpa dharmas*, so this language can state the ultimate truth about the external world.) For the first objection, imagine you are having the visual experience you would interpret as standing in front of a uniformly green field: you see a certain green with a certain shape. Why is it, asks Vasubandhu, that when you have the experience we interpret as taking a step, you continue to see the same green? To bring the point home, imagine you are having the experience we would interpret as seeing a piece of green paper on the ground: you see a similarly shaped green color. In that case you would not continue to see green after having the experience we call taking a single step. What explains the difference? The two property-particulars are the same color and the same shape, so there shouldn't be any difference between them, yet there clearly is. Of course we want to say there is a difference here: the first greenness *dharma* is bigger than the second. But to say one is bigger than the other is to speak of size, and that will bring up exactly the problem the property-particulars theory was trying to avoid. For if something has size, then it is made of parts and so cannot be a *dharma*.

While the first objection involves the sense of vision, the second involves touch. Suppose you are having the experiences we call holding a banana in your hand. This will involve your seeing a certain yellow color, smelling a certain odor, and feeling a certain smoothness and a certain shape. Consider just the shape that you are aware of through touch. That shape has two ends, but at any one time you can be aware of only one and not the other. How can that be? The only plausible answer is that at any one time you are aware by touch of just one part of the banana shape. But of course to say this is to say that the shape has parts, and thus is not a *dharma*. So once again what is ostensibly a property-particular turns out not to be an ultimately real entity after all.

By now you should be able to work out on your own how the third and fourth objections go. The overall point of v.15 is clear. While the property-particulars theory of the *rūpa dharmas* seems to work in some cases, it cannot account for all our sensory experiences. There are some sensory experiences that seem to require the existence of things with size. And once we accept these, we fall back into the difficulties of infinite divisibility that beset the atomist. Is there any way around this problem? The Sautrāntikas, we might recall, deny that shape is a *dharma*. The present difficulty might help us understand why. All of Vasubandhu's objections to the property-particulars theory bring in shape in one way or another, so perhaps denying that shape is ultimately real might help the realist answer these objections. If for instance we can't say that the two greens we see have the same shape, then there is no reason to expect that our experience of the first will be just like our experience of the second. So the fact that after 'taking a single step' I still see green in the first case but not the second would not pose a problem. The question is whether it is possible to describe all of our sensory experience in a phenomenal language that does not mention shape, and so does not inadvertently bring in size. If so, then perhaps the realist can say that the object of perception is the external property-particular. This may be a possibility worth exploring. But at least initially it does not seem too promising. It is difficult to see how we could eliminate all talk of shape from our phenomenal language and still succeed in describing all the important features of our experience. For instance we classify leaves primarily on the basis of their shapes: we call these maple leaves and those oak leaves because of their common and distinct shapes. The realist has their work cut out for them if they want to rescue the view that the object of perception is an external object in the form of a property-particular.[5]

8.5

With this we will end our exposition of Vasubandhu's second major argument. In the remainder of *Viṃśatikā* he considers several more objections. We will examine just a portion of this final section:

[Objection:] It can be settled whether [the external object] is existent or non-existent by the employment of the means of knowledge. And of all the means of knowledge, it is perception which is the most important. Then if the external object is non-existent, how can there be the cognition, 'I am perceiving'?
[Reply:]
16. Perceptual cognition is just like in dreams and the like; moreover, when that [cognition] occurs,
      The external object is not seen; how can it be thought that this is a case of perception?
As was explained above [v.3], even in the absence of an external object [sensory cognition can occur].
      Moreover, when that [a perceptual cognition] occurs, the external object is not seen; how can it be thought that this is a case of perception? It is when the perceptual cognition occurs that one says, 'I am perceiving'. At that time, the external object is not seen, since judgment is only performed by mind-consciousness and since visual consciousness is then extinguished. How can it be said that this is a case of perception? Particularly as the external object is momentary, how much more so must its color or taste then be extinct?
      [Objection:] We do not remember that which was not experienced, and this requires the experience of an external object. This is none other than seeing. Thus it is that perception pertains to color-and-shape, etc., which are its intentional object.
      [Reply:] This remembering of experienced objects proves nothing, since
17. As has already been said, an impression bears the form of that [object]; memory arises from this;

---

[5]Another possibility that might be worth exploring is that shape is indeed a *dharma*, but in addition there are size *dharma*s. So each occurrence of a color *dharma* such as green is accompanied by some shape *dharma*, such as round. But one green *dharma* that is accompanied by a round *dharma* might be accompanied by a 'largeness' *dharma*, while another is accompanied by a 'smallness' *dharma*. Whether this can be made to work is the question. One concern might be that it will end up on the seriously 'heavy' side. This approach also fails to address the difficulty at the heart of the second objection.

In sleep the unawakened one does not ascertain the absence of a visual object.

As was said before, an impression of visual consciousness bearing the form of an external object arises even without there being an external object. From just such an impression there arises a memory-dependent mental impression, a representation of that, which is constructed in the form of color-and-shape, etc. Thus from the occurrence of memory the existence of external objects does not follow.

[Objection:] If just as in sleep so in the waking state as well the impression has an intentional object without there being a real external thing, then the world should realize of its own accord the non-existence of that [external object]. But it does not. Thus it is not the case that apprehensions of external objects are all, like sleep, devoid of external objects.

[Reply:] This cannot be allowed. For those who are awake, dulled as they are by the sleep of falsely constructed repetitive [karmic] influences, do not apprehend that when they perceive an external object it is unreal, precisely as in sleep. But when, through the attainment of the transcendent, non-conceptual cognition which is the contrary of that, one [truly] awakens, then by reason of the manifestation of the purified worldly cognition which is obtained in the wake of that [transcendent cognition], one correctly apprehends the non-existence of an external object. This is the same [as the case of sleep and ordinary awakening].

[Objection:] If the impressions of beings arise bearing the representations of external objects solely because of distinctive transformations in [the beings'] own mental streams, and not because of distinct external objects, then how can it be shown that the impressions of beings are determined by association with good and bad friends, and by hearing true and false doctrines, since neither the good and bad friends nor those teachings exist [according to you]?

[Reply:]
18. There is mutual determination of impressions through reciprocal influence.
In sleep the mind is overcome by torpor; it does not have the same effect.

Mutual determination of impressions occurs among all beings suitably linked by means of reciprocal influence of impressions. 'Mutual' means between one another. Accordingly the distinct impression arises in one mental stream from some distinct impression in another mental stream, not from a distinct external object.

[Objection:] If as in sleep so in the waking state as well the impression has no external object, why is it not the case that good and bad conduct have the same desirable and undesirable future [karmic] results whether one is asleep or not?

[Reply:] Because 'in sleep the mind is overcome by torpor; it [one's good and bad conduct] does not have the same effect.' It is for this reason, and not because there are real external objects.

[Objection:] If all this is just impressions, and there are no such things as bodies and voices, how is it that for instance sheep can be chased and killed by shepherds? Or if that death is not caused by them, how is it that the shepherd earns the fate of a murderer?

[Reply:]

19. Death is an alteration caused by another's distinct impression, just as
    By the mental powers of demons there occur loss of memory and the like
        in others.

Just as because of the mental powers of demons, etc., there occur in others such alterations as loss of memory, dreams, being seized by evil spirits, and the like. Because of the mental powers of sorcerers as well. Or again as in the case of Kātyāyana's powers causing Saraṇa to dream. Or when Vasumitra was defeated by another [in battle] because of the mental anger of a forest ascetic. In the same way through the power of a distinct impression of one person there occurs some action which harms the life-force of another, and thus death, that is, the cutting off of the stream of resembling [*dharmas*], occurs – thus should it be known.

Notice that in v.16 Vasubandhu gives a compressed form of the time-lag argument. When we first encountered that argument (Chapter 6) it was used to support representationalism. Here Vasubandhu uses it differently. The opponent has objected that perception is the most important of our means of knowledge, and since the opponent thinks perception involves cognition of external objects, they do not see how an impressions-only theorist can agree that perception is a means of knowledge. How can an idealist be an empiricist? But this objection clearly presupposes a direct realist account of perception. The opponent only thinks impressions-only is incompatible with empiricism because they think that when we perceive, we are directly aware of external objects. Vasubandhu uses the time-lag argument to show that direct realism is false. All we are ever directly aware of in sensory experience are mental images. When we first encountered the time-lag argument, it was being assumed that physical objects exist. Given that assumption, the time-lag argument could be used to support representationalism. But once this assumption is called into question, the argument can only show that the intentional object in sensory experience is something inner or mental; it cannot be used to prove the existence of physical objects. Notice that Vasubandhu also gives an explanation of some of the differences between waking sensory experience and dream experience. Because mental acts are less forceful in sleep, the actions one performs in dreams don't have the kinds of karmic consequences that waking actions can have. He might use the same device to explain why the dream experience of eating a meal is not typically followed by the experience of fullness.

Now notice the objection that precedes v.18. By 'distinctive transformations in mental streams' the opponent means the ripening of seeds that is supposed to give rise to impressions. So the opponent is saying Vasubandhu can't explain how one person can influence another person's experiences. A 'good friend' here is someone who teaches the Dharma to others, a 'bad friend' is one who leads others astray, for instance by causing them to live lives devoted to the pursuit of sensual pleasure. But the point is quite general, and can be illustrated with a much simpler example. If I greet you and shake your hand, we want to say that your sensory experiences of hearing my greeting and feeling my handshake were caused by my desires, not by your karma. So far, Vasubandhu has only mentioned one source of sensory experience, the ripening of karmic seeds. So it looks as though his theory cannot account for the facts about those of our sensory experiences that come through interpersonal interaction.[6]

Vasubandhu responds by telling us that there are actually two sources of impressions. In addition to the ripening of karmic seeds, impressions can also be caused in a mental stream by the occurrence of a distinct impression in another suitably linked mental stream. Your experience of hearing my greeting and feeling my handshake were caused by my desire to make you feel welcome. Now this desire must have a certain strength if it is to produce this effect in you. But this is just the difference between a mere wish and an effective decision. Our two streams must also be 'suitably linked'. All this means is that the prior histories of each stream must have led to certain similarities in present experiences. We say that you won't hear my greeting and feel my handshake unless our bodies are in close proximity. Vasubandhu denies we have bodies, but he agrees that an effective desire to make you feel welcome will only produce the auditory and tactile impressions in you if our streams currently contain the sorts of similar impressions that we interpret as standing together in the same place. A similar account will explain how one person can murder another (or a shepherd can kill a sheep) if there are neither weapons nor bodies. Under suitable circumstances an effective desire can bring about the utter disruption of a distinct mental stream. (If there is rebirth, the mental stream continues under radically altered circumstances; if there is no rebirth, then the 'disruption' consists in the cessation of that mental stream.) Once again, a mere wish won't do. But we know the difference between the fleeting thought, 'I wish they were dead', and the determined volition that leads to active planning and execution. The laws governing the production of impressions are such that only the latter can lead to the serious disruption of a series of impressions.

To our ears this will sound bizarre. We think the only way one person can cause another to have experiences is through a physical medium: my lips move, your eardrums oscillate, and you hear my voice. Vasubandhu's account tells us one mind can act directly on another. This will sound to us like he is attributing special psychic powers to mental streams. And unless you believe in demons and other sorts of magical beings, this will seem quite mysterious and highly implausible.[7] Now an idealist could go on the offensive and say that if anything is mysterious here, it is the realist's claim that something mental can bring about something physical. We suppose

---

[6]Indeed you might be wondering if the impressions-only theorist is not also committed to solipsism, the view that there is only one mental stream, namely your own. If there are no external objects, are there other mental streams, or is mine the only one that exists? Vasubandhu is not a solipsist, but he gives no argument for the existence of other minds. Among later Yogācārins, though, there was a debate over the existence of other minds.

[7]Vasubandhu and his audience probably did. That is why his text mentions demons and sorcerers: because they agreed that some beings have such powers, it would not have seemed quite so odd to them that all beings might. Still we do not, so it is worth asking how else this view might be defended.

it is my desire to greet you that causes my hand to extend to yours. But how does this desire, which is something mental, bring about the physical activity? We already accept that one mental event can cause another, at least in a single mental stream. My desire to solve some problem causes me to focus my awareness intently on the issue. Consequently we understand how it might be that a desire in one mental stream could cause an impression in another. For here we are at least talking about one mental event causing another mental event. But, an idealist might say, the realist's claim that mental events can cause physical ones (and vice versa) is quite incomprehensible.

An idealist might say something like this. The British idealist Berkeley did. But Vasubandhu does not. Nor to my knowledge does any other Yogācārin. The reason for this is probably that it would not occur to most Buddhists to think it odd that a mental event could cause a physical one, or vice versa. And this is because Buddhists generally understand causation as no more than invariable concomitance.[8] The Buddha's formula of dependent origination was: 'whenever this occurs that occurs, in the absence of this there is the absence of that'. Here there is no mention of some occult power or force that brings the effect into existence; there are just the two events, cause and effect. So it will not seem odd that an event of one sort could bring about another event of a very different sort – not so long as we observe constant conjunction between the two kinds of event. It is only when we think of causation as requiring something like power to link cause and effect that mental-physical interaction might seem peculiar.[9] What Vasubandhu could say is just that direct mental causation between distinct mental streams seems odd to us only because we are used to thinking in naive realist terms. Once we have learned to see through the realist interpretation we have superimposed on our experience of impressions, we will see that there is nothing really odd about intersubjective mental causation. For (unless we believe there really are demons and sorcerers) it will still be true that one mind can cause experiences in another only under those circumstances we would ordinarily describe as one body acting on another. While there are no bodies, there are those circumstances that common sense interprets as one body acting on another. And these are just the ones that Vasubandhu describes as mental streams 'suitably

---

[8]As we will see in Chapter 9, the Mādhyamika will argue not only that anything more than this is unwarranted, but even that this view of causation cannot be ultimately true.

[9]Here is a rather different reason to be skeptical about mind-body interaction. Suppose we believed that every physical event may be explained in terms of some law of physics. And suppose we also believed that the laws of physics only mention physical events. Then we would believe that every physical event has some other physical event as its cause. Suppose we also believed that desires are mental, and not physical things (such as brain events). Then explaining the physical event of my hand reaching out to shake yours, by saying it was caused by a mental event like my desire to greet you, would be superfluous; there would already be a complete explanation of this event in terms of some physical event (such as a brain event). But this argument is based on the assumption that appropriately scientific causal laws could only link physical causes with physical effects. A Buddhist realist could say we have no special reason to believe this – unless we already believe that physical powers are required to bring about physical effects.

linked by means of reciprocal influence of impressions'.

This raises a general point. It is tempting to think that everything would be different if Vasubandhu were right and there were only impressions. What we have just seen is that in a sense, nothing would be any different. That is, our experience would go on exactly as it always had. All that would change is our interpretation of that experience. It would still be true that only under certain circumstances could I cause you to hear something I want to say to you. We now interpret this fact in terms of causal interactions of bodies with other bodies and with minds. If there are only impressions, we should interpret it in terms of direct mental causation between suitably linked mental streams. But it is exactly the same experiences to which we give these two quite different interpretations. One surprising result of this is that an impressions-only theorist could still do science. In doing science we are seeking to find those regularities that help us explain and predict the course of our experience. We are used to thinking that these are to be expressed in terms of laws about the behavior of physical objects. The impressions-only theorist will say they must instead be put in terms of laws governing the transformation of mental streams. But the data to be explained are the same in either case. They are just what can be expressed in a purely phenomenal language. The laws will take different forms, and employ different nomenclature. But they will still be laws concerning how our sensory experience goes.

There is, though, one new twist that arises from Vasubandhu's claim concerning direct intersubjective mental causation. This requires that the causal laws the impressions-only theory uses to explain and predict our sensory experience be considerably more complicated than we initially thought. Our experience of inanimate natural objects like mountains and rivers will still involve causal laws that connect past desires with karmic seeds, which in turn ripen under appropriate conditions to produce our present impressions. But at least some of our sensory experiences of other persons will be explained in terms of causal laws linking a desire in one mental stream with an impression in a suitably linked distinct mental stream. And now consider our experience of artifacts, useful objects intentionally created by persons. An artifact like a pot is the result of a desire on the potter's part, so the impressions-only theorist will want to explain our experience of it not in terms of karmic seeds, but in terms of a desire in a distinct mental stream (namely the potter's). But our sensory experience of the pot isn't confined to just those times when we are 'suitably linked' with that mental stream. We can continue to have pot experiences when the potter isn't around anymore, for instance when the potter has died.[10] Now the hypothesis of karmic seeds was meant to explain how something in the remote past could be the cause of a present effect when everything is momentary.

---

[10]If you believe in rebirth, you could say that that potter's mental stream continues all the same. So desires in that series could still be the cause of our pot-experiences. But suppose it were an enlightened potter whose pot we are seeing. The mental stream of an enlightened person ceases upon their death, so there is still a problem.

The idea was that the cause produced a seed, which produced another seed, etc., in an unbroken series, until conditions bring about the ripening of a seed to produce an impression. And this makes sense when the remote cause and the seed series and the impression all belong to the same mental stream. But it isn't clear how the seeds hypothesis could work in the case of our experience of artifacts. The seeds couldn't be in the potter's mental stream, since we can have pot-experiences after that stream has ceased. So did the potter's pot-making desire cause seeds in the mental streams of those who now see the pot? Suppose the pot I see now was made ten years ago. Then the potter's desire would have caused a seed in 'my' mental stream ten years ago, and that seed would have been replicated in an unbroken series up to the present, when I finally have the experiences that count as the ripening conditions (such as the experience we call walking into a ceramics gallery). But how did the potter's desire 'know' to plant a seed in my mental stream? Did it already 'know' that in ten years I would be interested in ceramics? Or is it rather that the potter's desire causes seeds in every mental stream, and only those mental streams with the right experiences ever have that series of seeds ripen to produce a pot-impression? In that case there are going to be an awfully large number of seeds in each mental stream. Things get even more complicated when someone decides to smash the pot. That means that seeds in some mental series that would otherwise have ripened to produce pot impressions now are not going to. How is that to be explained?

The point here is not that the impressions-only theorist could not explain all these facts about our experience of artifacts. Where there are genuine regularities in our experience, they can always explain them using causal laws that connect only mental events. The point is rather that in order to do so, they will need to make the causal laws of their theory extremely complex. At a certain point the realist opponent might say it is no longer clear that the impressions-only theory is just as good as the realist theory at explaining and predicting our sensory experience. One thing we ask of our theories is that they employ relatively simple and straightforward laws. And it may no longer be clear that the impressions-only theory does this. Might this be a way for the realist to respond to Vasubandhu's argument from lightness? This could be worth exploring. Suppose, though, that it worked. Would this be a vindication of common sense? Notice that then one would in effect be saying that we should believe physical objects exist only because this theory gives the simplest way to make sense of the patterns in our experience. This might be a way to defend realism, but it would leave us a long way from the direct realism of common sense.

8.6

We will end our examination of Vasubandhu's arguments for impressions-only here. There is still the question what the soteriological point of all this is supposed to be. Why should coming to believe that there are no physical objects, only impressions in a mental stream, help us overcome suffering and attain nirvāna? It is sometimes thought that the point must be to eliminate objects of attachment and clinging. The idea is that we would stop suffering if we no longer believed there are material things. But this cannot be right. Suppose I coveted a shiny new sports car. Learning that there are only impressions need not eliminate my craving. For even if the car doesn't exist as something independent of my mental stream, there are still the impressions that we (wrongly) interpret as, for instance, driving the car. I can still desire to have those impressions. And given the way the causal laws seem to work, I can only have those impressions if I first have the impressions we interpret as handing the salesperson a large amount of money. Once again, the truth of impressions-only would not change the nature of our experience, only how we interpret it. So if the point of the theory were to make us less 'materialistic' in the sense of desiring material things, it wouldn't work.

In the part of *Viṃśatikā* that we skipped over, Vasubandhu tells us what the point actually is. This part of the text begins with the opponent asking Vasubandhu why, if there are no physical objects, the Buddha talked about the *āyatanas* or sense-spheres, such as the visual sphere of color-and-shape. Vasubandhu replies that the Buddha was using his expedient pedagogical methods (*upāya*) and giving a teaching that works on two distinct levels depending on the audience. For ordinary followers this is a way of making the point that the *skandha*s are devoid of self.[11] But for the more advanced, this teaching may be interpreted in such a way as to make the point that all *dharmas* lack a falsely imputed essence. Understood on the first level, the Buddha is teaching that the person is devoid of self or essence, on the second, that *dharma*s are devoid of intrinsic nature (they are empty). So the first represents the Abhidharma understanding of the Dharma, the second represents the Mahāyāna understanding. Here is how he puts it:

> 10. Thus there is the intimation that the person is devoid of self; again, in another way,
>   The teaching is the intimation that *dharma*s are devoid of essence, by way of a falsely constructed essence.

Teaching this, it is intimated that the person is devoid of self. 'From the two [types of *āyatana*, object and sense] the six [types of consciousness] are produced, but there is no one thing that is the seer, [hearer, smeller, taster, feeler,] thinker' – knowing this, those who are to be instructed in the teaching of the selflessness of the person enter into the selflessness of the person. 'In another way' – namely by means of the teaching of impressions only. How does this intimate the essencelessness of *dharma*s? Knowing that this representation of color-and-shape, etc., arises only as an impression, that is, that no *dharma* bears the defining characteristic of color-and-shape, etc., then what [essence] exists?

[Objection:] If indeed no *dharma* exists anywhere, then this 'impressions only' does not exist either. How is it established?

---

[11]Namely by showing that consciousness must be impermanent. The doctrine of the twelve *āyatanas* was central to the Buddha's argument that consciousness must be radically impermanent. See Chapter 3, §3.

[Reply:] It is not the case that the essencelessness of *dharma*s is intimated by saying that no *dharma* exists anywhere. However, what is falsely constructed by the ignorant – such as the intrinsic nature of *dharma*s, what is to be grasped and the grasper, etc. – by means of that imagined essence [of impressions] their essencelessness [is intimated]; but this is not done by means of that inexpressible essence which is the object of cognition of the Buddhas. Since the essencelessness of impressions-only as well is intimated by means of a constructed essence of another impression, the essencelessness of all *dharma*s is intimated by the establishment of impressions-only, not by the denial of their existence.

As Yogācārins understand it, the distinctive Mahāyāna teaching that all *dharma*s are empty is to be understood as the claim that they all lack the intrinsic natures that we wrongly superimpose on them. In the case of *rūpa dharma*s, Vasubandhu holds, this falsely imputed nature includes being external. Why would it be important to overcome this false superimposition? When we wrongly imagine there to be external objects we are led to think in terms of the duality of 'grasped and grasper', of what is 'out there' and what is 'in here' – in short, of external world and self. Coming to see that there is no external world is a means, Vasubandhu thinks, of overcoming a very subtle way of believing in an 'I'.

The eighteenth-century German philosopher Immanuel Kant sought to refute Berkeley's subjective idealism, claiming that we must suppose there are physical objects existing independent of our consciousness. His argument was that without the notion of something permanent and mind-independent (that is, an objective world of physical objects), we could never arrive at our concept of an 'I' that is the subject of different experiential contents. In short, there can be no sense of subjectivity or the 'in here' without a sense of objectivity as the 'out there'. Vasubandhu would agree, but he and Kant draw diametrically opposed conclusions. Kant thinks that since we must believe in an enduring subject of consciousness, we must also believe that there are physical objects. Vasubandhu instead thinks that once we see why physical objects can't exist we will lose all temptation to think there is a true 'me' within. There are really just impressions, but we superimpose on these the false constructions of object and subject. Seeing this will free us from the false conception of an 'I'.[12]

This point is made in a commentary on the other part of Vasubandhu's *Vijñaptimātratāsiddhi*, the *Triṃśikā* ('30-versed'). For this text, which is more soteriological and less philosophical in its orientation than *Triṃśikā*, we no longer have Vasubandhu's commentary on the verses. But here is how the later commentator Sthiramati explains a point Vasubandhu makes in v.28:

---

[12]Note that this does not constitute an argument for the Yogācāra view. To say that the impressions-only theory helps eliminate suffering is not to give a reason why one should believe it. The belief that there is a large balance in my checking account might alleviate my suffering over my financial situation, but that's no reason to believe it is true. All we are doing at this point is asking what soteriological significance impressions-only would have if it were true; we are not now inquiring into its truth.

'Because there is no grasping in the absence of what is to be grasped'. There is a grasper if there is something to be grasped, but not in the absence of what is to be grasped. Where there is no thing to be grasped, the absence of a grasper also follows, there is not just the absence of the thing to be grasped. Thus there arises the extra-mundane non-conceptual cognition that is alike without object and without cognizer.

But why would the resulting cognition be 'non-conceptual'? And what did Vasubandhu (in the commentary on *Viṃśatikā* v.10 that we were just examining) mean by an 'inexpressible essence' that is cognized by the enlightened? Are we brushing up against the mystical here? Are we being told to take on faith what only yogins can actually know through their faculty of non-rational intuition?

Perhaps not. At this point in *Triṃśikā*, Vasubandhu has just explained the Yogācāra doctrine of *trisvabhāva*, the doctrine that there are three intrinsic natures, each with its own type of emptiness. This represents the Yogācāra interpretation of the doctrine of emptiness. Remember that this doctrine – that all *dharmas* are empty of intrinsic nature – is supposed to be definitive of Mahāyāna, and Yogācāra is a Mahāyāna school. But if we take the teaching of emptiness literally, then given what *dharmas* are supposed to be (namely, things with intrinsic nature), it seems to rule out their very existence. And this is something of an embarrassment for Yogācāra, which claims that there are ultimately real things in the form of impressions. The doctrine of *trisvabhāva*, of three natures and three kinds of emptiness, is their way of trying to reconcile the impressions-only doctrine with the teaching of emptiness. The *trisvabhāva* or three intrinsic natures are the imagined (*parikalpita*) intrinsic nature, the dependent (*paratantra*) intrinsic nature, and the perfected (*pariniṣpanna*) intrinsic nature. Let us look at how these are explained in Vasubandhu's verses (and Sthiramati's commentary). First he says what each of the three natures is, then he will explain in what sense each of them can be said to be empty.

> 20. Whatever is discriminated by means of whatever concept,
>   That is the imagined intrinsic nature; it is not real.

He says 'by whatever concept' to show the infinity of concepts available through the distinction between what is internal and what are discriminated as external things … Whatever thing is the object of conceptualization and thus is not real due to lack of existence, just that thing is what has the imagined intrinsic nature; it does not have intrinsic nature since it is due to causes and conditions. For [if it did have intrinsic nature and so were real] then there would be a multiplicity of mutually contradictory concepts [such as 'having size' and 'having no size'] applicable to a single thing and its absence. [But a concept applies to a real thing only if it corresponds to the intrinsic nature of that thing.] And it is not possible for there to be a multiplicity of mutually contradictory intrinsic natures with respect to a single thing or its absence.

> 21ab.   Dependent intrinsic nature is the concepts that originate in dependence
>   on conditions.

The meaning is that whatever is governed by distinct causes and conditions originates depending on something distinct.

21cd.   The perfected is whatever there is of that [dependent] that is forever devoid of the prior [imagined].

There being a concept, the imagined intrinsic nature has the nature of [the duality of] grasped and grasper. The imagined intrinsic nature is called 'imagined' because, there being a concept, an unreal grasped-grasper (subject-object) nature is constructed. The perfected intrinsic nature is whatever of the dependent is forever and always free of that grasped-grasper [dichotomy].

22ab.   Hence it [the perfected] is not just simply identical with that [dependent], it is neither distinct from that nor is it non-distinct.

The perfected is the dependent's being forever free of the intrinsic nature of the imagined. And that nature of being free is not correctly said to be either distinct or non-distinct [from the dependent nature].

22cd.   It [the perfected] should be declared to be just like impermanence, etc., [the dependent] is not seen when that [perfected] is not seen.

[The perfected is like impermanence:] Just as impermanence, suffering and non-self are not distinct from the predispositions etc., nor are they non-distinct. If impermanence were distinct from the predispositions, then the predispositions would be permanent. But if they were non-distinct then the predispositions would be of such a nature as to be annihilated, like impermanence ... When it – the perfected intrinsic nature – is not seen, that – the dependent intrinsic nature – is not seen. If the perfected intrinsic nature, which is to be apprehended through an extra-mundane non-conceptual cognition, is not seen, understood, witnessed, then the dependent is not grasped through that cognition, since this purified worldly cognition is obtained as a consequence of that.

23.   With respect to the threefold intrinsic nature there is a threefold lack of intrinsic nature,
The lack of intrinsic nature has been taught with respect to all *dharma*s collectively.

24.   First there is being devoid of its very defining characteristic; next there is Its not having a nature through itself, finally there is [the ultimate] lack of intrinsic nature.

25ab.   That is the ultimate truth of *dharma*s, for that is also thusness.

The first is the imagined intrinsic nature, this is devoid of intrinsic nature just by its defining characteristic, for its defining characteristic is imputed, as is the defining characteristic of *rūpa* to *rūpa*, that of experience to feeling, etc. Thus since it lacks its own form, like the sky-flower, it is devoid of its very own-form. The next is the dependent intrinsic nature. With respect to it the nature is not through itself, as with a magical apparition, since it arises in dependence on other conditions. Hence since its origination is not in accordance with how it is manifested, with respect to it there is said to be the lack of intrinsic nature through origination. 'That is the ultimate truth of *dharma*s, for that is also thusness'. The meaning of that is that it is the ultimate extra-mundane cognition because nothing exceeds it. Or the *pariniṣpanna* intrinsic nature is said to be the ultimate truth because like space it is everywhere homogeneous and pure. Since the perfected intrinsic nature is the ultimate nature of all *dharma*s that are dependent by nature,

the perfected intrinsic nature is the ultimate emptiness, for it has as its intrinsic
nature the absence of the perfected. [Triṃś. 20–25]

We may think of the *trisvabhāva* as three different ways in which reality can be
experienced. Each type of emptiness then represents a form of misinterpretation that
must be stripped away from that way of taking our experience. The imagined
represents the common-sense way of understanding the world: thinking of it as
involving objects, each with their own natures, being grasped by a conscious subject.
The subject-object dichotomy that structures this interpretation of experience
requires the use of concepts. When I think of my experience as that of feeling a hot
coffee cup, this requires applying the concept of a physical object to one aspect of the
experience, and the concept of a feeling (as a subjective state, a state of 'me') to
another aspect. But if impressions-only is correct, these are misattributions. We
wrongly impute distinctive natures to our experiences when we think of them in this
way. To realize this is to see experience in the dependent way, as just the flow of
impressions dependent on prior causes and conditions. The dependent is what is left
when we strip away from the imagined what is wrongly imputed through our use of
concepts and the subject-object dichotomy. But to the extent that we are thinking of it
at all – even if only as the non-dual flow of impressions-only – we are still
conceptualizing it. So if, as the Mahāyāna *sūtras* seem to hold, conceptual
proliferation (*prapañca*) is the most fundamental expression of ignorance, then there
remains something to be stripped away from the dependent. Thus we arrive at the
perfected mode of taking our experience, which is just pure seeing without any
attempt at conceptualization or interpretation. Now this is also empty, but only of
itself as an interpretation. That is, this mode of cognition is devoid of all concepts,
and so is empty of being of the nature of the perfected. About it nothing can be said or
thought, it is just pure immediacy. Notice though that this is not to be understood as
the experience of some different realm. The perfected and the dependent are not
ontologically distinct; the former is just the latter stripped of what it is actually empty
of. This is important because an enlightened person could not live for long totally
immersed in the perfected mode of cognition. To get around in the world one must
employ concepts. The dependent represents for Yogācāra a kind of 'purified worldly
cognition' in which an enlightened person can use ordinary concepts while
recognizing them for what they truly are – the products of ignorance.

This sheds some light on what Vasubandhu meant when he said in *Viṃśatikā* v.10
that the teaching of impressions-only intimates the emptiness of all *dharma*s without
lapsing into the nihilism of saying that no *dharma*s whatever exist. He was
contrasting his Yogācāra interpretation of emptiness with that of Madhyamaka. The
Yogācāra *trisvabhāva* reading is to be preferred, he thinks, because it leaves in place
some underlying nature – some thing-ness (*dharmatā*) or thus-ness (*tathatā*) – as the
ground on which ignorance has superimposed its false constructions. But why
exactly is what is left 'inexpressible', why must all conceptualization be
transcended? In his comments on *Triṃśikā* v.20, Sthiramati seems to be saying that

concepts could apply to real things only if those things had the natures expressed by the concepts. So the concept 'color' could apply to real *dharmas* only if there were real things that had the nature of being colored. But, he says, since each real thing is the product of many causes and conditions, there would have to be as many different (and often mutually incompatible) concepts applicable to a given real thing as there are causes and conditions for its existing. And in that case a given thing would have a multiplicity of distinct intrinsic natures. That is clearly impossible. Only a conceptual fiction could have a complex nature, and what we are looking for is the ultimately real. So if the reasoning is sound here, we can see why ultimately real things would have to be beyond conceptualization and thus inexpressible in nature. But it is still not entirely clear why anything that was in any way conceptualizable would have to have a complex nature. A full account of this point will have to wait until Chapter 10.

Further Reading

Two recent discussions of Yogācāra that give a different account of its relation to Madhyamaka than the interpretation given here are Ian Charles Harris, *The Continuity of Madhyamaka and Yogācāra in Indian Mahāyāna Buddhism* (Leiden: E.J. Brill, 1991), and Gadjin M. Nagao, *Mādhyamika and Yogācāra*, ed. and trans. L.S. Kawamura (Albany, NY: SUNY Press, 1991).

For an account of the Nyāya response to impressions-only see Chapter 7 of B.K. Matilal, *Perception: An essay on classical Indian theories of perception* (Oxford: Oxford University Press, 1986). See also Joel Feldman, 'Vasubandhu's Illusion Argument and the Parasitism of Illusion upon Veridical Experience', *Philosophy East and West* **55** (2005): 529–41.

For the classic Western formulation of idealism see George Berkeley, *A Treatise Concerning the Principles of Human Knowledge*. A good treatment of Berkeley's overall system is found in the relevant portion of Jonathan Bennett, *Locke, Berkeley, Hume* (Oxford: Oxford University Press, 1971).

For the origins and development of the doctrine of karmic seeds and the related theory of 'storehouse consciousness' (*ālaya-vijñāna*) see Lambert Schmithausen, *Ālayavijñāna: on the origin and the early development of a central concept of Yogācāra philosophy* (Tokyo: International Institute for Buddhist Studies, 1987).

CHAPTER NINE

Madhyamaka: The Doctrine of Emptiness

The view that all things are empty, or devoid of essence, is definitive of philosophical Mahāyāna. In the last chapter we examined how Yogācāra tried to defend this doctrine by giving it an idealist reinterpretation. It is now time to see whether the doctrine of emptiness is philosophically defensible when taken literally. This is what the Madhyamaka school claims. In this chapter we will examine some key arguments of the Mādhyamikas for the claim that all things are empty.[1] We will also look at some key objections to the Madhyamaka view. And as always we will be exploring the soteriological consequences of the view we are examining. But before we do any of this we need to be clear about the difficulties facing anyone who takes the doctrine of emptiness at face value. This will enable us to sort out the various ways that Madhyamaka might be interpreted, and why some interpretations might be more plausible than others.

9.1

The Madhyamaka school traces its origins to Nāgārjuna, who was of South Indian origin and is generally thought to have been active around 150 CE. Nāgārjuna is the author of the foundational Madhyamaka text *Mūlamadhyamakārikā* (MMK), as well as several other works. Nāgārjuna's disciple Āryadeva (*ca.* 200 CE) extended the kinds of analyses Nāgārjuna had given in MMK to new areas. But then there is a gap. It is not until the sixth century CE that we again see Mādhyamikas engaging in sustained philosophical activity. We then have three major commentaries on MMK, those of Buddhapālita (active around 500 CE), Bhāvaviveka (*ca.* 500–570 CE) and Candrakīrti (*ca.* seventh century CE). Why the gap? One possibility is that it took Mahāyāna philosophers that long to appreciate the power of Nāgārjuna's arguments. During the intervening three centuries, much energy went into developing the alternative Yogācāra understanding of emptiness. Perhaps it was not until this had been thoroughly explored that some began to suspect Nāgārjuna was right after all to take the *Prajñāpāramitā* doctrine of emptiness at face value.

To see why this scenario might be plausible, we need to remind ourselves of what the doctrine of emptiness says, and what the interpretive options are. As Nāgārjuna understands it, to say of something that it is empty is to say it is devoid of intrinsic nature (it is *niḥsvabhāva*). Yogācārins would agree. (See Chapter 8, §6.) The claim

---

[1]The practice among scholars has been to refer to the school as 'Madhyamaka' and its members as 'Mādhyamikas'.

we find in the early Mahāyāna sūtras was actually that all things are devoid of essence (*nairātmya*). But the move from 'devoid of essence' to 'devoid of intrinsic nature' is easy to explain. According to Abhidharma's mereological reductionism, an ultimately real thing has just a single nature. Abhidharma also holds that ultimately real things have their natures intrinsically; they don't borrow their natures from other things, as the chariot borrows its size, shape and weight from its parts. So the essence of an ultimately real thing would have to be whatever single property is intrinsic to that thing. Thus if something ultimately real is devoid of essence, it must lack intrinsic nature.

Suppose we were persuaded by the Abhidharma argument for mereological reductionism. We agree that wholes are mere conceptual fictions, and that only things with intrinsic natures could be ultimately real. Suppose the Mādhyamikas then gave us a set of persuasive arguments to the effect that nothing could actually have an intrinsic nature. What would our options be? Two are immediately apparent. The first is to embrace metaphysical nihilism. We could say that ultimately nothing whatever exists. This is unpalatable. And as we will soon see, Nāgārjuna explicitly rejects it. Still it is an option. The second option could be called the 'reality is ineffable' strategy. The thinking that leads to this option is this: if what is ultimately real cannot be described as either partite or impartite, then perhaps the fault lies with the concepts we use to try to describe ultimate reality. Maybe the nature of reality simply transcends the conceptual capacities of finite beings like ourselves.[2] If so, then we might avoid the nihilist conclusion. We might say that there does exist something that is ultimately real; it just cannot be described – at least not by us. (Yogācāra adopted a variant of this option.)

These might seem to be our only two options. But perhaps not. For we encountered a similar situation once before. In Chapter 4 we looked at the question whether the nature of nirvāna can be described. We saw that when the Buddha was asked whether or not the enlightened person exists after death, he rejected each of the four possible answers. Some have taken this to mean that the state of cessation without remainder ('final nirvāna') cannot be described. But this was not the point the Buddha was making when he rejected all four possibilities. Instead he was indicating that they all share a common, false presupposition. Here we find the same type of seeming deadlock: what is ultimately real cannot be described as having intrinsic nature, being devoid of intrinsic nature, being wholes, being partless parts, being utterly non-existent, etc. Should we thus conclude that the ultimately real is ineffable? There is a presupposition shared by all the possibilities here – including metaphysical nihilism and the 'reality is ineffable' option. This is the presupposition that there is such a thing as the ultimate truth. For any of these possibilities to be correct, there would have to be such a thing as the way that things absolutely objectively are. If we were to

---

[2]This leaves open the possibility that the ultimate nature of reality can be known through a kind of immediate intuition that does not employ concepts. Some Mahāyāna Buddhist thinkers embraced this possibility.

embrace the 'reality is ineffable' option, we would be accepting that presupposition. We would be assuming that it makes sense to ask how things are, independently of concepts that reflect our needs and interests. And this presupposition might be false. It might be that the very idea of the ultimate truth is incoherent. So this is a third option. If the Madhyamaka arguments for emptiness turn out to be good, we might take them to show that there can be no such thing as the ultimate truth. Now Mādhyamikas hold that the ultimate truth is that all things are empty. So we could put this third option as: 'The ultimate truth is that there is no ultimate truth.' Of course this sounds paradoxical. We'll return to this later.

Broadly speaking, then, there are two types of interpretation of the doctrine of emptiness, metaphysical and semantic. A metaphysical interpretation takes the doctrine to be an account of the ultimate nature of reality. Our first and second options are both of this sort. The third option is not. It is a semantic interpretation, that is, it takes the doctrine to be saying something about truth.[3] In particular, it takes the doctrine of emptiness to be the rejection of the idea that the truth of a statement must depend on the ultimate nature of reality. That is the idea that the Abhidharma conception of ultimate truth is based on. So on the semantic interpretation, the doctrine of emptiness is the rejection of the idea of ultimate truth. You will recall that Abhidharma claimed there are two kinds of truth, ultimate and conventional. We could accordingly say that Abhidharma has a dualist conception of truth. And then on the semantic interpretation of emptiness, Madhyamaka might be described as semantic non-dualism. For it says there is only one kind of truth.

At this point you might be wondering how truth could be strictly semantic, and not at all metaphysical. Doesn't the concept of truth involve the idea of how things really, objectively are? Doesn't it involve the idea that there is such a thing as the ultimate nature of reality? Take the statement, 'There's a soft-drink machine in the lobby.' For it to be true, doesn't there have to be a machine downstairs? Of course there really aren't any machines. 'Soft-drink machine' is just a convenient designator for parts put together in a certain way. But those parts (or the parts of those parts) would have to be there, arranged in that way, wouldn't they? Perhaps not all the statements that we commonly accept as true actually correspond to reality. The statement about the soft-drink machine doesn't, for it's based on the assumption that there are soft-drink machines when there really aren't. It uses a concept that is molded by our interests and our limitations. But that statement is useful for us, it helps us achieve our goals. And to explain this fact, don't we have to assume that something is objectively there? If the Mādhyamika is saying there is no ultimate truth, how can they explain the conventional truth? Why is it useful to be told there's a soft-drink machine downstairs? Why does it lead to successful practice?

These are good questions. But the semantic non-dualist will reply that they all presuppose the very point that is at issue. They assume that in order for any of our

---

[3]Semantics has to do with linguistic meaning. Truth is considered a semantic concept because to understand the meaning of a statement you need to be able to say what would make it true.

statements to be true, there must be such a thing as how the world itself is, independently of concepts molded by our interests and limitations. The semantic nondualist takes the arguments for emptiness to show that this assumption is false. They also claim that truth can be explained in purely semantic terms, without bringing in metaphysics. But this is not the place to go into how that might work. At this point we are just exploring what our options might be if the arguments for emptiness are good. And we now know that the metaphysical options – nihilism and the 'reality is ineffable' strategy – are not our only ones. We now need to look at the arguments themselves. Once we have done that, we may be in a better position to resolve the dispute between the metaphysical and the semantic interpretations of emptiness.

9.2

There is no one Madhyamaka argument for emptiness. Nāgārjuna and his followers give us many different arguments on many different topics. In MMK, for instance, there are arguments concerning the causal relation, motion, the sense faculties, the relation between fire and fuel, the relation between a thing and its nature, and many other subjects. But these arguments all share a common form. They start from the hypothesis that there are ultimately real things, things with intrinsic natures, and they then show that this assumption has unacceptable consequences. They are all, in other words, *reductio ad absurdum* arguments, arguments that reduce the hypothesis in question to absurdity. The argument concerning causation, for instance, shows that if what is ultimately real had intrinsic nature, then there could never be causation, so things could never come into existence. This one argument does not prove that all things are empty. Someone who thought there are things with intrinsic natures could claim that they are not produced. But then the Mādhyamika will have other arguments meant to show that other absurd things follow from that view. The idea is that eventually the opponent will see that any possible move to salvage their view about the ultimately real is blocked. So they will give up their view that there are non-empty things. They will agree that all things are empty.

In the second chapter of MMK, Nāgārjuna tries to show that it cannot be ultimately true that there is motion. We will look at just the first part of MMK II. Now MMK is written in the same concise verse style that is used in the foundational sūtras of other schools of Indian philosophy. This makes it difficult to understand without a commentary. But the existing commentaries are often quite complex and hard to follow. So we will here relax our rule of giving only the original text. We will supply our own modern commentary to the verses of MMK. This commentary is based on the original Sanskrit commentaries, though. So your readings on Madhyamaka will still be quite close to the thinking of the Mādhyamika philosophers themselves.

1. In the first place the [path] gone over is not [now] being gone over; neither is
    the [path] not yet gone over being gone over.
   The [path] presently being gone over that is distinct from the [portions of
    path] gone over and not yet gone over is not being gone over.

If motion is possible, then it should be possible to say where the activity of going
is taking place. It is not taking place in that portion of the path that is already
traversed, since the activity of going has already occurred there. Nor is it taking
place in the portion not yet traversed, since such activity is still to come. And
there is no third place, the presently being gone over, where it could take place.
(This argument of the three times, to the effect that an event cannot occur in past,
future or present, serves as the model for several other arguments.) The argument
here is the same as that of Zeno's paradox of the arrow. Like that paradox, it relies
on the assumption that space and time are both infinitely divisible.

2. [The opponent:] Where there is movement there is the act of going. And
    since movement occurs in the [path] presently being gone over,
   Not in the gone over nor the not yet gone over, the act of going occurs in
    the presently being gone over [path].
3. [Response:] How could it be right to say that the act of going is in the [path]
    being gone over
   When it is not at all right to say there is presently being gone over without the
    act of going?

For something to be the locus of present going there has to be an act of going.
And something x can't be the locus of something else y unless x and y are distinct
things. In the ensuing vv.4–6 Nāgārjuna will use this point to show it cannot be
right to locate going in the present.

4. If you say the act of going is in the [path] presently being gone over, it
    follows
   That the [path] being gone over is without the act of going, since [for you]
    the [path] presently being gone over is being gone over.

Since the locus of present going and the going are distinct (v.3), the locus itself
must be devoid of any activity of going.

5. If the act of going is in the [path] presently being gone over, then two acts of
    going will follow:
   That by which the [path] presently being gone over [is said to be such], and
    moreover that which [supposedly exists] in the act of going.

For the locus to serve as locus of the act, it must itself be something whose nature
is to be presently being gone over. But this requires an act of going, since
something can't be being gone over without there being an act of going. So we
now have two acts of going: the one for which we are seeking a locus, and the one
that makes this the right locus for the first.

6. If two acts of going are supplied, then it will follow that there are two goers,
   For there cannot be an act of going without a goer.

Since this is an absurd consequence, the opponent's hypothesis of v.2 that led to
it must be rejected. Note that there is no reason to stop at two goers; the logic of
the argument leads to an infinite regress of goers. [MMK II.1–6]

There are two different arguments here, that of the three times (v.1), and an argument to the effect that identifying a locus where going takes place would require a second going (vv.3–6). The first argument is fairly clear. If the present is a dimensionless instant, how can anything be moving in the present? Nāgārjuna will later (in v.12) use the same reasoning to raise difficulties for the notion that something could begin to move. Beginning is a change, and changes require time to occur: a change involves something being one way at one time and another way at a later time. So something couldn't begin to move in the present, since the present is just a dimensionless instant. Likewise for the three times argument of v.1: motion involves being at one place at one time and at another place later, so motion isn't something that could occur at the present instant. It can only occur over two distinct instants, such as a past moment and the present. You might wonder why it couldn't still be true that motion occurs, even if we have to say it occurs between past and present. The answer is that it could then be conventionally true that motion occurs, but not ultimately true. For one thing, there would have to be a single thing that existed at the two different places, first at the earlier time and then at the later time. And if everything is momentary, then nothing exists from one instant to the next. (This was the reasoning behind the Sautrāntika denial that anything moves, which we examined in Chapter 6.) But deeper still, this analysis shows that motion involves mental construction. Motion involves how things are at two distinct moments. And only the mind can bring those two moments together. Motion could not be an intrinsic nature; it could not be ultimately real.

The second argument is more puzzling. It could be put as claiming that there is an inadmissible relation of mutual dependency between the locus of going and the act of going: neither can be what it is without the other, so neither could be ultimately real. Suppose there is a path with three segments, A, B and C. Suppose a goer has already traversed A, has not yet traversed C, and is presently traversing B. Can we say that B is where its going is taking place? The question then is how B comes to have this nature of being the locus of going. Nāgārjuna says this would require that there be a second act of going, separate from the going whose locus we are looking for, something that gave B the nature of a locus of going. But suppose we were to say that B's nature is just to be a place, something that might or might not be a locus of going. Then when the goer comes along and does its going there, this makes it a locus of going; but it could exist perfectly well without any going. In that case there wouldn't be any need for a second act of going to identify it as a locus of going; a single act of going would be perfectly adequate. Why can't we say this?

The problem Nāgārjuna sees with this proposal is that it gives B two natures – that of being a place, and that of being the locus of going – with the first being its essence (what it really is) and the second being a contingent nature it just happens to get. We are then treating B as a substance that bears both essential and contingent properties. And we already know that nothing that is ultimately real could be like this. Something with this sort of compound nature is not 'findable under analysis'. If it is ultimately true of B that it is a locus of going, then this must be its intrinsic nature. The difficulty is that it could get this nature only in dependence on an act of going.

How could something be a locus of going unless there were some going occurring there? And to supply a second act of going to fulfill this need is clearly absurd. The only alternative is to say that it is the original act of going that makes B a locus of going. Yet we've already seen that there can't be a going unless there is a locus in which it takes place. If going is dependent on a locus, we can't make the locus dependent on the going – at least not if they are to be ultimately real. So it looks like this strategy won't work.

Nāgārjuna gives several more arguments in MMK II. Like the two arguments we've just considered, they try to show it could not be ultimately true that things move. But we will end our examination here. The results may not seem all that far-reaching. The Sautrāntikas had already argued that ultimately there is no motion (see Chapter 6, §4). But it was worth looking at the first two arguments of this chapter in some detail. For we will see the strategies he uses – that of the three times, and that of showing mutual dependence–repeated elsewhere.

9.3

In MMK III, Nāgārjuna examines the doctrine of the twelve *āyatanas*. We saw in Chapter 3 that these are the six sense faculties and their respective objects. Since the Buddha made use of this classification, it was assumed in Abhidharma that these are ultimately real things. Nāgārjuna's examination focuses on vision and the visible, but as he will point out in v.8, the same line of argument will apply equally to the other ten *āyatanas*:

1. Vision, hearing, taste, smell, touch and the inner sense (*manas*)
   Are the six faculties; the visible etc. are their fields.
2. Not at all does vision see itself.
   If vision does not see itself, how will it see what is other?
By the anti-reflexivity principle, vision does not see itself. It is then said to follow that vision does not see things other than itself either (i.e., vision does not see anything at all). Why should it follow from the fact that vision does not see itself that it sees nothing else? If seeing is the intrinsic nature of vision, then vision must manifest this intrinsic nature independently of other things. This means that vision should be able to see even in the absence of any visible object. For otherwise its seeing would be dependent on the existence of the visible object. But seeing requires that there be something that is seen, and in the absence of any visible object, only vision itself could be what vision sees. Vision does not see itself, however. Hence seeing could not be the intrinsic nature of vision, so it could not be ultimately true that vision sees visible objects.

   Objection: the anti-reflexivity principle does not hold, since there are counter-examples: a fire, while burning its fuel, also burns itself. Hence it has not been proven that vision does not see itself.
3. [Reply:] The example of fire is not adequate for the explanation of vision.

Indeed that, together with vision, is refuted by [the analysis of] 'present-being-gone-over, gone-over, and not-yet-gone-over' [in MMK II].

The commentary *Akutobhayā* explains, 'Just as the act of going is not found in the gone-over, the not-yet-gone-over, or in the present-being-gone-over, so the act of burning is not to be found in the burnt, the not-yet-burnt, or the present-being-burnt.' The reply is thus that since no account may be given of how an ultimately real fire could burn anything, fire cannot be said to burn itself. Consequently it can't be used as a counter-example to the anti-reflexivity principle.

4. When there is no vision whatever in the absence of seeing,
    How can it be right to say 'Vision sees'?

If vision were ultimately real, its intrinsic nature would be seeing. So it makes no sense to suppose that vision might exist in the absence of any seeing. Note that to attribute the *capacity* for seeing to a vision that is not actually seeing is to make vision's nature of seeing dependent on something else. In that case seeing would not be its *intrinsic* nature.

5. Vision does not see, nor does non-vision see.
    The seer is also to be understood in the same way as vision.

6. There is no seer with vision or without.
    If the seer is non-existent, how will there be what is to be seen and vision?

Something is a seer through possessing vision. But vision can make something a seer only if vision sees. Since (by the result of vv.1–4) vision does not see, and non-vision obviously does not see, there appears to be no acceptable analysis of how something could be a seer. If we then define the visible as what can be seen by a seer, it is unclear how the visible could be ultimately real. The same reasoning applies to vision.

7. Due to the non-existence of vision and what is to be seen, the four, consisting of consciousness etc.,
    Do not exist. How, then, will appropriation, etc., come to be?

'The four' are consciousness, contact, feeling, and desire. In the twelve-linked chain of dependent origination these are identified as successive steps leading to appropriation (*upādāna*), which is the affective stance of taking the elements of the causal series as one's own. So the argument is that in the absence of vision there cannot be, with respect to visual experience, the sense of ownership that is relevant to the origination of suffering. The assumption that vision is ultimately real is incompatible with the Buddha's four noble truths.

8. One should know that hearing, smelling, tasting, touch, and the inner sense are explained
    By means of vision; as well as indeed the hearer and what is heard, etc.

The same reasoning applies to the other five sense faculties and their respective objects. Thus the conclusion of v.7 extends to all possible experience. [MMK II]

Notice that the argument turns on the claim that there is a relation of mutual dependence between a sense faculty and its objects. So this is another example of the mutual dependence strategy. A different strategy is used in the argument against the six *dhātus*, found in MMK V. The six *dhātus* are earth, air, water, fire, space and consciousness. This is another Abhidharma classification, like that of the five *skandhas*. These are thus supposed to be ultimately real entities. Nāgārjuna takes the *dhātu* of space as the subject of his examination, but the argument will once again be generalized to the other five *dhātus*:

1. Space does not at all exist prior to the defining characteristic of space.
   If it existed prior to its defining characteristic, there would result the absurdity of something's being without defining characteristic.

As a *dhātu*, space is held by Ābhidharmikas to be ultimately real. This means it must have its own intrinsic nature, which is here called a defining characteristic (*lakṣaṇa*). The defining characteristic of space is said to be non-resistance: if there is a space between the desk and the wall, then we can put something there without the space resisting. The subject of Nāgārjuna's examination will be the relation between space and its defining characteristic. Since these are said to be related (through the characterizing relation), the question arises how these two things come to be so related. Is it that space, as the bearer of the defining characteristic, is in itself a bare something that is devoid of defining characteristic? On this view the bearer would in itself be a bare substrate, something that comes to be *space* (that which is non-resistant) through being characterized by the defining characteristic of non-resistance. Nāgārjuna rejects this view on the grounds that it would require there to be something that is devoid of defining characteristic.

2. Nowhere does there at all obtain an existent without defining characteristic.
   An existent devoid of defining characteristic being unreal, where would a defining characteristic function?

Abhidharma holds that real things must have their own natures. It might seem that we can make sense of the idea of a bare stuff that then takes on the nature it is given by its defining characteristic. When we think this, though, we are covertly attributing a defining characteristic to this bearer: the defining characteristic of 'bare-stuffness'. If a 'bare stuff' could not exist without even so minimal a characteristic as 'bare stuffness', then this would suggest that the idea of a character-less bearer is indeed incoherent.

3. There is no functioning of the defining characteristic where the bearer is without defining characteristic, and where it is with defining characteristic.
   And it does not function anywhere other than where there is or is not a defining characteristic.

The function of a defining characteristic is to characterize its bearer. In the case of space this would mean making it something whose nature is to be non-resistant. Now this function requires that there be a bearer, and either that bearer is (prior to the functioning of the defining characteristic) itself without a defining characteristic or something with a defining characteristic. Since there is no such thing as space that is devoid of defining characteristic (that is, that lacks even the characteristic of 'bare stuffness'), the first possibility is ruled out. The commentator Candrakārti sees two problems with the second:

(1) A defining characteristic would then be superfluous. Since space would already have a nature, why would it need something else to make it be the sort of thing it already is?

(2) An infinite regress results. To explain how non-resistance$_1$ functions to characterize space, we suppose that space already has a defining characteristic, non-resistance$_2$. But now we can ask the same question about non-resistance$_2$ that we asked about non-resistance$_1$: does it characterize a bearer that is without defining characteristic, or a bearer already with its own defining characteristic? The former has been ruled out. The latter means we must supply a non-resistance$_3$. And the regress shows no sign of stopping here.

4. And if there is no function of the defining characteristic, it makes no sense to speak of a bearer of defining characteristic.

And if a bearer of defining characteristic cannot be asserted, a defining characteristic is likewise impossible.

5. Therefore neither a bearer of defining characteristic nor a defining characteristic exists.

And certainly no existent whatever occurs devoid of both bearer of defining characteristic and defining characteristic.

Space cannot be an ultimately real existent, since we can make sense of neither space as bearer nor of non-resistance as defining characteristic.

6. When the existent is not real, with respect to what will there come to be non-existence?

And who is there who, lacking the nature of either an existent or a non-existent, cognizes what is both existent and non-existent?

To deny that space is an existent is not to affirm that it is non-existent. To affirm the latter, one would need to be able to say what space is, and the argument so far has been that this cannot be done. Moreover, there is no third possibility apart from saying that space is existent and saying that space is non-existent. So apparently no statement about space could be ultimately true.

7 Therefore space is not an existent, not a non-existent, not a bearer of defining characteristic, nor indeed a defining characteristic.

The other five *dhātus* are the same as space.

The argument generalizes to the other *dhātus* as well.

8. But those of little intellect who take there to be existence and non-existence with respect to things,

They do not see the auspicious cessation of what is to be seen. [MMK V]

Notice the difficulty that the last two verses create for the nihilist interpretation of emptiness. The argument has supposedly shown that since there is no intelligible account of the relation between existent and defining characteristic (or intrinsic nature), there can be no such thing as an ultimately real existent. This might sound like metaphysical nihilism. But metaphysical nihilism is the claim that ultimately there are no existents. And as Nāgārjuna points out in v.7, this claim would make sense only if we could meaningfully talk of existents. If the argument against space and the other *dhātus* has succeeded, what it shows is not that nothing whatever exists. What it shows is rather that there can be no ultimately true account of the nature of reality (including metaphysical nihilism).

Does the argument succeed, though? It is based on the assumption that bearer and defining characteristic (e.g., space and non-resistance) are distinct things that have to be put into relation. What if we denied this assumption? What if we said that this is a mere conceptual distinction, that the bearer and the defining characteristic are really one and the same thing? This is, after all, what Sautrāntikas say about the *dharmas*. They could say that an occurrence of space just is an occurrence of non-resistance. But there is a problem with this view. Suppose there are three earth atoms A, B and C in a row, with a space between each. We'll call the space between A and B space 1, and that between B and C space 2. What is it that makes space 1 distinct from space 2? Note that this is not the question how we tell them apart. It's rather the question what makes them be two distinct things. If space is just its defining characteristic, then each of them is just an occurrence of non-resistance. And non-resistance is a general nature, something that can occur in many distinct loci. What makes non-resistance 1 distinct from non-resistance 2? You might think the answer is obvious: the first is the one that is between A and B, while the second is the one between B and C. But this answer presupposes that A, B and C are distinct earth atoms. And if there is no difference between bearer and defining characteristic, then A, B and C are all just solidity (the defining characteristic of earth). So what is it that makes these solidities distinct? Solidity is, after all, a general nature, just like non-resistance. It is one thing that can be repeated in many different loci. If the individuation of 1 and 2 involves A, B and C as distinct things, then there had better be some answer to the question what individuates A, B and C. The obvious answer is that B is the solidity that has 1 between itself and A, and 2 between itself and C. The trouble with this obvious answer, though, is that it presupposes an answer to the question of what individuates space 1 and space 2. And that is precisely the question with which we started. We have just gone round in a circle. What the circle shows is that on this account, neither space nor earth would have its nature intrinsically. Each would borrow its nature from the other.

So the argument of the chapter is defensible. And it appears to effectively rule out the nihilist interpretation. If we can't say what it is for something ultimately real to exist, we can't meaningfully say that ultimately nothing exists. It does not, though, rule out the 'reality is ineffable' interpretation of emptiness. Indeed passages like v.8 have led some interpreters (both classical and modern) to understand the doctrine of emptiness in this way. On the other hand, the verse could also be understood in a semantic non-dualist way. It could be taken to mean that when one understands that all things are empty, one abandons the idea of an ultimate nature of reality – thereby abandoning the view that it is beyond words. But nothing in the verse or the commentaries helps us choose between these two interpretations.

A passage in MMK XIII is more helpful. There Nāgārjuna is responding to the objection that in order for anything to be empty, there must be ultimately real things. For, the opponent says, emptiness is a property, and there can't be a property unless there is some real property-possessor. (This is meant to show that not everything could be empty.) In his reply Nāgārjuna agrees that for it to be ultimately true that all things are empty, there would have to be an ultimately real bearer of emptiness. But he does not withdraw the claim that all things are empty. Instead he says it's a mistake to take this claim as ultimately true:

7. If the non-empty existed, then something that could be called the empty might
somehow come to be.
Nothing whatever exists that is non-empty; then how will the empty come to
be?

8. Emptiness is taught by the Conquerors as the expedient to get rid of all
[metaphysical] views.
But those for whom emptiness is a [metaphysical] view, they have been called
incurable.

The word translated here as 'expedient' literally means something that expels or
purges. So emptiness is being called a sort of purgative or physic. In his
commentary on this verse, Candrakīrti quotes a discussion between the Buddha
and Kāśyapa in the *Ratnakūṭa Sūtra*: "'It is as if, Kāśyapa, there were a sick
person, and a doctor were to give that person a physic, and that physic which had
gone to the gut, having eliminated all the person's bad humors, was not itself
expelled. What do you think, Kāśyapa, would that person then be free of
disease?" "No, lord, the illness of the person would be more intense if the physic
eliminated all the bad humors but was not expelled from the gut."' [MMK
XIII.7–8]

It would be a mistake, Nāgārjuna says, to take emptiness to be a metaphysical theory,
something that claims reality is ultimately a certain way. But this is just what the
'reality is ineffable' interpretation of emptiness does. It says that emptiness reveals
that reality is forever beyond our conceptual grasp. So it assumes there is such a thing
as how the world is independently of the ways in which we happen to think about it.
And this is the assumption that Nāgārjuna says emptiness is meant to purge. On the
'reality is ineffable' interpretation, emptiness rids us of competing metaphysical
views by installing itself as the correct view. But then we would not be fully purged
of metaphysical views, and so not really cured. Instead, Nāgārjuna says, we must
abandon the very idea of an ultimate truth.

9.4

So far we have looked at arguments against motion, the sense faculties, and the
relation between bearer and defining characteristic. None of these proves that all
things are empty. If they show anything, it is just that certain particular views about
the world could not be ultimately true. A more ambitious argument seeks to show that
nothing produced by causes and conditions has intrinsic nature. If we agreed that
everything arises in dependence on causes and conditions, this argument might then
show that all things are empty. The core of the argument is given in two verses:

1. The occurrence of intrinsic nature cannot be by means of causes and
conditions.
An intrinsic nature that was produced by causes and conditions would be a
product.

Candrakīrti explains the argument as follows. The intrinsic nature of a newly arisen thing cannot have already been in the causes and conditions that produced that thing. The heat of fire, for instance, cannot already be in the fuel. For if it were, its production would have been pointless: if there is already heat in the fuel, why bother to start a fire to obtain heat? So the intrinsic nature would have to be a product of the causes and conditions. But this creates a difficulty.

2.   And how could there ever be an intrinsic nature that is a product?
      Indeed intrinsic nature is not adventitious, nor is it dependent on something else.

The difficulty is that the two terms 'product' and 'intrinsic nature' are mutually contradictory. Candrakīrti explains that we say the heat of hot water, and the red color of a flower that is normally white, are not their intrinsic natures because these properties are products of distinct causes and conditions. Hot water is hot because of the proximity of fire; the flower is red because of the excess iron in the soil in which it was grown. The water and the flower get these properties in dependence on causes and conditions that are adventitious, or extraneous to the existence of the water and flower. But in v.1 it was argued that intrinsic nature would also have to be a product of causes and conditions. The fire would have to acquire its heat in dependence on the fuel, air and friction. So heat, as a product, could not be an intrinsic nature of fire. [MMK XV.1–2]

To this it could be objected that the cause of the heat is not extraneous to the existence of the fire in the way that the cause of the red color is extraneous to the existence of the flower. What Nāgārjuna seems to have in mind is that the fire must be thought of as existing distinct from the property of heat, since otherwise the heat could not be thought of as something the fire 'owns', something it receives from the causes and conditions and takes as its own. And some Ābhidharmikas did think of *dharmas* in this way, as substances that have their intrinsic natures as properties. But not all did. The Sautrāntikas did not. So they could say the causes and conditions of the fire just are the causes and conditions of the heat. The argument given here would not show that there is a problem with their position. It would not show that fire then 'borrowed' its nature from its causes and conditions. Another argument would be needed to refute the Sautrāntika view.

Indeed it might be objected that here the Mādhyamika commits the fallacy of equivocation: using a word that has two different meanings as if it had only one. The word in question is 'compounded' (*saṃskṛta*). This word gets used in two different ways, which we can distinguish as follows:

• compounded$_1$: composed of several distinct things;
• compounded$_2$: produced by causes and conditions.

These two different uses of the word are connected. Something that is compounded$_1$, such as a chariot, can also be said to be compounded$_2$, in that it is produced by the coming together of those distinct things. In fact Nyāya would say that the atoms of which the chariot is constituted are its cause.[4] Now Buddhism's mereological reductionism means that anything that is compounded$_1$ is a mere conceptual fiction. It must be something that borrows its nature from its causes, hence it must lack intrinsic nature. But given the ambiguity of the word 'compounded', we cannot simply argue that because something is compounded it must lack intrinsic nature. Consider these two arguments:

A 1. The chariot is compounded.
    2. Anything compounded lacks intrinsic nature.
    Therefore the chariot lacks intrinsic nature.
B 1. Fire is compounded.
    2. Anything compounded lacks intrinsic nature.
    Therefore fire lacks intrinsic nature.

Argument A is good, but argument B commits the fallacy of equivocation. In both premise A2 and premise B2, 'compounded' is being used in the sense of compounded$_1$. In premise A1 the word is also used in this sense, so argument A works. But in premise B1, 'compounded' can only mean 'compounded$_2$'. For while it is true that fire is the product of causes and conditions (fuel, air, spark, etc.), we don't know that every occurrence of fire is made up of other things. Perhaps there are fire atom *dharmas* that are really impartite. So while argument B might look just as legitimate as argument A, it is really fallacious. Has Nāgārjuna committed this fallacy?[5] Or does he have an argument that proves anything compounded$_2$ must lack intrinsic nature?

Perhaps such an argument could be developed out of what Nāgārjuna says about the causal relation in MMK I:

1. Not from itself, not from another, not from both, nor without cause,
    Never in any way is there any existing thing that has arisen.
Nāgārjuna begins with the conclusion for which he will argue in this chapter: ultimately real existents do not come into existence as the result of causes and conditions. There are four possible ways in which this might be thought to happen, and he rejects all. The argument against the first is given in v.3, while the argument against the second takes up the rest of the chapter. There is no separate argument against the third or fourth possibilities. But since the third combines the first and second, it must be rejected if each of those is. As for the fourth, the commentators explain that existents do not arise without cause, since then it would follow that anything could be produced from anything at any time.
2. There are four conditions: the primary cause, the objective support, and the
          proximate condition,
    And of course the dominant condition; there is no fifth condition.

---

[4]Specifically, they are what Nyāya calls the inherence-cause of the chariot.
[5]He is accused of doing so by Richard Hayes in 'Nāgārjuna's Appeal', *Journal of Indian Philosophy* **22** (1994): 311–14; and also by David Burton, in *Emptiness Appraised* (Richmond, Surrey: Curzon, 1998), pp. 90–94.

This classification of four kinds of condition represents the view of the Ābhidharmika opponent. (1) The primary cause is that from which the effect is thought to have been produced, e.g., the seed in the case of a sprout. (2) Only a cognition has an objective support, namely its intentional object, that of which it is conscious. A visual cognition has a color-and-shape *dharma* as its objective support, an auditory cognition has a sound, etc. (3) The proximate condition is that entity or event that immediately precedes the effect and that cedes its place to the effect. (4) The dominant condition is that without which the effect would not arise.

3ab.   The intrinsic nature of existents is not found in the conditions etc.

The first half of v.3 gives the basic argument against production from itself, the first of the four possibilities mentioned in v.1. If the effect is produced from itself, then its intrinsic nature is already present in its cause (perhaps in unmanifest form). As Candrakīrti explains the argument, 'It would not thus be possible [for the effect to exist] before that arising. If it were, then it would be grasped, and arising would be pointless. Thus the intrinsic nature of existents is not in the conditions, etc.' We wish to know the cause of fire because we want something with its intrinsic nature, heat. If that nature were already present among its causes, then it would be pointless to produce fire.

3cd.   The intrinsic nature not occurring, neither is the extrinsic nature found.

The second half of the verse begins the argument against 'production from another' (which is the Abhidharma view). To say that the effect is produced from another is to say that it derives its nature from something else. We just saw that the natures of cause and effect must be distinct. So on this view cause and effect are distinct things with distinct natures, such as milk (liquid) and curds (solid). But now the question is why it should be milk and not clay or a seed that gives rise to curds. For clay and seeds are equally distinct from curds, with equally distinct natures. If this question cannot be answered, then there would be no connection to ensure that particular causes will only produce some effects and not others.

Candrakīrti sets the stage for v.4 by having the opponent answer 3cd as follows: 'Then, those who claim that origination is by means of conditions having been contradicted, it is claimed that origination is by means of an action (*kriyā*). The conditions such as vision and color-and-shape do not directly cause consciousness [as effect]. But conditions are so-called because they result in a consciousness-producing action. And this action produces consciousness. Thus consciousness is produced by a condition-possessing, consciousness-producing action, not by conditions, as rice [is produced] by the action of cooking.' So the opponent is proposing that a kind of causal force is what connects a cause with its effects. The next verse then points out the difficulty with this proposal.

4.   An action does not possess conditions, nor is it devoid of conditions.
     Conditions are not devoid of an action, neither are they provided with an action.

The action is supposed to be the causal force that makes the causes and conditions produce the right kind of effect. It is supposed to explain why only when a seed is planted in warm moist soil does a sprout appear (and why a sprout doesn't arise from a stone). But why does just this kind of action result from the seed in warm moist soil? What explains the production of the right kind of action from the causes? By the logic of the opponent's response to 3cd, the only possible answer is that there is another action that comes between the causes and conditions and this action. And this leads to an infinite regress.

5. They are said to be conditions when something arises dependent on them.
   When something has not originated, why then are they not non-conditions?
6. Something cannot be called a condition whether the object [which is supposedly the effect] is [already] existent or not [yet] existent.
   If non-existent, what is it the condition of? And if existent, what is the point of the condition?

Suppose that the effect arises from distinct causes and conditions. Then on what basis are these said to be the cause of the effect? Presumably this is because they produce the effect, but now it is asked just when this production takes place: after the effect has already come into existence, before it has come into existence, or at some third time? Obviously not the first, since production then would be superfluous. Nor the second, since a productive cause must produce something, and when the effect does not yet exist it is nothing. And there is no third time between the time before the effect exists and the time when it does exist. If the effect is ultimately real, then either it does exist or it does not. This is another case of the argument of the three times, which we already encountered in MMK II.

7. Since a *dharma* does not operate when existent, non-existent, both existent and non-existent,
   How in that case can there be an operative cause?

Candrakīrti explains that by 'operative cause' is meant primary cause, the first of the four kinds of conditions identified in v.2. So here Nāgārjuna is applying the reasoning of vv.5–6 to this type of cause. In subsequent verses he will raise similar problems for the other types. [MMK I.1–7]

Nāgārjuna is probably right when he dismisses (v.3) the view that the effect already exists in the cause. As far as ultimate reality is concerned, it seems more plausible that the effect is distinct from its causes and conditions. But what are we to make of his arguments against this second possibility? There are two: the argument that invoking a causal force to connect cause and effect results in an infinite regress; and an argument from the three times. The first is like an argument given by the nineteenth-century British idealist F.H. Bradley against relations in general: in order for relation R to link a and b, there will have to be a distinct relational tie R_1 linking a to R, another relational tie R_2 linking R to b, yet another tie R_3 linking a to R_1, etc. Bradley thus claims that belief in real relations leads to an infinite regress. This argument invites the response that it is of the nature of a relation to relate things, so R stands in no need of any further relations to link a and b.[6] Perhaps this response is not decisive. But it would be up to someone who remains impressed by the Bradley

---

[6]Nyāya gave a similar response to the Advaita Vedāntin philosopher Śrī Harśa when he criticized the Nyāya category of inherence along similar lines. See Stephen Phillips, *Classical Indian Metaphysics* (LaSalle, IL: Open Court, 1995), pp. 221f, 230f.

regress to explain why any extra relational ties are needed. Nāgārjuna's first argument says that extra causal forces would be needed to link the cause *c* and the effect *e* to the causal force F. If we were to say that it is just the nature of F to link *c* and *e*, could he explain why further causal forces F_1, F_2, etc. would be needed? Here it's important to remember why a causal force was posited in the first place. This was in response to the challenge from those who think the effect already exists in its cause. They pointed out that on their view we can explain why a given effect can only be produced from certain causes and not from others. When milk is heated and a clabbering agent stirred in, curds are produced. Why must we start with milk, and not clay or beeswax? And why is the result curds, and not a pot or a candle? To say that the curds are already in the milk in unmanifest form is at least to propose an answer to this question. How will we answer the question if we deny that the effect exists in the cause?

If you are familiar with David Hume's account of causation, you will appreciate the force of the last question. Hume also assumed that cause and effect are distinct things: first there is the collection of milk, heat, clabbering agent and stirring motion, then there is something new, the curds. The one ceases and the other comes into existence in its place. Because we see this succession time and again, we say that the one is the cause of the other. But when we say this, we mean more than just that this is how it has always gone, or even that it will continue to go this way in the future. We mean that it must go this way – that when causes and conditions are properly assembled, they make it necessary that the effect come into existence. And what, Hume asked, is the source of this idea that there is a necessary connection between cause and effect? We certainly don't observe such a connection. All we observe are the cause and the effect as distinct things in succession. Why, then, do we suppose there is a causal force or power that makes just this effect happen given the causes and conditions? Hume concluded that we do this because we are projecting our feeling of expectation onto the world. In the past we have seen milk, heat and clabbering agent, followed by curds. Having seen this succession often enough, just like Pavlov's dogs we come to expect that the one will always be followed by the other. When we now observe a clabbering agent being stirred into hot milk, we anticipate the appearance of curds. Our idea of necessary connection between cause and effect is just this feeling of anticipation projected out onto the world.

Nāgārjuna's first argument helps us see how Hume reached this conclusion. Nāgārjuna begins by asking whether cause and effect are identical or distinct. If they are identical, then we can understand why clabbering the hot milk causes curds. What we cannot understand is why, if the curds already exist in the milk, we needed to do anything to get them. If they are distinct, then we can see why something had to be done. But now we cannot see why you get curds only from milk and not from plaster or gold, and why you can't get figurines or gold rings from milk. The posit of a causal force was meant to address that question. But the logic of the situation means we are headed for an infinite regress. For we can now ask why the causal force should be just the sort that brings curds into existence. This is just as much of a mystery as the question we began with, why the milk produces the curds. As long as we think of what produces the effect as distinct from it, the same question will arise.

Objection: 'But we do know why milk produces curds – or at least science can tell us why. Maybe a scientist would explain that the acidity of the clabbering agent makes the particles in the milk start clumping together to form curds, or some such thing. Nāgārjuna and Hume just didn't have the scientific knowledge we have today; maybe that's why they had trouble understanding causation.' The problem with this objection is that the appeal to scientific explanations can only put off the inevitable for so long. At some point the explanations of science will bump up against the same unanswered question: why does this kind of cause produce that sort of effect? It's supposedly a basic law of physics that when two particles collide at very high speed, a certain amount of matter goes out of existence and a certain amount of energy comes into existence. Here the cause and the effect are distinct things: the matter has determinate mass and spatial location, while the energy has neither. So why does the one produce the other? Since they are distinct, we can't say that the energy was already present in the matter. So why does the energy come into existence when the matter goes out of existence? To say that this is a fundamental law of physics is just to say that the question has no answer. We're back to saying cause and effect are connected by a causal force. Science can't help us avoid the regress that results when we say cause and effect are distinct.

Some are also suspicious of the argument of the three times. It says there is no time when the cause produces the effect. Of course we can't say the cause produces the effect when the effect already exists, or when the effect doesn't yet exist. But couldn't we say the cause produces the effect during the time the effect is coming into existence? True, if cause and effect are distinct, they don't both exist at the same time. But couldn't it be that first the cause exists, initiating a process of production, at the completion of which the cause ceases to exist and the effect stands forth as a new existent? The difficulty with this proposal is that it requires there to be a time when the effect is neither existent nor non-existent, but is somehow between the two – in the process of coming into existence. Now this idea makes sense when we apply it to things like chariots. Putting all the parts of a chariot together takes some time. So we could say that between the time the first two parts are put together and the time the last part is attached, the chariot is undergoing production. We might then say that during that period the chariot is no longer simply non-existent, but is not yet truly existing either. And this, we might say, is when the cause of the chariot is doing its job of being productive. But we can say this precisely because the chariot is a whole made of parts, a conceptual fiction. We couldn't say it about anything that is ultimately real. For things with intrinsic nature there is no third time.

The underlying point here is deceptively simple, but with profound implications. If cause and effect are distinct and both ultimately real, then they must exist at distinct times. There is no time when they both exist. How, then, can there be any such thing as a real causal relation between them? Only the mind can bring them together. In this respect the argument is just like the three times argument against motion. Causation, like motion, is something that occurs over time. To say that something moves, we must construct a stretch of time consisting of several moments. Likewise to say that something causes something else, we must hold together two distinct moments: the moment when the causes and conditions obtain, and the moment when the effect exists. For the Mādhyamika this shows that causation must be a conceptual construction. Only with the help of the mind's aggregating activity can it appear as if there is real causal connection in the world.

Suppose this is right. What are the consequences? Apparently there is no real causal connection. Does this mean that the world is a thoroughly random place, that absolutely anything can happen at any moment? Nāgārjuna doesn't think this follows. Remember that in verse 1 he denies four distinct ways in which things could be said to originate. The fourth of these is 'without cause'. So from the fact that things do not originate from themselves or from distinct causes, he does not think it follows that things come into existence for no reason at all, completely at random. But maybe he's wrong about that. Why shouldn't it follow? There are several reasons. First, it's crucial to remember that all this concerns the ultimate truth, how the world is apart from the concepts we happen to use to get around in the world. So nothing in the argument rules out the possibility of its being conventionally true that clabbering milk causes curds. And indeed it is conventionally true. That is, accepting this statement invariably leads to successful practice: if you want to make curds, this is what you have to do. Second, if there were ultimately real things, there is no reason to think they would pop into existence utterly at random. Nothing in our experience behaves like that, and the ultimately real is supposed to be what underlies and explains how ordinary experience goes. Third, we need to avoid the trap of thinking this is our only remaining option. Nāgārjuna has argued that existing things cannot be produced from themselves, nor from things other than themselves. Since neither of these options works, it won't work to say that an existing thing is produced from a cause that is both identical with and distinct from it. It might then seem as if there's just one possibility left, that things come into existence for no reason at all. But the fact that this is option number four might remind us of the Buddha's use of the tetralemma. Remember that he rejected all four logical possibilities (for instance with respect to the question of what happens after an enlightened person dies; see Chapter 4, §1). There it also seemed like there could only be the four possibilities. The Buddha rejected all of them though, because they share a common false presupposition. So here too we have the option of rejecting all hypotheses about how existing things originate. Perhaps they also share a false presupposition – that there are ultimately real things that might originate.

There is one last point about the arguments of MMK I that should be mentioned. What these are meant to show is that causation is not a feature of ultimate reality. This should not be confused with the very different claim that we can never know whether something is really the cause of something else. You will sometimes hear it said that just because we've seen clabbering produce curds a thousand times, we don't really know it will work the same way the next time. To say that something is the cause of something else is to say the one thing will always be followed by the other. And sometimes it's just a coincidence that the two things have occurred together. So the fact that they have occurred together up till now in our experience is no guarantee that they always will. Hence, some conclude, we can't really know that the one causes the other. Now this may or may not be a good argument. The point, though, is that it is not what Nāgārjuna is saying. He is not talking about whether we can know when there is causal connection. He is talking about whether there is such a thing as causal connection. That's a very different matter.

We started with the question whether Nāgārjuna commits the fallacy of equivocation when he claims that a product of causes and conditions must be empty. We can now see that he does not need to give a fallacious argument to support this conclusion. The arguments of MMK I will do the job. If they are good arguments, then they show that the causal connection is a conceptual construction. So anything that is said to be the product of causes and conditions must also be a conceptual construction. Since it is not ultimately real, it lacks intrinsic nature; it is empty.

9.5

The following passage is from MMK XX, which examines the concept of an assemblage of causes and conditions. This idea of an assemblage, which was common to Nyāya and Abhidharma, has it that the effect is produced when the cause and all the conditions are assembled together. In the case of a sprout, for instance, the assemblage might include the seed, soil, moisture and warmth. Nāgārjuna's arguments here are similar to those we have seen him give in MMK I and elsewhere, so it should be possible to work out what they are on your own. No running commentary will be given here, but remarks from the commentators are provided in a few tricky spots. Test your understanding of Nāgārjuna by seeing if you can expand his statements into full-fledged arguments:

1. If the effect is produced from the assemblage of the cause and the conditions,
   And the effect exists in the assemblage, how will it be produced from the assemblage?
2. If the effect is produced from the assemblage of the cause and the conditions,
   And the effect does not exist in the assemblage, how will it be produced from the assemblage?
3. If the effect existed in the assemblage of the cause and the conditions,
   It would surely be perceived in the assemblage, and it is not perceived in the assemblage.
4. If the effect did not exist in the assemblage of the cause and the conditions,
   Then causes and conditions would be the same as non-causes and non-conditions.
5. If the cause, having yielded its causal character to the effect, were to cease,
   There would be a double nature of the cause, what is given and what is ceased.

6   And if the cause were to cease without having yielded its causal character,
    Its effect, being produced from an extinguished cause, would be without
    cause.

7. If the effect were to become manifest simultaneously with the assemblage,
    It would follow that it and the producer of which it is produced are
    simultaneous.

Buddhapālitavṛtti: Then how would there be the determination, 'Of these, this is
the cause, that is its effect'?

8. And if the effect were to become manifest before the assemblage,
    Then the effect, being devoid of cause and conditions, would be uncaused.

9. If it were held that, the cause having ceased, the effect was the transformation
    of the cause,
    It would follow that there is rebirth of a cause that had already been produced.

10. How can what is ceased and ended produce an effect that has arisen?
    How, on the other hand, can a cause that endures with its effect give rise to
    that with which it is connected?

11ab.   And if unconnected with the effect, what sort of effect will that produce?

Akutobhayā: And if the cause is really unconnected with the effect, what sort of
effect will it produce? If it is asked why this is, the effect is unproduced and
unreal, the effect does not have prior existence being unrelated to the cause.

11cd.   Whether [the effect is] seen or unseen, a cause would not produce the
effect.

Akutobhayā: The visual sense faculty, as cause of visual consciousness, could be
said to produce visual consciousness that has either been seen or has not been
seen. And neither of these obtains. Why? Of the seen, it is pointless, of the unseen
it is futile, due to the fact that what is unseen has no conditions on which it
depends.[MMK XX.1–11]

9.6

The critique of causal connection is clearly important to Madhyamaka, but it can be
misunderstood. It is tempting to take Madhyamaka as saying that things that are
caused have natures that depend on other things. If (as most Ābhidharmikas claim)
everything is caused, then wouldn't Mādhyamikas be saying that everything depends
for its nature on something else? And doesn't that mean that everything is connected
to everything else, that the nature of any one thing is tied to what the rest of the world
is like? While this might seem like a reasonable interpretation, it faces one major
obstacle. Earlier we looked at the first two verses from MMK XV, the examination of
intrinsic nature, where we found an argument that what is conditioned lacks intrinsic
nature. Here is the next verse, and remarks from two commentaries:

3. Given the non-existence of intrinsic nature, how will there be extrinsic
    nature?
    For it is said that extrinsic nature is the intrinsic nature of an other-existent.

Prasannapadā: Here is indicated that for the world, intrinsic nature is designated as 'other' in dependence on some other intrinsic nature. If indeed heat were the intrinsic nature of fire, then extrinsic nature would be designated in dependence on water as a substantial intrinsic nature. But as there is no intrinsic nature of anything analyzed by those seeking release, how could there be otherness? And since there is no extrinsic nature, it is proven that there is no intrinsic nature.

Prajñāpradāpa: Because it is called extrinsic nature due to dependence on the being of another – this is the argument. Intrinsic nature is the nature of its very own self; there is designation of extrinsic nature due to dependence on another. Hence [the non-existence of] extrinsic nature follows because of there being no intrinsic nature. It is due to itself that there is designation of the other. There is no establishing the reason [for saying extrinsic nature exists], since a verbal distinction [such as that between 'intrinsic' and 'extrinsic'] must have a real reason; and if its reality is denied, there is no example [to establish the reason], since [such examples as] 'long' and 'short' would be unestablished.

Bhāvaviveka's point in the second passage is clear enough. Just as it couldn't be right to call some things 'short' unless there were things that we could correctly call 'long', so a nature couldn't be 'extrinsic' or borrowed from another unless there were natures that were intrinsic. Candrakīrti's comments in *Prasannapadā* may need some explaining, though. He has in mind the stock example of extrinsic nature, the heat of hot water. Ābhidharmikas agreed that what we ordinarily call 'water' is a conceptual fiction because we think of water as something that must be wet, but that can be either hot or cold. To think of water this way is to think of it as something that exists independently of its having the property of heat. So it must have some nature other than heat that makes it be water, and then it has other properties like being hot or being cold. When it is hot, its heat is a nature that is extrinsic: it is borrowed from something else, something that has heat as its intrinsic nature (namely fire). This shows that water is conceptually constructed because it shows we have bundled together several different *dharmas* in coming up with our concept of water. An ultimately real water could only consist in a single *dharma*, such as wetness.[7] Now Candrakīrti understands Nāgārjuna's argument against extrinsic nature to be that for the heat of hot water to be extrinsic, there has to be some nature that is intrinsic to water (namely wetness). And the argument so far in the chapter has been that there are no natures that are intrinsic. The argument, in other words, is that *x* can't borrow a nature from something else *y* unless there already is an *x* there to do the borrowing. And there can't be an *x* unless there is some nature that is its own, that makes it be what it is. So there can't be extrinsic nature if there is no intrinsic nature. And this means it couldn't be ultimately true that everything depends for its nature on something else.

We saw earlier that Nāgārjuna calls emptiness an expedient to get rid of all

---

[7]This is just what Abhidharma has in mind when it talks of water atoms as ultimately real things – impartite occurrences of wetness. See Chapter 6.

metaphysical views. The view that all things are interrelated, that everything borrows its nature from other things, is a metaphysical view. It is a theory about the nature of what is ultimately real. It may be tempting to think this is what emptiness really means. What we have just seen, though, is another case in which a Madhyamaka argument shows a metaphysical interpretation of emptiness to be wrong. This is more evidence that metaphysical interpretations of emptiness won't work. Perhaps emptiness will have to be understood semantically. A semantic interpretation says that the point of establishing emptiness is to show the very idea of an ultimate truth to be incoherent – to show that the ultimate truth is that there is no ultimate truth.

But this raises some troubling questions. First, how could it be ultimately true that nothing is ultimately true? After all, if nothing is ultimately true, then the statement 'There is no ultimate truth' couldn't be ultimately true. No statement could be ultimately true. So saying it's ultimately true that there is no ultimate truth doesn't make any sense. But this paradox can be resolved if the word 'ultimate' is being used in two different ways. Mādhyamikas claim that in order to become fully enlightened we need to learn that all things are empty. So they might call emptiness an ultimate truth in the sense that this is the final truth one must apprehend for enlightenment. But this is different from the Abhidharma sense of the term 'ultimate truth'. We can dissolve the paradox by making this difference clear, as follows:

- ultimate truth$_1$: a fact that must be grasped in order to attain full enlightenment;
- ultimate truth$_2$: a statement that corresponds to the ultimate nature of mind-independent reality.

The semantic interpretation then takes the doctrine of emptiness to mean:

The ultimate truth$_1$ is that there is no ultimate truth$_2$.

So the Madhyamaka position is not self-contradictory when interpreted this way. But there is another question about the semantic interpretation that is more troubling. According to this interpretation, to say all things are empty is to say there is no ultimate truth. Presumably the Mādhyamika thinks it is true that all things are empty. If there is no such thing as the ultimate truth, though, how can there be any truth at all? Perhaps they will say it is conventionally true that all things are empty. Could there be conventional truth if there is no ultimate truth? Recall that conventional truth is supposed to be what works for us, given our interests and cognitive limitations. So our earlier statement about the soft-drink machine on the first floor is conventionally true because, although there really are no such machines, it's convenient for us to say there are when parts are arranged in a certain way. Doesn't this require that there be things that are not mere conceptual fictions, things that exist independently of those useful concepts that reflect our interests and limitations? If we grant that the soft-drink machine itself isn't really real, then in order to explain why it's useful to believe it does exist, it seems we have to say there are those really real things that we have bundled together under the convenient designator 'soft-drink machine'. And the way that those really real things are would be the ultimate truth. The objection, in other words, is that you can't have truth without a metaphysical theory about the ultimate nature of reality. So the semantic interpretation of emptiness doesn't make sense.

To this objection the Mādhyamika could respond with an analogy: giving up ultimate truth is like going off the gold standard. At one time, paper currencies like the dollar and the pound were backed by precious metals such as gold and silver. A dollar bill is just a piece of paper, but people accepted it as valuable because they knew it could be exchanged for a certain amount of gold. During the twentieth century, though, all the world's major currencies went off the gold standard. Understandably, many people were afraid that their paper money would become worthless when it could no longer be redeemed for precious metals. But of course no such thing happened. For what gives a piece of paper value is not its being backed by a certain quantity of precious metal. A currency note is not just a convenient marker for gold. Its value comes from the fact that people employ it as a medium of exchange. It is obviously useful that there be a medium of exchange. The alternative is barter, and satisfying our needs by barter would be difficult and time-consuming. We are infinitely better off if we all agree to buy and sell commodities using currency. Then when I have more eggs than I need but want some bread, I won't have to find someone with extra bread who wants eggs. Instead I can sell the eggs to anyone who happens to want them, and use the currency I received in exchange for the eggs to buy bread. The value of the currency derives from the convention of treating it as a medium of exchange. It derives from its role in a set of human practices.

The Mādhyamika could say that just as the value of a paper currency doesn't require backing by something with intrinsic value, so the truth of the statement about the soft-drink machine doesn't require grounding in things with intrinsic nature. Remember that the ultimate truth was supposed to be what the world is like independent of those ways of thinking about it that reflect our interests and limitations. Perhaps it was a mistake to suppose that something like that was needed to explain why the statement about the soft-drink machine works, why it helps us get what we want. Maybe the only explanation we need is that we have all agreed to call something that dispenses soft-drinks a soft-drink machine, and there's something that dispenses soft drinks on the first floor. Notice that this does not make it completely arbitrary which statements are true. The paper currency analogy may help us see why this is. The convention that gives a piece of paper a certain monetary value is one that we all have to accept; my saying a dollar bill is equal in value to your new car, or to a plane ticket to Tahiti, doesn't make it so. A currency has value only if we all abide by the same convention. This might go for those conventions that establish our linguistic practices as well. The conventions might work only if they reflect ways of thinking about the world that we can all agree on.

According to the semantic interpretation, the doctrine of emptiness says truth is non-dual: there is only one kind of truth. On this interpretation, the point of establishing emptiness is to establish semantic non-dualism, the view that there is only conventional truth. This makes the doctrine of emptiness something like what is currently called 'semantic anti-realism'. The semantic anti-realist view of truth is complex and extremely controversial. There is a great deal we would need to discuss before we could adequately assess it, and thus decide whether semantic non-dualism might be correct. We won't do that here.[8] But there is another question we can ask: is the semantic interpretation really the right way to understand Madhyamaka? Or might this instead be a case of reading some currently fashionable philosophical theory back into a classical Indian context where it has no place? So far the case for the semantic interpretation has been negative. It has basically been that rival interpretations of emptiness can't be right. Is there anything Mādhyamikas say that actually supports this interpretation?

There is. An important tenet of Madhyamaka is that emptiness is itself empty. Here are two verses in which Nāgārjuna affirms this:

> 'It is empty' is not to be said, nor that something could be non-empty,
> Nor both, nor neither; 'empty' is said only in the sense of 'conceptual fiction'.
> [MMK XXII.11]
> Dependent origination we declare to be emptiness.
> That [emptiness] is a dependent concept, just that is the middle path. [MMK XXIV.18]

To call emptiness a 'dependent concept' is to say that it lacks intrinsic nature. And of course no statement about something that lacks intrinsic nature (such as a chariot) can be ultimately true. So nothing we can say about emptiness can be ultimately true. But likewise no statement about non-empty things, things with intrinsic natures, is ultimately true either. And so on for the rest of the tetralemma. As we have seen before, when all the members of a tetralemma are denied, we need to look for a common presupposition they share that might be false. Here it looks like the only possibility is the assumption that there is such a thing as the ultimate truth. To say all things are empty is to say that there is nothing that is the kind of thing that ultimately true statements would be statements about. To say that emptiness is also empty is to say that no statement about emptiness could be ultimately true either. The upshot is that the very idea of an ultimate truth is empty.

9.7

All this leads to our final question about emptiness: what is the soteriological point?

---

[8]For more on the anti-realist conception of truth, see essays 3, 6, 10, 11 and 32 in *The Nature of Truth*, edited by Michael Lynch (Cambridge, MA: MIT, 2001). For a critical survey of the variety of anti-realist positions see Gerald Vision, *Modern Anti-Realism and Manufactured Truth* (London: Routledge, 1988).

This question is especially acute if (as has been argued here) emptiness is best interpreted semantically. It would be one thing if emptiness had some metaphysical implications, such as that everything is somehow connected to other things. Then we could imagine that realizing the emptiness of all things might undermine the boundaries we draw between ourselves and others. Perhaps that would make us less selfish as a result. We saw why this sort of interpretation seems unlikely. But it is harder to see how realizing emptiness could transform our lives if this realization only concerns the nature of truth. How could giving up the idea of an ultimate truth help us overcome suffering? The concept of truth simply seems too abstract for any changes in our conception of it to have life-altering consequences.

There are several things that might be said in response. The defender of semantic non-dualism might say that realization of emptiness was never intended to do all the work in enlightenment. Much of the work is still to be done by the Buddhist doctrine of non-self. The doctrine of emptiness simply serves as a corrective to certain tendencies that can emerge when we try to realize non-self. Remember that the Buddhist project is to eliminate suffering by overcoming the notion that there is an 'I' for whom life can have meaning. The idea of an absolutely objective ultimate truth is useful in helping us do this. We all know how projecting our wants onto the world gets us in trouble. Believing there's lots of money in my checking account because it makes me feel good is a recipe for disaster. The idea of an ultimate truth is just the idealization of this point. It's the idea of what remains after we subtract what are the mere products of our interests and limitations. And seeing the world in these terms may be the most effective way for us to come to believe that there really is no person for whom life could have meaning, that the 'I' is just a useful fiction. The one difficulty with this way of realizing non-self is that it may lead to a subtle form of clinging. This is revealed by a telling gesture on the part of those who believe there is an ultimate truth. Faced with evidence that there may be different perspectives on some phenomenon, such people will often pound the table. This is more than just a way to call attention to incontrovertible facts (such as the solidity of the table). Pounding the table is also a form of self-assertion. In this case it's a subtle form of self-assertion. If I insist that there is an absolutely objective way that things are, I claim that the way the world is is independent of your interests and limitations – and mine as well. So my table-pounding may seem self-effacing. But I am nevertheless claiming that the truth is on my side. Such behavior may be an obstacle to genuine realization of non-self. This may be why the Mādhyamika thinks that in addition to realizing the essencelessness of persons, we must also realize the essencelessness of *dharmas*. The latter realization robs us of the grounds for a notion of the ultimate truth. It thus represents, they may think, the culmination of realizing non-self.

But this response may lead to a new concern. Suppose the initial complaint – that semantic non-dualism is too abstract to have soteriological significance – has been dealt with adequately. The question is whether, in achieving that soteriological significance, Madhyamaka has not gone too far. The point of emptiness is, we are told, to make it impossible for us to be dogmatic. Not being dogmatic sounds like a good thing. But in this case it may come at the price of being a relativist about truth. Without the notion of ultimate truth, how do we resist the conclusion that what is true is relative to the interests and limitations of an individual or a society? To be a relativist about truth is certainly a way to be undogmatic. If I hold that any given statement might be true when said by me or my group, but false when said by you or your group, then I'm certainly not going to pound the table when you deny what I affirm. But what if the statement is 'There is no self', or 'Everything is empty'? What can the Mādhyamika say to an individual or a whole society that insists there are selves, and things with intrinsic natures? If there is no unique best way of describing the world, how can one description be better than another?

Here is where the hard philosophical work begins. Madhyamaka does claim that some ways of thinking about the world are better than others. The belief that there is no self is, in the end, more likely to lead to successful practice than the belief that there is a self. True, Nāgārjuna does say that neither belief is ultimately true (at MMK XVIII.6). So the Buddha might teach non-self to some audiences, while he will teach others in a way that leads them to believe there is a self. In both cases the Buddha is simply using expedient pedagogical methods. He is asserting what he judges will best lead to the cessation of suffering given the beliefs and capacities of his audience. But as the commentaries on this verse make clear, there is thought to be a progression involved here. The audience that is led to believe there is a self is one that does not yet know of karma and rebirth, and lives solely for present sensual gratification. They are not yet ready for the teaching of non-self. The Buddha is preparing them for this teaching by getting them to accept karma and rebirth, and thus begin to practice the moral virtues. (See Chapter 4, §4 for how this is supposed to work.) Someone in this audience is not as far along on the path to nirvāna as is someone who is prepared for the teaching of non-self. So the Mādhyamika would say that while it is not ultimately true that there is no self, as far as conventional truth is concerned it is better to believe non-self than to believe there is a self.

The question is how this can be. How can there be better if there is no best? Perhaps what the Mādhyamika has in mind is that the idea of an ultimate truth, the ideal of absolute objectivity, is a useful fiction. The thought is that while there is only conventional truth, only what 'works' in a given situation, still anyone's overall picture of the world can always be improved upon. We can always do better by taking into account how others see things. But we're unlikely to do this if we're relativists about truth. If we think the same statement can be true when said by one person and false when said by another, then we are unlikely to try to resolve our disagreements when others see things differently. So we're better off if we think 'The truth is out there', that there is a genuinely objective way things are that transcends how things might appear to us. This would explain why we think that when it comes to truth, there has to be a best for there to be better and worse. If the Madhyamaka arguments for emptiness are good, then there is no best, no ultimate truth. Still, it could be claimed, we are better off pretending that there is.

Whether the position we have just sketched is coherent is a complicated question.

This is clearly not the place to explore all the issues involved, or try to resolve them. What is worth noting is just how deep are the issues raised by the Madhyamaka doctrine of emptiness. This is rather remarkable given how bizarre that doctrine initially sounds. The long silence with which Nāgārjuna's arguments were first received suggests that other Indian philosophers thought they could be readily dismissed. The current state of the debate suggests otherwise.

Further Reading

Currently the best English translation of *Mūlamadhyamakakārikā* is that of Jay Garfield, *Fundamental Wisdom of the Middle Way* (New York: Oxford University Press, 1995). This translation is from the Tibetan and not from the Sanskrit original. Garfield's running commentary on the verses is usually reliable.

For a discussion of an important dispute over Madhyamaka methods, see the essays in *The Svātantrika-Prāsaṅgika Distinction*, edited by Georges Dreyfus and Sara McClintock (Boston: Wisdom, 2003).

The classic statement of the 'reality is ineffable' interpretation of emptiness is that of T.R.V. Murti, *The Central Philosophy of Buddhism* (London: Allen & Unwin, 1955). A more recent formulation is in David Seyfort Ruegg, 'The Uses of the Four Positions of the *Catuṣkoṭi* and the Problem of the Description of Reality in Mahāyāna Buddhism', *Journal of Indian Philosophy* **5** (1977): 1–71.

A charitable nihilist reading of Madhyamaka may be found in Thomas E. Wood, *Nāgārjunian Disputations: A Philosophical Journey through an Indian Looking-Glass*, Monographs of the Society for Asian and Comparative Philosophy (Honolulu: University of Hawai'i Press, 1994). A hostile nihilist interpretation is in David Burton, *Emptiness Appraised* (Richmond, UK: Curzon, 1999).

A study of post-Nāgārjuna Madhyamaka and its relation to Yogācāra is: Tom Tillemans, *Materials for the Study of Āryadeva, Dharmapāla and Candrakīrti: the Catuḥśataka of Āryadeva, chapters XII and XIII, with the commentaries of Dharmapāla and Candrakīrti*. Wiener Studien zur Tibetologie und Buddhismuskunde vol. 24.1 and 24.2 (Vienna: Arbeitskreis für Tibetische und Buddhistische Studien Universität Wien, 1999).

For an accessible formulation and defense of anti-realism, see Hilary Putnam, *Reason, Truth and History* (Cambridge: Cambridge University Press, 1981).

CHAPTER TEN

The School of Diṅnāga:
Buddhist Epistemology

The Buddhist schools and movements we have examined so far have all had their own distinctive names: early Buddhism, Abhidharma, Mahāyāna, Theravāda, Vaibhānṣika, Sautrāntika, Yogācāra, Madhyamaka. Not so the school that is the subject of this chapter. Since it was founded by the logician Diṅnāga (480–540), modern scholars often refer to it as the school of Diṅnāga. But it is also called 'Yogācāra-Sautrāntika', and sometimes just 'Buddhist logic'. Scholars don't have a single name for it because there is no one name that classical Indian Buddhists used for all the thinkers in this tradition. This is probably because it was a school in a different sense than those we have looked at so far. Its goal was not to articulate a distinctive path to nirvāna. Instead it set about developing philosophical tools that it hoped would be of use to people following any one of a number of different paths.

The schools we've examined up to now have all had their own distinctive metaphysical views. Sautrāntika, for instance, teaches that all things are momentary, while Yogācāra has its claim that only impressions exist. As the alternative name 'Yogācāra-Sautrāntika' suggests though, the school of Diṅnāga does not take a stand on at least one important metaphysical issue – whether there are physical objects. After all, Yogācāra denies that there are, while Sautrāntika affirms their existence. So someone could be a 'Yogācāra-Sautrāntika' only by refraining from entering into this controversy. The teachings of the tradition that starts with Diṅnāga are meant to be compatible with both positions. This must mean that they don't actually answer an important question about what reality is like. And a Buddhist path to liberation is supposed to be based on an account of the nature of reality. This does not mean the members of the school of Diṅnāga were not interested in nirvāna. Nor does it mean they thought philosophy is irrelevant to attaining nirvāna. Instead they seem to have thought that the dispute over certain metaphysical issues like the existence of an external world would never be resolved to everyone's satisfaction.[1] Philosophy could still contribute to liberation, though, if it could at least tell us what constitutes a means of knowledge. What Diṅnāga and his followers did was develop a Buddhist answer to Nyāya epistemology. Their thought was that if this epistemology was acceptable to both Sautrāntika realists and Yogācāra idealists, then it would help people progress toward liberation regardless of their stance on the metaphysical issue. So this school

---

[1]To say this is not to say that members of the tradition did not have their own views about these issues. Dharmakīrti, for instance, was probably an idealist. He and others are careful to formulate their epistemology in a way that is compatible with a variety of metaphysical positions. But this does not mean they held there is no correct answer to such questions as whether there is an external world.

does not offer a total package – a complete picture of the world, plus advice about how we should act based on that picture. It can be thought of as a group of philosophical specialists who leave much of that work to others. It sees its job as just equipping them with the best epistemological tools available.

To say this is not to say that there are no metaphysical doctrines whatever in the school of Diṅnāga. As we are about to see, this school can be thought of as the culmination of the Abhidharma project. And that project was one of developing the metaphysics of empty persons. It is rather to say three things: that Yogācāra-Sautrāntika does not teach a distinctive path to nirvāna, that any metaphysical teachings it contains are grounded in its epistemological views, and that its epistemology is meant to be acceptable to all Buddhists regardless of their views on certain metaphysical issues. So with this in mind, let's look at what they actually have to say. The obvious place to start is with their account of the means of knowledge.

10.1

Where Nyāya says there are four means of knowledge, Yogācāra-Sautrāntika says there are just two: perception and inference. The other two are, they claim, just special cases of inference. In the case of testimony, for instance, they say we cognize a fact by inferring it from the utterances of a qualified expert. But this is not the most important difference between Nyāya and Diṅnāga's school over the means of knowledge. Far more important is Diṅnāga's claim that each means of knowledge cognizes its own distinctive object. This differs from the Nyāya view, that one and the same fact may be cognized using different means of knowledge. Suppose, for instance, that things like smoke, fire and hills exist.[2] Suppose that from down in the valley I see smoke on the hill, and then infer that there is fire on the hill. Suppose that while I'm down below, you are up on the hill, where you see and feel the fire. Nyāya would say that you and I are cognizing one and the same thing. The fire that you perceive is the very fire the occurrence of which I infer. The Yogācāra-Sautrāntikas disagree. They claim that your cognition and mine actually have distinct objects. What you perceive is a real particular. What I infer, though, is not that very fire itself. I cognize something more abstract, something more like 'fire in general'.

Diṅnāga calls the object of perception the 'particular nature' (*svalakṣaṇa*), and the object of inference the 'general nature' (*sāmānya-lakṣaṇa*). But he holds a view like

---

[2]Of course most Buddhists would deny this. They would point out that hills and the like are wholes made of parts, so they could only be conceptual fictions. Still our talk of hills can, they believe, be explained in terms of the occurrence of *dharmas* that are ultimately real. And such non-Buddhist philosophers as the Naiyāyikas think there really are such things as hills. So Buddhist logicians use hills and the like as examples when discussing the means of knowledge. That way their opponents can understand what they are talking about. Since a hill can always be reductively analyzed into a collection of *dharmas*, these examples could always be replaced with examples of things that Buddhists think are ultimately real. So there's no harm in using conventionally real things like hills as examples.

that of Sautrāntika concerning what is ultimately real: there is no real difference between a nature and the thing whose nature it is. And the object of perception is supposed to be ultimately real. So it would be wrong to think of the 'particular nature' as the nature of something. Like the *dharmas* of Sautrāntika, it is just a particular that is a nature. In order to keep this clear, we'll call it a particular. In the case of the object of inference, on the other hand, we don't need to worry about superimposing on it our idea that a nature has to be the nature of something. The object of inference is not ultimately real, it is a conceptual construction. And part of what the mind puts into it when the mind constructs the object of inference is the idea that a nature always belongs to something. So it isn't a mistake to think of this as something that has a general nature. Let's then agree to call it the object-in-general.

What we perceive are particulars. What we know through inference are objects-in-general. The particular is ultimately real. The object-in-general is a conceptual fiction. These are Diṅnāga's claims. What you see up on the hill is an ultimately real particular. What I infer down below is a conceptually constructed object-in-general. We cognize different things. Maybe we can see what Diṅnāga is getting at when we think about the difference between being told about the grandeur of the Himālayas and actually seeing them. (Remember that Yogācāra-Sautrāntika classifies learning through testimony as a kind of inference.) From another person's description we might be able to form a general conception of what it's like. But no matter how accurate our conception, it still lacks the concrete immediacy of the visual experience. A well-informed blind person might be able to say any number of true things about the colors and shapes we see when we look out from Kathmandu on a clear day. But they will never have the sensory experiences that their words accurately describe.

Why, though, does this mean that you and I cognize different things when we both cognize fire? Why not say instead just that we cognize one object in two different ways? This is what common sense says – and Nyāya agrees: you cognize the fire directly (because your sense of vision is in contact with it), I cognize it only indirectly (by way of the smoke that is a sign of its presence). It's the same real particular that we both come to be aware of. Our awareness may feel different. The fire may be much more vividly present to you than it is to me. But that needn't mean that we're aware of distinct things. Why does the Yogācāra-Sautrāntika reject this counsel of common sense?

Moreover, the fire that you cognize is said to be ultimately real, while the fire I cognize is only a mental construction. But Diṅnāga says that both perception and inference are means of knowledge. And something is a means of knowledge only if it invariably leads to successful practice. If you were cold up there on the hill, your cognition of the fire could lead you to success in your efforts to warm up. But the same goes for me down in the valley. It would take me longer to reach the fire and get warm, but the result would still be the same. In both cases there is successful practice. How can it then be that what you cognize is ultimately real while what I cognize is not?

The answer to the first question turns on the way in which we cognize things through inference. Recall how Nyāya explains this. (See Chapter 5, §2.) I see that the hill has smoke on it. And because I have previously seen smoke and fire together (in places like the kitchen), and I've checked to see if places that I know lack fire (like the lake) also lack smoke (what I see there in the morning is just mist), I know that smoke is pervaded by fire – that wherever there's smoke there's fire. So I know there has to be fire on the hill. Now the Yogācāra-Sautrāntika points out that the fire whose presence on the hill I thereby infer is something that is present wherever smoke is present and whose absence is never found where smoke occurs. But what sort of fire is it that is present in all those different locations, and whose absence is always found together with the absence of smoke? A fire that can be present in many different places and be absent in many others is not the particular fire that you see up on the hill. The fire you see exists in just one place – on the hill. The fire that I cognize by inference is not the particular fire, but fire-in-general.

So why did Nyāya think that we both cognize the same fire? The answer, in a word, is that Nyāya accepts universals. In the Nyāya categorial scheme, the fire is a substance. A substance is a particular thing, something that occurs at some particular place and time. On their account, though, what you see is not just the substance, the fire that is on the hill. You don't just see that particular thing. You see that particular thing as something: as an instance of fire. You see the substance and you see the universal that inheres in it. You see fire-as-inhered-in-by-*fireness* . This is why when you see it you can identify it as fire, a kind of thing you've seen elsewhere. Universals also play a role in my inferential cognition of fire. What I see is the smoke on the hill. But in seeing this smoke I also see the *smokeness* inhering in it. And because of my past experience with smoke and fire, I know that *smokeness* is pervaded by *fireness*. So when I see the *smokeness* in this smoke, I am also in contact with the *fireness* that pervades it. *Fireness* in turn inheres in every fire, including the one on the hill. So by cognizing the smoke and also the pervasion of *smokeness* by *fireness* , my cognition is in contact with the fire on the hill. My cognitive contact is less direct than yours. Mine goes: smoke-inherence-*smokeness*-pervasion-*fireness*-inherence-fire. Your cognitive contact is directly with the fire that's at the end of my chain. That would explain why your cognition is more vivid than mine. But it is one and the same fire (as inhered in by *fireness*) that we both cognize.

Notice the role that universals play in the Nyāya story. It is because Naiyāyikas believe things like *fireness* and *smokeness* are out there in the world that they can claim my inference puts me in cognitive contact with the same particular substance that you perceive. If we believe universals aren't real things, but just mental constructions, the story will be very different. You, being up on the hill, would still be in contact with the particular fire. But my contact with the smoke on the hill could not reach that fire by way of connections out there in the world. It could only reach fire by way of a connection between smoke and fire that has been made in my mind. And while the mind can do all sorts of wonderful things, it isn't magical. It can't all by itself reach out and touch the fire on the hill. So how do I come to be aware of there being fire on the hill? According to Yogācāra-Sautrāntika, the fire that is cognized when I infer the existence of fire on the hill is an idea or mental image. Specifically it is the mental image that is associated with the word 'fire'. It is something that can be present whenever smoke is present, and something in whose absence smoke will always fail to be found. It is something that can be present in many places, absent from many others. If there are no universals, if every real thing is particular, then nothing in reality can be like this. But a mental construction can. We can come to treat a mental image as standing proxy for any and all individual fires. When we do so, that mental image plays the role of fire-in-general. That is what I cognize standing down in the valley.

10.2

It was this line of thought that led Diṅnāga to conclude that the object of perception and the object of inference are two distinct types of thing. We still haven't answered the second question we asked, why inference would 'work' if its object were not ultimately real. Perhaps you can now see how Yogācāra-Sautrāntika answers that question. But we'll have to postpone a full discussion of it until we've dealt with some other matters. There's another question we need to attend to now: why shouldn't we believe there are universals? We just saw that the Yogācāra-Sautrāntika claim that perception and inference have distinct objects is based on their rejection of universals. They hold the view known as nominalism: the view that the universal is a 'mere name' and not something with mind-independent reality. But what reason is there to accept nominalism, and not the realism about universals championed by Nyāya?

This might seem like an odd question. To many people it seems obvious that only particular things are real, and that one thing could not be in many different places at one time. But if you think about the role that universals play in the Nyāya theory of knowledge, it might no longer seem quite so obvious that there aren't any universals. When we see a cow we are able to say that it is a cow. When we see a patch of red we are able to say that it is red. To say these things is to say that what we now see goes together with other things that are also called by the same name. How is that possible if there isn't something that they all share in common? What makes Flossie go together with Bossie and Daisy, if there is no such thing as *cowness* in each of them? How do we know that the color of the tomato, the ripe apple, and Santa's suit all go by the same name, if there isn't some one thing *redness* they all share? While it may seem easy to say that *cowness* and *redness* are just 'abstractions', just 'ideas', it has proven surprisingly difficult to say how we could form such 'abstract ideas' if there weren't some real basis for our applying the words 'cow' and 'red'. This is what is known as the problem of the One over the Many. Because it seems to many people that real universals would be very peculiar things, the problem has often been overlooked. But ignoring a problem is not the same thing as solving it.

We can see an example of this in Abhidharma. The Abhidharma schools were all officially nominalist. They denied the existence of universals on the grounds that real universals would have to be eternal. So their existence would conflict with the Buddha's claim that everything is impermanent. Denying universals helped Ābhidharmikas in their effort to replace Nyāya's seven categories with just one, that of the *dharma*. Not only would this eliminate the category of universals, it also renders inherence and individuators superfluous. The difficulty is that at the same time that the Abhidharma schools denied the existence of universals, they also said that *dharmas* naturally form kinds or classes. Some *dharmas* fall under *rūpa skandha*. Some of these are visible-object *dharmas*. And some of these are red, some are yellow, etc. If there are no universals, though, what is it that makes many visible-object *dharmas* all naturally belong to one kind, red? They didn't say.

But is there really a problem here? Maybe we can explain how these *dharmas* form natural kinds by using the fact that they all resemble one another. Could that be why the Ābhidharmikas thought they could ignore the One over Many problem? No. To see why not, consider the following. Let's call the tomato *dharma* T, the apple *dharma* A, and the Santa *dharma* S. We judge that T resembles A, A resembles S, and S resembles T. Are these three resemblances or just one? If we say they are all one and the same resemblance, then we are back to invoking a One over Many. We've smuggled universals into our picture without acknowledging it. If they are three, then why do these resemblances make T, S and A all red? After all, the taste of a mango resembles the taste of a papaya, yet we don't call either taste red. So there must be different resemblances. What makes the resemblance among T, S and A the kind that makes something red? It looks like the only answer we can give is that these are all resemblances in respect of being red. But then we haven't explained what it means for something to be red. Resemblances won't help us avoid universals.

On this point, then, Abhidharma was inconsistent: it denied the existence of universals, but didn't explain how we can get by without them. The school of Diṅnāga attempts to work out the basic Abhidharma project in a consistent way. Where Abhidharma sees its ultimate reals, *dharmas*, as falling into natural kinds, Yogācāra-Sautrāntika says its ultimate reals, the particulars, are each unique and thus indescribable. If the ultimate nature of reality is how the world is independently of all mental construction, and shared natures like *redness* are mental constructions, then no real entity can be ultimately like any other. The reals are just unique particulars. In Chapter 8 we saw Yogācāra make a similar claim. So here Yogācāra-Sautrāntika seems to be honoring the Yogācāra side of its heritage. Diṅnāga and his followers are also saying that the true nature of reality is inexpressible. This is not just because we humans can't describe things carefully enough, or in fine enough detail. Any words that were used to describe reality would falsify it. To describe something is to attribute to it some property that other things might also have. If the real particulars are genuinely unique, they can never be described. We are aware of them in perception. But because they don't have shared natures, we could never express the content of our awareness in words.

But this all depends on the rejection of real universals. And we have yet to answer the question we began with. Now that we see just how useful real universals can be, why should we deny they exist? The basic answer has already been hinted at several times: because they would be eternal. But is there any problem with eternal things other than the fact that the Buddha seems to have said there aren't any? The Yogācāra-Sautrāntikas think they can show that there is. Their argument goes like this:

1   Only what is causally efficacious is real.
2   To be causally efficacious is to produce an effect at a particular time.
3   Something eternal would be unchanging.
4   There would be no reason for an unchanging thing to produce an effect at any one time and not another.
5   Hence nothing eternal could be causally efficacious.
    Therefore no existing things are eternal.

Premise (1) says that for something to exist is for it to make a difference to how things are in the world. The idea behind (2) is that an effect involves an event, something that happens. As such it must occur at some particular time. If it always existed then there wouldn't be an event involved. So anything that is the cause of an effect has to produce that effect at some particular time. Premise (3) is based on the idea that anything eternal would have to be simple or impartite. Anything that's compounded can always have its parts rearranged in a way that brings about its destruction. And something that is simple could not continue to exist while undergoing qualitative change. For that requires that there be one part that changes and another part that does not. Premise (4) then points out that if our eternal entity is unchanging, it cannot be what brings about an effect at some particular time. To say it produces an effect is to say that the way that it is explains the occurrence of the effect. Since it would always be the way that it is, if it produced anything it would always be producing it. And that idea is incoherent. To produce something is to make something happen at a particular time. So an eternal entity couldn't be the cause of any effect, from which we can conclude that such a thing couldn't exist.

There are questions that might be raised about this argument, but we will not take them up here. We have seen that there are reasons to think there could not be any eternal entities. Since universals would have to be eternal, this gives us some reason to believe that there are no universals. In that case Diṅnāga would be right to hold that the objects of perception and inference are distinct kinds of things: the object of perception is the ultimately real unique particular, that of inference is the mentally constructed object-in-general. But we've also seen that the nominalist must pay a steep price for their ontological economy. If there are no universals, then why does it seem like we can express our perceptual experiences in language? And why is inference a means of knowledge, something that helps us attain our goals? The answers to these two questions turn out to be connected. We turn now to the

Yogācāra-Sautrāntika answer to the first question, concerning perception. Their answer to the second, concerning inference, will eventually emerge out of their account of perceptual judgments.

10.3

We saw earlier (in Chapter 5) that according to Nyāya there are two stages in a perceptual cognition: there is the conceptual stage, in which we are aware of the object as being a certain way; but this is always preceded by a non-conceptual stage in which we are aware of the constituents of a perceptual judgment individually, without being aware of them as forming a relational complex. Suppose we see Flossie the cow. It is the conceptual stage that is expressed as the perceptual judgment that Flossie is a cow. This expresses the content of a conceptual cognition, because the object of this perception is Flossie as inhered in by *cowness*. But Nyāya claims we can have this cognition only after we first cognize Flossie, *cowness* and inherence individually. Only after being aware of them individually can we be aware of them as making up the relational complex. The stage of non-conceptual cognition cannot be expressed in words. To express something in words is to make a judgment, to attribute a character to something. On the Nyāya account all the elements of this judgment are out there in the world, none is constructed by the mind. But the mind must first be aware of them by themselves before it can be aware of the relational complex they make up.

Now Yogācāra-Sautrāntika disagrees with many details of this picture of perception. But they do agree with Nyāya that perceptual cognition involves two stages, the non-conceptual and the conceptual. They also agree that perceptual judgments involve attributing some general nature to an object. They don't accept universals, though, so they have to deny that perceptual judgments reflect what exists outside the mind. Only non-conceptual perception can do that. This is what Diṅnāga is getting at when he calls perception 'cognition that is free of conceptual construction'. My conceptual cognition of Flossie as a cow involves attributing *cowness* to the real particular out there. But while the world contains real particulars, it does not contain universals like *cowness*. So if perception puts us in touch with the world, then the conceptual stage of perceptual cognition is not perception. We may call it a 'perceptual judgment', for it is always preceded by what is properly called 'perception'. But it is a judgment, something involving concepts. And that makes it a kind of inference.

It strikes many people as odd to say that seeing Flossie as a cow involves an inference. It certainly doesn't feel like we have to stop and reason our way to the conclusion that Flossie is a cow. Seeing Flossie as a cow feels like something we just do when we see Flossie. This is what Nyāya is getting at when it says we see universals like *cowness*. But if there are no universals out there where Flossie is, there must be some process of mental construction involved in our seeing her as a cow – a process that we are not ordinarily conscious of. Diṅnāga started with the idea that this mental process involves associating what we actually see – the unique particular Flossie – with a word, in this case 'cow'. His real insight comes when he says that knowing what word to call something involves an inference. To know that what I see is called a cow, I need to know that anything like this is called a cow, and I need to know that anything that isn't called by that name is not like this. And this is just like what I need to know to infer that there's a fire on the hill: that anything that's like this hill in having smoke also has fire, while nothing that lacks fire has smoke. So if seeing Flossie as a cow is a matter of associating what I see with the word 'cow', then seeing Flossie as a cow must involve a kind of inference. We aren't aware of performing this inference because we do it so quickly and automatically. It's something we learned to do when we learned to talk, and ever since then we've been doing it constantly. So it's not surprising that we are unaware of doing it, just as we're no longer aware of all we're doing when we stand upright and walk.

According to Yogācāra-Sautrāntika, two things happen in rapid succession when you are on the hill and see the fire there. First you have a non-conceptual cognition in which you are visually aware of that unique particular located on the hill. This is what is properly called 'perception'. You then very quickly perform a kind of unconscious inference whereby you judge that what you see is the kind of thing that is called a 'fire'. This results in the conceptual cognition that may be expressed as 'This is a fire.' We can call this cognition a 'perceptual judgment'. But it is important to remember that for Diṅnāga and his school it is not perception, for it is about fire-in-general, which is not really out there. This does not make your cognition erroneous. Quite the opposite. Now that you are aware of the fire as a fire, you can use your knowledge about fire-in-general. One of the things you know about fire is that it can warm you when you are cold. Since you are cold and want to warm up, your perceptual cognition of the fire helps you satisfy your desire. We said above that a means of knowledge must be able to lead to successful practice. Even though your judgment is about a mental construction, not something in the world, it still leads to successful practice. So it counts as a means of knowledge. It just turns out that it's an inference. It's just like my cognition of fire-in-general through the inference I perform down in the valley.

Perception is also a means of knowledge. But because it is non-conceptual, Yogācāra-Sautrāntika claims it does not give rise directly to successful practice. You can only know that the particular you see will warm your hands after you have conceptualized it as fire. And that involves inference. So why is perception a means of knowledge? Because it leads you to construct fire-in-general, and that construction leads to successful practice. Both perception and inference (including perceptual judgment) are means of knowledge because both bring about veridical cognitions. A veridical cognition is one that is not falsified by subsequent experience. And a cognition is falsified by bringing about unsuccessful practice. Suppose I wrongly took the smoke on the hill as a sign of an impending volcanic eruption. I might try to save my life by running away. But this would not meet with success. Running away would be pointless, since no volcanic eruption threatens my life. This is a case of a faulty inference. Its faultiness lies in its leading to unsuccessful practice. Perceptions don't give rise to actions; they only lead to perceptual judgments. So a perception can't be directly falsified by an action. It can only be falsified by leading to a judgment that itself is falsified through its leading to unsuccessful practice.

10.4

Inference is the second means of knowledge. It is the reliable cause of indirect veridical cognition. That is to say, it is what regularly causes us to have true beliefs about facts that we cannot apprehend directly by perception. Dharmakīrti defines inference as 'the cognition of an inferable due to a reason with the triple mark'. By a reason is meant a property that serves as an instrument for the indirect cognition of something else. In the inference of fire on the hill, the property of having smoke is the reason. My true belief that there is fire on the hill is brought about by my perceptual judgment of smoke, something 'having the triple mark'. The triple mark is:

1 being in the subject of inference
2 only being present when the *sādhya* (the property to be proved) is present
3 never being present when the *sādhya* is absent.

So in the case of the fire inference, smoke has to be present on the mountain (which is the subject of the inference), it must always occur together with fire (the *sādhya*), and it must never occur where there is no fire. Cognition of a reason with these characteristics is a reliable cause of cognition of the subject's having the *sādhya*. Because there is smoke on the mountain, smoke is only present where there is fire, and smoke is never present where there is no fire, my belief that there is fire on the hill is correct.

It was Diṅnāga who first formulated this definition of inference. Buddhist logicians after him all followed his basic approach. To this his commentator Dharmakīrti[3] added a classification of three types of reason: effect, identity and non-cognition. The reason of effect is used in inferring the occurrence of the cause from cognition of its effect. The fire inference is an example of this. Smoke serves as its reason because fire is the cause of smoke. The general idea is that if *x* is the cause of *y*, then knowing that *y* has occurred enables us to infer that *x* must have occurred. Note that it doesn't work the other way around. I can't safely infer the effect from the cause. To say fire is the cause of smoke is to say that all smoke is the effect of some fire. But this does not mean that every fire causes smoke. There can be smokeless fires. So if I see a fire I

---

[3]Dharmakīrti (late sixth or early seventh century CE) is no ordinary commentator. While purporting to explain Diṅnāga's thought, he actually introduced enough innovation that he could be called the second founder of the Yogācāra-Sautrāntika school.

cannot infer that there must be smoke. Likewise if I see a sprout coming up from the soil, I can infer that a seed must have been planted there. But seeing a seed planted doesn't entitle me to conclude that a sprout will appear later. For instance, toxins in the soil might prevent a sprout from forming.

A reason of identity is a reason whose occurrence in the subject is in fact identical with the occurrence there of the *sādhya*. Suppose, for instance, that I judge what I see to be a maple. I might then infer that it is a tree. The reason I use in this inference is the property of being a maple. Dharmakīrti calls this a reason of identity because, he claims, the tree's being a maple is actually identical to its being a tree. To see why he would claim this, consider the fact that according to Yogācāra-Sautrāntika, only the unique particular is real. From this it follows that whatever makes it true of the particular I am looking at that it is a maple can only be that particular itself. And the same goes for what makes it a tree. Since it is one and the same particular's being what it is that makes it both a maple and a tree, its being a maple and its being a tree are essentially identical.[4]

Now you might think that a reason of identity involves what philosophers nowadays call an analytic truth. To say of a statement that it is analytic is to say that it is true by virtue of the meanings of the words it is composed of. The stock example is 'All bachelors are unmarried.' This is said to be true just because 'bachelor' means an unmarried adult male. Those who believe there are analytic truths say they can be known *a priori*: we don't need to do any empirical investigation in order to know that bachelors are unmarried, we know it just by knowing what the words mean. So the statement 'All bachelors are unmarried' doesn't actually tell us anything new. But Dharmakīrti would disagree. He holds that inferences like 'This is a tree because it is a maple', and 'He is unmarried because he is a bachelor' can be informative. Otherwise they would not count for him as means of knowledge. Like other Indian epistemologists, he builds an informativeness requirement into his idea of a means of knowledge. This is why memory, for instance, is not a means of knowledge. No matter how accurate a memory might be, it can never make us aware of something we have not already cognized. But Dharmakīrti says we can infer that the maple is a tree, so he must think we can learn something new by performing this inference. Dharmakīrti, like Quine, does not believe that there are things we can know *a priori*.[5]

The third type of reason, reason of non-cognition, is used in knowing of something's absence. Yogācāra-Sautrāntika rejects the Nyāya position that absences are real. But I am able to know such things as that there is no money in my wallet.

---

[4]Wouldn't this also license the invalid inference of 'This is a maple' from 'This is a tree'? No. The identity of being a maple and being a tree has only to do with this particular (which is both a maple and a tree). There are other particulars where the property of being a tree is identical not with the property of being a maple but with that of being a willow. So from the fact that something is a tree it is not legitimate to infer that it is a maple. How the identity of a property can vary like this is the subject of the theory of *apoha*, discussed below.

[5]See W.V.O. Quine, 'Two Dogmas of Empiricism', *Philosophical Review* **60** (1951): 20–43.

And this looks like a case of cognizing the absence of money from my wallet. If absences aren't real, how can I know such a thing? Dharmakīrti explains that this involves a kind of inference. When I look in my wallet I see both sides of the interior. Since my eyes are working properly and the light is adequate, if there were any money in there I'd see it. My seeing both sides of the interior is incompatible with my seeing money. So I can infer that there is no money in my wallet. My cognition of something that is incompatible with the presence of something else I would have cognized had it been there entitles me to infer the absence of that something else.[6]

Dharmakīrti claims that all inferences involve one or another of these three kinds of reason. It would be interesting to test this claim. Is there any sound reasoning that does not follow one of these three patterns? But there is another question that is more pressing. All these inferences involve pervasion. I couldn't infer that the hill has fire unless smoke were pervaded by fire. I couldn't infer that what I see is a tree unless being a maple were pervaded by being a tree. And I couldn't infer that there's no money in my wallet unless the visibility of the inside of the wallet were pervaded by incompatibility with the presence of money. Now pervasion looks like a relation between universals. The tree inference, for instance, seems to involve the fact that the maple is a species of tree. And this looks like a relation between what is common to all maples, *mapleness*, and what is common to all trees, *treeness*. Yet Yogācāra-Sautrāntika denies there are any universals. It denies there is anything real that is common to all the particulars we call maples, and likewise for all the particulars we call trees. So how can the inference work? How can the fact that this particular is correctly called a maple be a reason to also call it a tree? Maybe all the maples I encountered in the past were also trees. But if there is nothing that all maples share in common, then why would what was true of those past ones have any bearing on this one in front of me now?

For that matter, what could make it right to call what I am now seeing a maple? When I learned the meaning of 'maple', I was shown some other particular and told to call it by that name. This is a different particular I'm seeing now. If there is no universal that's common to that particular and this one, why is it right to call this one a maple too? And my being able to call it by the right name is the test of my perception being veridical. For remember that in order to count as a means of knowledge, a sensory cognition must be able to lead to successful practice. And this, we saw, goes by way of the perceptual judgment that associates the content of the cognition with a word. The test of my perception's being veridical is my judging that what I see is a maple. For then I can bring to bear what I know about maples, such as that they are a source of firewood. If my perception is correct, then it could lead to successful practice such as warming my hands in front of a fire. Maybe when I learned the word 'maple', I learned that a maple is a tree and that it's made of wood,

---

[6]Most Naiyāyikas also hold that absences are known by inference. Their dispute with Yogācāra-Sautrāntika concerns whether absences exist, not how we cognize them.

which is a source of fuel. And maybe all those things were true of the particular that I saw then. But if that particular and this one do not have a shared nature, why should it be true of this one too? How can there be any successful practice with respect to the real things we perceive, if these are unique particulars? The Yogācāra-Sautrāntika has some explaining to do.

10.5

The explanation comes in the form of the theory of *apoha*, or 'exclusion'. According to the theory of *apoha*, the meaning of a word is 'the exclusion of the other'. What does this mean? Take a kind word (that is, a word for a kind of thing) such as 'fire' or 'yellow'. To know the meaning of a word is to know how to use it. So we would think that to know the meaning of 'fire' is to know what things that word applies to. But this approach leads straight to the idea that there must be something all those things have in common that makes it right to apply the same word to them. This approach leads straight to the idea that there must be universals. The insight that led Diṅnāga to his *apoha* view is that we know how to use the word 'fire' if we can distinguish between the things that are called fires and the things that are not. To learn to use a word is to learn to draw a certain distinction. It is to learn to carve up the world in a certain way: all these things go here, all the other things go over there. Now the approach that leads to universals assumes that we can only learn to draw such a distinction if there is something common to 'all these things'. Diṅnāga's idea was that we can also learn to draw the distinction the other way round, by focusing on 'those others'.

To learn to use 'fire', for instance, we must learn to tell the difference between the things that are correctly called 'fire' and those that are not. Now the class of all those things that are not fire is enormous, and enormously heterogeneous. It includes everything from earth and ice to cows, cats, and colors. No one would expect there to be a single real universal, non-*fireness*, that is present in all the members of this class. But the fires are just those things that are left over once we have excluded this class. So even if there is nothing common to all the things called 'fire', they still form a discrete class by being distinct from the non-fires. Even if all the fires are unique particulars with no shared nature, they still form a distinct class: the class of things that are not non-fire. And this is not based on their having a shared nature. This is just a case of overlooking difference. Each fire is a unique particular, utterly unlike anything else in the universe. We collect them all together by overlooking the particularity of each, seeing them as united in their difference from the non-fires. This is how we construct fire-in-general.

This was the basic intuition behind Diṅnāga's claim that the meaning of a kind term is the exclusion of the other. If everything is unique, then the nature of a particular is just its difference from everything else. Its nature is to exclude all other particulars. Still certain particulars might be grouped together under a kind term if we could overlook their mutual differences and focus instead on their shared exclusion of some group that is 'other'.[7] But there is an obvious objection to this strategy. How are we supposed to tell when to call something a fire? The *apoha* theory says we don't need to find what's common to all the fires (there isn't anything that is), we just overlook the ways they differ from one another and focus on their common difference from the non-fires. But we can't do that unless we already know which things are non-fires. And there isn't anything the non-fires have in common – except their being different from fire! So it looks like we can't tell which things are non-fires unless we already know how to tell whether something is a fire. And that's exactly what the theory was supposed to explain. It seems like we've just gone around in a very tight circle.

Here is how Yogācāra-Sautrāntika answers this objection. The first and second passages are from the Perception chapter and auto-commentary of Dharmakīrti's major work *Pramāṇavārttika*, while the third is by Śāntarakṣita and his commentator Kamalaśīla:

PV III. 73. Though there be a difference, a plurality is determined by means of intrinsic nature, there being the establishing of a single meaning through the cognition, etc., of the object of a single conception, as with the senses and the like.

As [according to us] the sense faculty, the object, light and attentiveness, or [according to you Naiyāyikas] the self, the sense faculty, mind and contact with its object, even though there is no universal that determines their nature, cognize a single color consciousness, so the different *śiṃśapa* trees etc. likewise, though mutually unrelated, bring about the conception of a single nature and a single form, or as wood, according to the convention of being effective for obtaining fire and the like. And this is not the case in different things such as water and the like, or cognition of color and the like through hearing, etc.

74. Or the many herbs that, together or separately, cure fever etc., though they be of many different kinds; and this is not so of others.

While the *gudūcī, musta*, etc., bring about one effect, whose defining characteristic is curing fever, etc., they do not depend, in this, on a universal, they being distinct, for that is their nature. Nor is this found in what lacks this distinguishing mark, such as clabbered milk. [Pandeya, pp. 209–10]

PV III. 82. There [in the case of the many particulars] what is many is [treated as] having a single causal capacity when it comes to designation and cognition – worldly treatment as one [kind of thing] has as its basis their all being distinct from everything lacking capacity for that [goal]. [Pandeya, p. 214]

TS 1034. But whenever a plurality is considered to be the cause of a single effect, then a single word is applied [to them] by the imposition of a single property.

---

[7]This is like the strategy that has often been used to create a sense of national identity among people with very different interests: foster a sense of *we* through shared opposition to a common enemy *they*.

TSP: Though there be no universal, it is still determinate, in accordance with a rule pertaining to universal terms, when there is the performing by many of a single function. Though many, some things by their nature all perform one function. In order to express their capacity for a single function, by imposing a single form for the sake of lightness for agents, a single word is applied. As the word 'pot' is applied to what have many colors, etc., when they have the capacity to fulfill the definitive function of holding honey, water etc.

We can see how this is supposed to work if we think about the example of the medicinal herbs. There are several different herbs that can all be used to lower a fever. Because they come from different plants, they work differently. But all of them produce an effect in which we take an interest, *viz.*, lowering a fever. And so we come up with a single word to designate them all: 'anti-pyretic'. Our use of this single word leads to the sense that they must all share something in common. But this is just like the conviction that a chariot is a single thing. It results from our projecting our interests onto the world. Just as our interest in means of transportation leads us to see the chariot parts as making up a single whole, so our interest in fever abatement leads us to see the different herbs as having a common nature. And just as there really is nothing but the chariot parts assembled in a certain way, so there really is nothing but the different herbs, each acting in its own distinctive way.

Yogācāra-Sautrāntika claims that something similar happens when we learn the convention for a kind term like 'maple'. We might think it's obvious that all the maples have a common nature, and that that's why we call them all maples. But Buddhist logicians say it's really just the other way around. They seem to resemble one another because we have learned to call them all by one name. And we have one word for them all because each can, in its own distinctive way, satisfy a certain desire, such as the desire for syrup or for firewood. We overlook their individual differences, and learn to see them as all alike, because we have come to see them as a group that stands over against all those things that do not satisfy the desire. This explains why Dharmakīrti thinks it's informative to infer that what I see is a tree from the fact that what I see is a maple. Suppose I learned to call a 'maple' everything not falling into the class of things that fail to satisfy a desire for syrup. And suppose I learned to call a 'tree' everything not falling into the class of things that fail to satisfy my desire for firewood. As it happens, what is in front of me now will satisfy both desires. But I don't necessarily know that when I identify it as a maple. For my way of telling whether something is a maple need not involve my desire for firewood. To know that it is a tree, I may have to recollect facts about my past experience with syrup and firewood. Those facts concerned other particulars than the one I now see. So even if this one fits into the same pattern as them, I'm still learning something new about this one.

In our discussion of the theory of *apoha* so far we've been talking about what it is that we learn when we learn to use a kind term. But it may not be clear that we actually could learn to use kind terms on this theory. So it might be useful to see how the learning process is supposed to go. Suppose we are teaching a child to use the word 'fire'. We won't have succeeded until the child can make the same judgments we do about whether something is a fire. According to the theory, the meaning of 'fire' is given by the formula, 'not non-fire'. How does the child learn to apply this formula? It obviously starts with us showing her a fire and pronouncing the word. Her perception of the fire causes the occurrence of a mental image, and that mental image is something that can be copied and repeated. (This is what happens when we remember an experience and then replay it in our mind.) What we want is for her to form a mental image that she can use in the future to determine whether the word applies. She will do this by calling up that mental image and comparing it to what she is then experiencing. But the comparison can't be a matter of looking for resemblance. There is no resemblance. The comparison can only be a matter of looking to see if the present perception is incompatible with the recalled mental image. If it is, if the present perception is excluded by the recalled mental image, then what she is seeing is non-fire. If it is not excluded, then what she is seeing is not non-fire. So it would be correct to call it fire.

How, though, does she form this image? The perceptual image formed by the fire in front of her when we are teaching her is just as particular as the fire that caused it. Since the fire is a unique particular, it is different from everything else. So the image it causes in her will exclude every other perception – including those caused by other fires. If that were the image that she learned to associate with 'fire', then she'd never call anything else by that name. What we must do is help her form an image that is incompatible with all the non-fires while not excluding those images caused by perceiving other fire particulars. Here is where the satisfaction of desire comes in. Suppose the fire we're using is on a cold hillside. Its presence will then satisfy her desire to be warm. We can then lead her to other parts of the hillside and point to all the non-fires that do not satisfy that desire. This way we can bring her to form and retain an image that excludes on the basis of failure to satisfy the desire to be warm. Then when she perceives other fire particulars in the future, the perceptual images they cause will not be incompatible with the image she has learned to associate with 'fire'. So she will know that they can also be called by that name.

The theory of *apoha* is the Yogācāra-Sautrāntika solution to the problem of universals. It represents a kind of nominalist semantics: a theory of how words can have meaning in the absence of real universals. The problem of universals has been debated in Western philosophy at least since the time of Plato and Aristotle. But there is nothing in the Western tradition anything like the theory of *apoha*. Does the theory work? Does it show us how we can make do without those peculiar entities known as universals? It would be right to be suspicious, for the solution it proposes seems almost too simple. It has the look about it of a kind of logical trick. Still it's one thing to be suspicious, and another to find a flaw. To test the theory you need to look for a real flaw. The way to do this is to look for someplace where the theory might have smuggled universals in when nobody was looking. Is there anywhere in the theory where this happens? One thing that might bear looking into is the use the theory makes of causal relations. It relies on the idea that, for instance, the different herbs can each cause fever abatement. Can there be causal relations if there are no universals? We might also want to give more thought to the claim that a language learner can form an image and then reproduce that image later. If there are no universals, what makes an image I have now a copy of one I had earlier? Buddhist logicians gave considerable thought to both these questions. So it's possible they have good, consistent answers to them. Still it's always useful to try our hand at putting a philosophical theory to the test.

10.6

Buddhist logicians beginning with Diṅnāga distinguish between two different kinds of inference: inference for oneself, and inference for others. The definition of inference that we discussed earlier actually applies to the first and not the second sort. Since an inference for others is meant to persuade other people that some statement is true, it must be laid out in more detail than an inference for oneself, much of which is done 'in the head'. The texts of the Buddhist logicians typically devote a separate chapter to each kind of inference. In such a work, the chapter on inference for others will give a definition that is meant to set out all that must be said to provide a sound argument. We won't go into the details of such a definition here. But these chapters typically give what are intended to be models of properly formulated philosophical reasoning. And these can be quite interesting, for they show us how Yogācāra-Sautrāntika thought the epistemological tools they developed could be used to defend some key Buddhist claims. Let's look at one such sample of argumentation, taken from a twelfth-century student manual of Buddhist logic by Mokṣākaragupta.

Our example is a defense of the answer Diṅnāga gave to the following question: How is cognition known? Much of Indian epistemology is taken up with questions concerning how cognition knows various objects. But we can only ask such questions if we know there is such a thing as cognition. So the question arises how this is known. Different schools gave different answers. Nyāya, for instance, claimed that a particular cognition is known by a subsequent act of introspective reflection. After seeing something, I can 'look within' and be aware of the perceptual event that just occurred. Another school (the Bhāṭṭa Mīmāṃsā) held that we infer that a cognition must have occurred from the fact that the object is cognized. Knowing that the cow I'm seeing is cognized, I infer that there must be a cognition that did the cognizing. Both answers hold that cognition is only known indirectly. The school of Diṅnāga rejects such answers. It claims that cognition must be self-cognizing. Take the example of perception of blue. Recall that for Yogācāra-Sautrāntika perception is not awareness of an external object. What I am aware of in the perception of blue is a mental image: for Sautrāntika a representation, for Yogācāra an impression. This mental image has the form of blue. But, claims Diṅnāga, this blue-formed mental image is not something distinct from the cognition that is aware of it. The occurrence of my perception is just the occurrence of a self-cognizing blue-formed cognition. It is because my perception is structured this way that I can be aware not only of blue, but also of my cognition of blue. This is how, in general, cognitions are known. Now there is an obvious objection to this view. It looks like a flagrant violation of the anti-reflexivity principle. Let's look at how the Yogācāra-Sautrāntika author Mokṣākaragupta formulates the argument for Diṅnāga's view and tries to answer this objection:

> The Justification of Self-cognition
> All consciousnesses and mental concomitants cognize themselves, they are self-cognizing. A consciousness is a cognition that grasps just the object. There being consciousness, there are mental concomitants; they grasp the distinctive form of the object and are characterized by pleasure, pain and indifference. Self-cognition is said to be perception, free of conceptualization and non-erroneous, because it is productive of direct awareness of its own form; with respect to all consciousnesses and mental concomitants, it is that which itself cognizes that form by which it is characterized.
>
> Here some object, saying that self-cognition of consciousnesses and mental concomitants is not possible, since it is contradictory for something to carry out an operation on itself. A dancer, be he ever so well trained, still cannot mount his own shoulder. The blade of a sword, no matter how sharp, does not cut itself. A leaping fire, no matter how intensely blazing, does not burn itself. Thus how is consciousness or mental concomitant to cognize itself? For the relation between cognizable and cognizer is just an instance of the relation between object and agent. And it is universally acknowledged that object and agent are distinct, like the tree and the carpenter.
>
> To this it is replied that in a cognition the cognizing of the cognizable does not occur by means of the object-agent relation. How then? By means of the relation between what is to be manifested and that which makes manifest. As a light illuminates itself, so cognition as well, unlike inert objects, arising with the intrinsic nature of illuminating from its own cause, is determined as self-cognizing. And so it has been said:
> Consciousness arises with a nature that is opposed to that of inert matter,
> Its being non-inert is just its consciousness of itself.
> But its self-cognizing is not by means of the object-agent relation,
> Since something that is unitary and not partite in form cannot have three aspects.
> [TS 2000–2001]
> It was also said by the author of *Alaṅkāra* [Prajñākaragupta]:
> Object, agent and the like are conceptually constructed and not ultimately real;
> It is explained that the self destroys itself by itself alone. [PVBh III.369]

The 'three aspects' referred to here are agent, object and action, that is, the cognition, what it is aware of (such as blue), and the act of cognizing (the perceiving by the cognition of the blue). We usually understand cognition to involve all three. Diṅnāga claimed, though, that we think this only because we impose conceptual distinctions on what is actually a single unified thing. The two quotations are claiming that since cognition is something that is ultimately real and thus impartite, it should not be thought of as actually analyzable into these three aspects. They merely reflect a useful way for us to think about cognition. But the anti-reflexivity principle applies only to cases where we can apply the agent-object distinction, such as the case of the carpenter and the wood that is the object of the carpenter's action of cutting.

> Moreover, it cannot be right that consciousness and mental concomitant are illuminated by another cognition. For it is not possible for another simultaneously existing cognition to illuminate consciousness and mental concomitant, since there is no relation of supporting cause and effect [between simultaneously existing things], as with the left and right horns of a cow. Nor could it be illuminated by something existing at a distinct time, for since things are momentary, what is to be illuminated would not then exist. Also, if there were no self-cognition, it would be difficult to see how there could be the awareness that the object is cognized, due to the reasoning, 'Awareness of what is qualified does not occur unless the qualifier has been grasped'. Here the object is what is qualified, being cognized is the qualifier, and what is cognized is qualified by means of cognition. If cognition is not thought in the form of what it is itself aware of, then how will the object that is qualified by cognition be thought of? It is not possible to perceive a stick-holder without perceiving the stick.
>
> And as for what was said by [the Naiyāyika] Trilocana: 'Just as one is aware of visible color without perceiving the eyes, so it will be possible to be aware that the object is known even though one is not aware of cognition', that is wrong. For that [example] is irrelevant to the present subject. The eye is not a qualifier of color. What is, then? Visual consciousness. If visual consciousness is not cognized, how will color be known? And so [our] doctrine is utterly unscathed.

Suppose I perceive blue, and I am also aware that I am aware of blue – that I cognize the cognition by which I perceive blue. The opponent holds that it is a distinct cognition that is aware of the perceptual cognition c_1 that cognizes blue. Then either this distinct cognition c_2 occurs simultaneously with cognition c_1, or it occurs subsequent to the perceptual cognition. Suppose c_1 and c_2 are simultaneous. Since c_2 is a cognition, and it is possible to be aware of any cognition, on the opponent's view this would have to be some distinct cognition that is aware of c_2. If it is a simultaneously existing third cognition, we have embarked on an infinite regress. The only way to avoid the regress is to have the original c_1 be the cognition that cognizes c_2. But then we have two simultaneously existing things in a relation of mutual causal dependence. And this makes no sense. It would not be sensible to claim that the left horn of the cow is the cause of the right horn, and at the same time the right horn is the cause of the left.

Suppose c_2 is subsequent to c_1. Since cognitions are momentary, this means c_1 no longer exists when I come to be aware of it. But we cannot perceive what does not exist. And introspection is a kind of perception; it is a kind of 'inner looking'. So this means my awareness of the perceptual cognition is not by introspection. Then it must be by means of either memory or inference. Mokṣākaragupta does not discuss the case of memory, but this may be because Diṅnāga had already supplied the argument against memory: since we do not remember what we did not previously experience, we could only remember our cognizing the blue if we had earlier cognized our cognizing the blue. So this approach would require that cognition cognize itself.

Suppose my awareness of the earlier c_1 is by inference. The subject of the inference will be the blue, the reason will be cognizedness, and the *sādhya* (the property to be proven) is cognition. The reason will be of the effect type: being cognized is an effect of cognition. This will be a good inference provided we can ascertain the presence of the reason in the subject. How am I aware that the blue is qualified by cognizedness? The only plausible answer would seem to be that there is this blue in my awareness, and I reason that there would not be this blue unless it were qualified by cognizedness. But I couldn't be aware of the blue as something that is qualified by cognizedness unless I were aware of cognizedness. I couldn't be aware of someone as 'the person holding a stick' unless I were aware of the stick. Likewise I couldn't be aware of the blue as something qualified by the property of having been cognized unless I were aware of the cognition whereby the blue is cognized. So the inference can't get off the ground without self-cognition. The Naiyāyika Trilocana objects that although the eyes are a cause of one's seeing blue, I am aware of blue without being aware of my eyes. By the same token, even though cognition is the cause of the blue's being cognized, it should be possible to be aware that the blue is cognized without being aware of the cognition. Mokṣākaragupta's reply to this objection is a good example of the sort of attention to detail that is a hallmark of the method of logicians.

Mokṣākaragupta next turns to the views of certain members of the Mīmāṃsā school, who claimed that a cognition cannot be perceived but only cognized by inference:

> Then again there is what was said by [Kumārila] Bhaṭṭa to prove that cognition is imperceptible: 'Just as there is proof of the existence of the senses by means of the fact that otherwise the illumination of color and the like is unexplained, so the existence of cognition is established in the same way.' On this the [commentary] *Bhāṣya* says, 'In the absence of a cognized object, no one perceives [their] awareness. An object being known, however, it is known by inference.' And the *Vārttika* says, 'Its cognition is due to cognizedness [of the object].' And cognizedness is said to be the manifestation of the object.
>
> This is also incorrect. For with respect to this manifestation also, there is inertness in the appearance of the form of the object apart from cognition, and illumination does not belong to the inert. And if it were something other than the object, it would still be inert, and would not be able to illuminate itself. If illumination were by another manifestation there would be an infinite regress. And there is also the absurd consequence that manifestation, something whose intrinsic nature is cognition, is imperceptible. Thus it must be asserted that cognition is self-cognizing. Self-cognition is given in experience, why deny it? This was said [by Dharmakīrti]:

> There can be no seeing of the object when the perceiving is not perceived.

And the author of *Alaṅkāra* [Prajñākaragupta] said:

> If the cognition is imperceptible, then how will there ever be awareness of its cognizedness?
> Who can define the nature of that which is imperceptible?

Once again, the inferential explanation of our awareness of our cognitions won't work without supposing that cognitions cognize themselves. To see the argument for this, we need to think carefully about what it is like to have a perceptual cognition. The blue that I am aware of is 'inert', lifeless, not the sort of thing that could disclose or illuminate itself. My awareness of blue is an experience of the manifestation or disclosure of this inert object. It seems, then, that I am aware not just of the object, but of the element of disclosure or illumination as well. The question is how I could be aware of that unless cognition cognized itself:

> If, however, all cognitions are self-cognizing and thus are perceptions, how will it not be the case that a conceptual cognition such as 'This is a pot' is non-conceptual, and that a cognition like that of the yellow conch-shell will be non-erroneous? To this it is replied that even a conceptual cognition is, taken just in itself, non-conceptual. By means of the judgment 'That is a pot', the external object alone is conceptualized, not [the cognition] itself. It was said [by Dharmakīrti]:
>
> If something grasps the meaning of a word there [in the object], in that case the cognition is conceptual,
> It is not intrinsic [to a cognition] that the meaning of a word [be the object], hence it [cognition] is completely perceptible.
> Moreover, what is erroneous is in itself non-erroneous, for it appears only through being self-illuminating. And something is said to be an error due to having an unreal object. It was said:
>
> With regard to its own form every cognition is non-erroneous, error is with regard to the form of another.
> Thus it is to be agreed that since otherwise there would be no accounting for illumination, if they illuminate, then existing things illuminate having arisen from what by nature illuminates just because of its own cause. [TB I §13, pp. 22–24]

Suppose Mokṣākaragupta has convinced us that all cognitions are self-cognizing. Now self-cognition looks like a kind of perception. For it is the immediate awareness of something (namely a cognition); it does not involve conceptualization; since the sense organs are not involved in cognizing a cognition, it could not be erroneous through faulty sense organs. But then inferential cognitions, and cognitions produced by faulty sense organs, will also turn out to be cases of perception. Take, for instance, my inferential awareness of fire on the hill. Suppose I have gone through the reasoning that leads me to the conclusion that there is fire on the hill. As a result I have a cognition of fire. This cognition, like all cognitions, is self-cognizing. But self-cognition is a kind of perception. Surely one and the same cognition cannot be an instance of both perception and inference. The reply is that taken in one way an inferential cognition is non-conceptual, taken in another way it is conceptual (and so inferential). What are these two ways? And does this really solve the difficulty?

Now take the cognition of yellow that the person with jaundice has when looking at the white conch-shell. This cognition is also self-cognizing, and self-cognition is a form of perception. If we follow Dharmakīrti and hold that a cognition must be non-erroneous to be perception, then it follows that this cognition is both perception and also mere pseudo-perception. For as a case of self-cognition it is non-erroneous. But because it is the result of disordered vision, it is erroneous. Here too the reply to this objection involves distinguishing between two different ways in which we might think about a cognition: as self-presentation, and as representation of some distinct object. The claim is that one and the same cognition might be veridical when taken in the first way, but non-veridical when taken in the second.

Here is a further question to ponder: does it make sense to call something a piece of knowledge if it's something that we are in principle incapable of being wrong about? Yogācāra-Sautrāntika says that self-cognition could never be non-veridical. And that seems right. How could a cognition go wrong in simply manifesting itself? Buddhist logicians worked very hard to show that self-cognition wouldn't violate the anti-reflexivity principle. We can now see that by self-cognition they don't mean the impossible act of an eye turning its gaze on itself. By self-cognition they mean something more like self-presentation, a cognition's illumination of its content through a kind of self-manifesting. The question that this raises, though, is whether self-cognition should really be thought of as a means of knowledge.

We will end our exposition of Buddhist philosophy at this point. There is much more to the school of Diṅnāga than we have been able to present here. And there are also interesting developments when Buddhist philosophy gets taken up in Tibet and in East Asia. A work such as this one cannot give an exhaustive survey of the entire Buddhist tradition. But perhaps it can equip those who want to explore further with the basic tools they will need.

Further Reading

There are now good translations available of four important Yogācāra-Sautrāntika works. The first and second of these are of single chapters of texts, while the third and fourth are of complete texts:

● Hattori Masaaki, *Dignāga: On Perception* (Cambridge, MA: Harvard University Press 1971).

● Tom Tillemans, *Dharmakīrti's Pramāṇavarttika: an annotated translation of the fourth chapter* (Vienna: Verlag der Österreichischen Akademie der Wissenschaften, 2000).

- Mrinalkanti Gangopadhyaya, *Vinītadeva's Nyāyabinduṭikā on Dharmakīrti's Nyāyabindu*, Indian Studies Past and Present **3** (Calcutta, 1971).
- Kajiyama Yuichi, *An Introduction to Buddhist Philosophy: an annotated translation of the Tarkabhāṣā of Mokṣākaragupta*, Wiener Studien zur Tibetologie und Buddhismuskunde **42** (Vienna: Arbeitskreis für Tibetologie und Buddhistische Studien, 1998).

Two somewhat dated book-length studies of Yogācāra-Sautrāntika are still useful. The first is by Theodor Stcherbatsky, *Buddhist Logic* (New York: Dover, 1962, reprint; first published in the *Bibilotheca Buddhica* series by the Academy of Sciences of the USSR, Leningrad, 1930). The second is Satkari Mookerjee, *The Buddhist Philosophy of Universal Flux* (Calcutta: University of Calcutta Press 1935).

An ambitious recent attempt to lay out Dharmakīrti's formulation of Yogācāra-Sautrāntika is John D. Dunne, *Foundations of Dharmakīrti's Philosophy* (Somerville, MA: Wisdom, 2004).

For an excellent study of the transmission of Buddhism from India to China, see Erik Zürcher, *The Buddhist conquest of China : the spread and adaptation of Buddhism in early medieval China* (Leiden: E.J. Brill, 1972).

For an account of the early history of Buddhism's entry into Tibet, see David Seyfort Ruegg, *Buddha-nature, Mind and the Problem of Gradualism in a Comparative Perspective: on the transmission and reception of Buddhism in India and Tibet* (London: School of Oriental and African Studies, 1989).

For a fascinating account of Tibetan Buddhist monastic education, see Georges Dreyfus, *The Sound of Two Hands Clapping* (Berkeley: University of California Press, 2003).

Index